North British Type 2 B-B Diesel-Hydraulic Locomotives, BR Class 22

6356, 81A Old Oak Common, 20 February 1971. The Class 22 quite rightly takes the centre of attention! (Anthony Sayer)

Front Cover: D6327, 85B Gloucester Horton Road, August 1970. (Norman Preedy [Kidderminster Railway Museum])
Rear Cover: D6302, 83D Plymouth Laira, 29 May 1963. (Alec Swain [Transport Treasury])

North British Type 2 B-B Diesel-Hydraulic Locomotives, BR Class 22

Volume 1 – Setting the Scene

ANTHONY P. SAYER

PEN & SWORD
TRANSPORT
AN IMPRINT OF PEN & SWORD BOOKS LTD.
YORKSHIRE – PHILADELPHIA

First published in Great Britain in 2024 by
Pen & Sword Transport
An imprint of Pen & Sword Books Limited
Yorkshire – Philadelphia

ISBN 978 1 39904 503 2

A CIP catalogue record for this book is
available from the British Library.

Typeset by Mac Style
Printed and bound by Printworks Global Ltd, London/Hong Kong.

Pen & Sword Books Limited incorporates the imprints of After the Battle, Atlas,
Archaeology, Aviation, Discovery, Family History, Fiction, History, Maritime,
Military, Military Classics, Politics, Select, Transport, True Crime, Air World,
Frontline Publishing, Leo Cooper, Remember When, Seaforth Publishing, The
Praetorian Press, Wharncliffe Local History, Wharncliffe Transport, Wharncliffe
True Crime and White Owl.

For a complete list of Pen & Sword titles please contact

PEN & SWORD BOOKS LIMITED
47 Church Street, Barnsley, South Yorkshire, S70 2AS, England
E-mail: enquiries@pen-and-sword.co.uk
Website: www.pen-and-sword.co.uk
or
PEN AND SWORD BOOKS
1950 Lawrence Rd, Havertown, PA 19083, USA
E-mail: Uspen-and-sword@casematepublishers.com
Website: www.penandswordbooks.com

CONTENTS

PREFACE

Coverage of the fifty-eight North British Locomotive Company Type 2 D63xx diesel-hydraulic locomotives has required two volumes to do the subject justice; these two volumes represent my seventh and eighth books in the Pen & Sword 'Locomotive Portfolios' series. This volume sets the scene and covers the ordering and introduction of the Class and associated financial considerations, technical aspects, appearance design and styling, delivery and acceptance testing, allocations, overhauls and repairs together with individual locomotive histories.

Volume 2 will include a discussion of the performance and operating issues associated with the Class, accident and fire damage incidents, general operations, detail differences (in some considerable depth), livery variations, storage, withdrawal and disposal, together with some concluding insights.

Extensive research work has once again allowed new material to be published on the Class, shedding additional light on the following key areas of their history:

- how the various Western Region Area Schemes, developed over the 1957-61 period, were used to define their Type 2 locomotive requirements,
- how NBL's financial difficulties during the early 1960s very nearly resulted in twenty additional locomotives being added to the fleet,
- how the Western Region attempted to tackle some of the technical problems which affected the fleet,
- how Classified body overhauls radically impacted the external appearance of the locomotives,
- how the National Traction Plans (1965-8) defined British Railways Type 2 requirements generally and the NBL Type 2 hydraulics in particular.

The first two 'bullet points' are dealt with in this volume, and the last three will be covered in Volume 2.

A multiplicity of information sources have again enabled the development of detailed histories for each of the fifty-eight locomotives (Chapter 8); space constraints have led to some abridgement but all information considered to be 'key' has been retained, specifically Swindon Works visits; the Works information helps to inform the timing and sequencing of the physical and cosmetic changes made to the class which will be dealt with extensively in Volume 2.

The generic and frequently used collective names for the D6300-57 fleet in the early days were the 'NBL Type 2s' or the '63-ers'. The D61xx locomotives were also NBL Type 2s but their sphere of operation was so geographically removed from the Western Region fleet as to make any distinction unnecessary. Locally, the Western Region defined the six 'Pilot Scheme' locomotives as the '6300' class and the fifty-two 'Production Locomotives' as the '6306' class, utilising the number of the first member of each sub-class as the title, a tradition carried forward from the WR steam era. Under the BR TOPS system the diesel-hydraulic Type 2s became Class 22s. Perhaps surprisingly no distinction was made between the two sub-series (i.e. Class 22/0 and Class 22/1) although this might well have occurred if physical re-numbering into the 22xxx series had taken place. In this book the descriptor 'D63xx locomotives'(or 'D63xxs') is used for the full class during the early years of their history, with 'Class 22' being introduced later, consistent with the introduction of the TOPS classification in 1968.

In my previous books the use of the terms 'No.1' and 'No.2' has been used to define the specific ends of locomotives. Swindon Works, however, used 'A' or 'B' to define the locomotive ends and this Western Region convention has been used in this book. 'A'-end equates to the No.1 end and 'B'-end to No.2. Traditionally the end nearest to the radiator has been defined as the No.1 or 'A'-end, but the central position of the radiator on the D63xx locomotives renders this 'rule' unusable. The 'A'-end of the D63xxs was the end where the engine was located but this position was not immediately externally apparent. The best visual determinant of the locomotive end, therefore, was the position of the boiler water filler door; if positioned to the right of the large radiator grille(s), then 'A'-end was to the left and 'B'-end to the right, and vice versa.

Anthony Sayer

ACKNOWLEDGEMENTS

Archive sources have provided a major input in developing the history of the D63xxs and I would personally like to thank the teams of people at The National Archive, the British Library, the Mitchell Library (Glasgow), and the National Railway Museum for their kind assistance.

My thanks are also due to the following individuals for their considerable help on specific topic areas: John Aitchison (Special Traffic Notices); Rob Aston (Bristol Marsh Junction storage); Ashley Butlin (Cashmore, Newport, scrapyard arrival dates); Amyus Crump (D6311 fire damage); Hugh Dady (Route Availability); Sean Greenslade (Exeter); Mike Hunt (all manner of things Technical); Doug Parfitt (Project 22 Society and Technical issues); Mark Parsons (in-depth Diesel-Hydraulic Technical, BICERI); Pete Nicholls (Paddington, Old Oak Common); Alan Whincup (works/bogie plates).

My continued use of the 'back to basics' approach has relied heavily on a massive amount of personal observations in various forms. I have made every attempt to credit everyone concerned in the Sources & References section (see Volume 2). Thanks to you all.

The two volumes have used over 300 images to support the text. My thanks go to the following organisations and individuals for the photographs used herein:-

- Colour-Rail, Online Transport Archive, Rail-Online, Rail-Photoprints, RCTS Archive, The Transport Library, Transport Treasury, Transport Topics, Historic Environment Scotland, and Old-Maps.co.uk.

- The Hawthorne Collection, Kidderminster Railway Museum, The Restoring & Archive Trust (Gloucestershire Warwickshire Railway)
- Rob Aston, Mark Bartlett, Jim Binnie, Stewart Blencowe, Adrian Booth, David Bromley, Jim Carter (Acton Wells Junction), Trevor Casey, Fred Castor, John Cosford, Amyus Crump, Eric Curnow, Trevor David, David Dunn, Derek Everson, Peter Foster, Peter Groom, Anthony Haynes, Robert Himsworth, Simon Howard, Mike Hunt, Dave Jolly, Mike Kirby, Andy Kirkham, Keith Long, Noel Machell, Colin Marsden, Ken Mumford, Terry Nicholls (courtesy Steve Nicholls), Ian Osborne, Mark Parsons, Brian Penney, David Quayle, Keith Sanders, Geoff Sharpe, David Smith, Steve Thorpe, John Grey Turner, Richard Vitler, Grahame Wareham, Alan Whincup, Pete Wilcox and Lindsay Young.

There are a small number of images from photographers where it has proved impossible to obtain the appropriate permission to use their photographs despite every endeavour being made to do so. In addition, there are a few images where the identity of the photographer is totally unknown; lack of any accreditation on slides or prints has prevented any possibility of determining their provenance. In both cases, anyone who feels that they have been inadequately credited should contact me via the publisher to ensure that the situation is corrected in future editions.

ABBREVIATIONS

BLC	Birmingham Locomotive Club.
BLS	British Locomotive Society.
BMJ	Bristol Marsh Junction.
BR	British Railways/British Rail.
BRB	British Railways Board.
BREL	British Rail Engineering Ltd.
BTC	British Transport Commission.
BTC SC	BTC Supply Committee.
BTC W&EC	BTC Works & Equipment Committee.
BTH	British Thomson-Houston.
CM&EE	Chief Mechanical & Electrical Engineer.
c.s.	Carriage Sidings.
DMU	Diesel Multiple-Unit.
e.c.s.	Empty coaching stock.
ER	Eastern Region.
FDTL	'Fires on Diesel Train Locomotives' Reports.
HCB	Headcode Boxes.
hp/bhp	Horsepower/Brake Horsepower.
LCGB	Locomotive Club of Great Britain.
LMR	London Midland Region.
MAN	Maschinenfabrik Augsburg-Nurnberg (engine manufacturer).
NBL	North British Locomotive Co. Ltd.
NTP	National Traction Plan.
P/E	Period Ending.
RCTS	Railway Correspondence and Travel Society.

rpm	Revolutions per minute.
RSL	Rolling Stock Library.
ScR	Scottish Region.
SLS	Stephenson Locomotive Society.
s.p.	Stabling point.
SPM	St. Philip's Marsh, Bristol.
SR	Southern Region.
STN	Special Traffic Notice.
S(s)/S(u)	Stored serviceable/unserviceable.
TOPS	Total Operations Processing System.
T&RS	Traction & Rolling Stock.
w/c or wc	Week commencing.
w/e or we	Week ending.
WR	Western Region.

Livery Abbreviations:

GNY	Green, no yellow ends.
GSY	Green, small yellow panels.
GFY	Green, full yellow ends.
BSY	Blue, small yellow panels.
BFY	Blue, full yellow ends.

Headcode-Box Abbreviations:

BO-HCB	Bolt-On Headcode-Box.
SI-HCB	Semi-Integral Headcode-Box

Chapter 1

CLASS INTRODUCTION

1.1 Western Region Diesel-Hydraulic Type 2s: How Many?

Fifty-eight North British Locomotive Company (NBL) diesel-hydraulic Type 2s were constructed. This fact is well known, as indeed is the fact that the fifty-eight were composed of six 'Pilot Scheme' locomotives and fifty-two Production locomotives. However, less well known is the fact that the Western Region (WR) only really wanted thirty-four of the Type 2s to meet their forecast requirements within the West of England Area Scheme submission to the British Transport Commission (BTC) in 1957; the other twenty-four were ordered as Type 1 substitutes in the absence of a suitable design in this power category at the time.

By the time of the authorisation of the next Area Scheme, Bristol, in 1958/59, BR and the WR had standardised on three diesel-hydraulic types, namely Type 1 (subsequently D95xx), Type 3 ('Hymek' D70xx) and a 'Super' Type 4 ('Western' D10xx). No further Type 2 requirements beyond the fifty-eight Types 2s already ordered were, therefore, envisaged. That is, until NBL started to run into severe financial difficulties during the early 1960s and an idea was hatched between NBL and BR for the supply of a further twenty Type 2s as a mechanism to bridge an impending hole in NBL's order book. Nothing came of this idea but there remains that little known possibility of D6358-77 trying to find useful employment somewhere on the WR.

All of these subjects are covered in greater detail in the following sections.

1.2 'Pilot Scheme' Diesel-Hydraulic Type 2s.

In a Memorandum to the Works & Equipment Committee (W&EC) dated 29 September 1954 and entitled *Diesel Locomotives with Hydraulic Transmission*, R.C. Bond (BTC Chief Mechanical Engineer) recognised that, with the exception of the Fell diesel-mechanical locomotive (10100), only electric transmission had thus far been used in diesel locomotives over 500hp on BR. In contrast, considerable development had taken place abroad with hydraulic transmission, notably in Germany, with deployment in locomotives across the full power range.

In 1953, NBL completed some mixed-traffic 625hp diesel-hydraulic locomotives for Mauritius Government Railways. Various test runs were carried out in Scotland prior to delivery and Bond participated in one test involving a pair of these locomotives between Glasgow and Edinburgh, commenting that they performed 'in a most satisfactory manner'.

During 1954, NBL completed preliminary designs and specifications for locomotives in the higher power ranges for potential sale abroad. Bond had a number of informal discussions with NBL who were looking for sales in the UK market, to act as a 'shop window' to the world. As part of the impending transitioning from steam to more modern motive power, Bond thought it 'very desirable' to undertake trials of diesel locomotives in the higher power categories to properly ascertain the relative merits of hydraulic and electric transmission. Bond recognised some of the potential generic benefits of hydraulic transmission which might accrue over the electric alternative, as follows:

- Lower locomotive weight per hp.
- Lower first cost.
- Lower maintenance costs.

In his September 1954 Memorandum, Bond proposed the construction of five locomotives for main-line passenger and freight services in the 2000hp-and-above range and six locomotives in the 1000-1250hp range to be used as twin units on heavy work or singly for lighter duties; he envisaged that these locomotives could be suitable for use throughout BR. He also recommended that his proposals be developed further with NBL with detailed designs and estimated costs obtained prior to a submission to the BTC.

The W&EC Meeting of 6 October 1954 (Minute 257/10) agreed with Bond's proposal. Whilst members of the team were keen to compare potential offerings from alternative suppliers, it was evident in 1954 that NBL were well ahead of the game having negotiated manufacturing licensing agreements with MAN and Voith for engine and transmission equipment respectively.

Following the Committee's approval, the Western Region were approached and they undertook to collaborate with

NBL on this project. The WR were aware that a major element of the forthcoming Modernisation Plan was the abolition of loose-coupled freight trains and the fitting of freight vehicles with continuous brakes and they therefore recognised that the dead weight of locomotives themselves would no longer be critical in the safe braking of such trains. Lightweight locomotives (with high-speed engines in conjunction with hydraulic transmissions) were therefore seen to provide the advantages of both lower initial cost of construction and reduced ongoing fuel consumption levels. In addition, WR management realised that fully-fitted freight trains running at higher speeds would allow a greater utilisation of the new diesels, further enhanced by adopting the philosophy of component replacement at depots (as opposed to major Works facilities required for exchanging the heavy low-speed engines and generators deployed in diesel-electric locomotives).

At a Technical Development & Research Committee Meeting on 11 November 1954 (Minute 83) Bond proposed a visit to the German Railways to inspect their hydraulic fleet of locomotives with a suitable support team to accompany him, including R.A. Smeddle, Chief Mechanical & Electrical Engineer (WR). The Committee agreed to the proposal and this visit took place during late-January and early-February 1955 and included visits to the MAN and Voith factories.

A Memorandum to the W&EC, dated 2 February 1955, covering the 1956 Locomotive Building & Condemnation Programmes, included a recommendation for the construction of thirty-one diesel locomotives including the eleven diesel-hydraulic locomotives proposed by Bond. These thirty-one locomotives were subsequently delivered as D1-10 (2300hp, diesel-electric), D200-9 (2000hp diesel-electric), D600-4 (2000hp diesel-hydraulic) and D6300-5 (1000hp, diesel-

D6305, 83D Plymouth Laira, 1960. (Keith Langstone [Rail-Photoprints])

hydraulic). Indicative prices were £84,000 and £50,000 each for the 2000/2300hp and 1000hp locomotives respectively. The W&EC subsequently requested approval from the BTC (W&EC Minute 357/40, 9 February 1955) and the order was authorised by the BTC on 17 February 1955 (Meeting Minute 8/74). These thirty-one locomotives were the first part of the 174-strong 'Pilot Scheme' fleet.

A Memorandum to the W&EC dated 18 March 1955 included details of NBL's design, cost and delivery proposals. Prices for the 2000hp and 1000hp locomotives were quoted as £86,000 and £53,000 respectively, the increase in prices being due to the proposed manufacture of engines/transmissions for D600/1 in Germany plus the provision of maintenance services by NBL for the first year. These proposals were accepted by the W&EC (Minute 386/25, 23 March 1955).

Order placement for the six Type 2s with NBL took place on 16 November 1955 (under Swindon Lot No.426). Details of the order as held within the *NBL & Constituent Companies Engine Orders 1879-1961* ledgers are listed below:

Date of Quotation	22 February 1955
Date of Order	16 November 1955
NBL Order No.	L77
Construction	Queen's Park Works, changed to Hyde Park Works 16/5/56 and back to Queen's Park Works 16/10/56.
BTC Contract No.	PRE/A/725/2
Order Details	Six (6) Diesel-Hydraulic Main-Line Locos. 1000bhp.
	Diesel Engine: NBL/MAN Type L12V17.5/21A. (*subsequently overwritten 'L12V18/21A.', where A = Aufladung [Supercharged]*)
	Hydraulic Transmission: L306r
	Locomotive Weight: 64 tons.
Delivery	To begin in 18 months from date of order at the rate of 2 locomotives per month.
NBL Progressive Nos.	27665-27670

To complete the diesel-hydraulic 'Pilot Scheme' story, three 2000hp locomotives (subsequently D800-2) were authorised by the BTC on 26 May 1955 (Minute 8/250) for construction at Swindon Works, giving fourteen diesel-hydraulics in total.

1.3 Post-'Pilot Scheme'.

1.3.1 Abandonment of the 'Pilot Scheme'.
The intention was for the 'Pilot Scheme' designs to be tested over a three-year period with the deliberate objective of determining a limited number of types for volume production commencing 1961/62 based on operational experience gained. However, facing deteriorating financial results, the BTC abandoned the three year trial period, and accelerated the introduction of diesel locomotives as fast as British production capacity allowed, believing that dieselisation and the consequent elimination of steam would dramatically improve the fiscal position. Thus, Minute 9/384 of the BTC Meeting of 26 July 1956 recorded:

The Commission ... discussed the purchase of additional main-line locomotives and agreed that they would be prepared to consider requests for a number of these without further trials, provided that there is sufficient technical evidence to show that the type of locomotive desired is fully and without doubt able to meet requirements ... in the service for which it is intended.

On 16 May 1957, a report entitled *Modernisation of British Railways: Report on Diesel and Electric Traction and the Passenger Services of the Future* was published. This report envisaged the ordering of 1,889 additional main-line diesel locomotives during the period 1957-62. The BTC at their Meeting on 23 May 1957 (Min. 10/212) approved the general concept of the extension and acceleration of diesel traction introduction as contained in the report, stating:

The Commission would be prepared to go further than they have already gone in regard to ordering diesel main-line locomotives, in spite of the risk of unsatisfactory performance in the early stages, if the Regions presented them with a limited number of firm plans for their use in specific areas (*so-called Area Schemes*), containing as clear a justification as possible.

1.3.2 Hydraulic v. Electric Transmission (1957 Position).
The dangers of giving up the trial period were made very clear by R.C. Bond, but BTC Chairman Sir Brian Robertson insisted that the Commission's decision was adhered to, subject to the specific conditions that reliable locomotives were introduced and that the number of different locomotive

designs was kept to an absolute minimum. These, as already mentioned, were the key objectives of the 'Pilot Scheme' process but it had now become necessary to recommend the smallest possible number of types without any experience having been obtained from the 'Pilot' locomotives. As a consequence, the only way of now achieving this was to base requirements on engineering judgement, knowledge of various firms' products and the operating experience of other railways.

The BTC Chairman's Conference held on 15 February 1957 included a debate on *Transmissions for Diesel Locomotives* in which R.C. Bond discussed the pros and cons of the various transmission types. Bond's submission critically analysed the generally accepted potential benefits of hydraulic transmission based on over two years of additional experience gained since his September 1954 report, summarised as follows:

- Lower locomotive weight per hp. Bond highlighted the fact that much of the weight saving with diesel-hydraulic locomotives was actually being achieved by marrying hydraulic transmissions with lightweight high-speed engines.
- Lower first cost. Bond's analysis indicated that the cost gap between electric and hydraulic transmissions was gradually closing over time as a consequence of technical developments in the industry.
- Lower maintenance costs. Bond was unable to prove or disprove this assertion; despite representations to the

German operator, detailed reports regarding maintenance costs had not been forthcoming.
- Improved reliability. No useful comparative data had been obtained in this area either. Bond was particularly worried about the reliability of cardan shafts and final drives deployed on high-powered diesel-hydraulic locomotives.

Bond's comments, whilst not condemning hydraulic transmission outright, certainly included some reservations which in his opinion could only be properly resolved by experience under British conditions.

1.3.3 WR Area Schemes and Diesel-Hydraulic Proliferation.
The abandonment of the 'Pilot Scheme' and the willingness to trial further diesel-hydraulic locomotives under British conditions paved the way for further orders of the Type 4 and Type 2 hydraulic designs under the umbrella of the BTC's 'Area Scheme' methodology.

1.4 Western Area Board Modernisation Plan.
The Western Area Board Modernisation Plan was presented to the BTC Chairman's Conference on 15 February 1957 (already referred to above with respect to R.C. Bond's *Transmissions for Diesel Locomotives* presentation); this envisaged the replacement of steam traction by diesel in four stages; the locomotive requirements for each of the stages was forecast as follows:

Area Scheme	Horsepower			Total	Completion by
	2000/2500	1000/1250	800		
No.1 West of England	72	34	24	130	1959
No.2 Bristol	86	42	62	190	1960
No.3 Gloucester & South Wales	353	120	182	655	1965
No.4 London, Birmingham & Chester	250	100	100	450	1968
Total	**761**	**296**	**368**	**1425**	

Given that fourteen main-line diesel-hydraulic locomotives had already been ordered for the WR as part of the 'Pilot Scheme' purchases, 116 further units were required to achieve dieselisation of the West of England Area. In addition, a further 190 locomotives would be required for Area No.2. Order placement for the 116 was considered urgent and within six to nine months for the 190 if the schemes were to be delivered on time. The Western Area Board explicitly stated their preference for hydraulic transmission.

The acquisition of 306 diesel-hydraulic locomotives without adequate 'Pilot Scheme' trialling was seen as a risk. However, delaying introduction would have meant that the higher cost

of operations associated with steam traction would continue for up to three further years, this against a backdrop of seriously deteriorating BR financial results. The Conference saw a future with all main-lines electrified, with diesels purely as a stop-gap measure; therefore, if diesel orders were delayed, then their revenue-earning life span would be reduced and pay-back impacted accordingly.

A key component of the Area schemes, in combination, was the requirement for 296 1000/1250hp locomotives (with six already ordered as part of the 'Pilot Scheme') plus 368 800hp locomotives. With respect to the latter Bond made the following comment in his Conference submission:

At a meeting held at Paddington on 29 April 1955, reference was made to the provision of diesel-electric locomotives (600-800hp) amongst the enquiries which BR had sent out to industry, and it was suggested it would be desirable to develop locomotives in this power range having hydraulic transmission, and proposed that Swindon should undertake the design for such locomotives for the Western Region.....This development is in abeyance for the time being because available design capacity at Swindon is fully occupied on the 2000hp ('Warship') locomotives.

Bond's view on the overall hydraulic subject was included in his own report as follows:

Whilst I have every hope and expectation that hydraulic transmission for high powers will be successful, I have consistently held, and still hold, the view that, if considerable numbers of diesel locomotives are to go into service before experience is gained with preliminary orders, such locomotives should have electric transmission, the characteristics and maintenance problems of which are, at present, far better known on BR than those which may arise with high power hydraulic transmissions.

Whilst I support the proposal to construct a further 116 diesel-hydraulic main-line locomotives for the WR, as an extension to the original orders ... I am not prepared to go further than this. I consider that no additional orders should be placed for high power diesel-hydraulic locomotives needed for Areas 2 and 3 until some

practical experience has been obtained with some of the locomotives now on order ...

... to adopt the course which I recommend might postpone the Area 2 scheme by about 12 months. I feel that this policy would be preferable to committing ourselves too extensively to a type of locomotive not fully proved under BR conditions.

Summarising the Conference discussion, the BTC Chairman stated that in view of the overall number of units required in the Western Area Board Modernisation Plan, the Commission would have to assess the magnitude of the risk involved in deploying locomotives with diesel-hydraulic transmission. The Chairman asked for the West of England submission to be brought to the Commission as soon as possible.

1.5 WR Area No.1 (West of England) Scheme.

Area No.1 covered the area west of Newton Abbot and the scheme included all principal main-line passenger services (including through trains to Bristol and London) and freight services.

A Memorandum to the W&EC dated 20 February 1957 recommended the construction of 116 locomotives (plus three shunters) as part of the 1958 Locomotive Building Programme (WR Supplementary Programme), to replace 206 steam locomotives. The 116 main-line diesel-hydraulic locomotives required were deliberately identical to the two types already under construction at Swindon and on order from NBL to avoid any proliferation of types, as follows:

Type of Locomotive	Total No. of Locomotives	Estimated Cost (Each)	Total
BR Workshops:			
2200hp (Maybach engines, Mekydro transmissions)	30	£86,000	£2,580,000
NBL:			
2200hp (MAN engines, Voith transmissions)	34	£86,000	£2,924,000
1000hp (MAN engine, Voith transmission)	52	£53,000	£2,756,000
Gross Outlay	116		£8,260,000

The W&EC Meeting (Minute 848/14, 27 February 1957) accepted the proposal and recommended approval by the BTC. Authority was given by the BTC on 28 February (Meeting Minute 10/81). At the latter meeting the BTC Chairman referred to the WR requirement for 190 diesel locomotives for Area 2 and stated that the Commission were likely to take the view that these should have electric transmission, echoing Bond's earlier remarks at the Chairman's Conference.

The following additional factors regarding Area No.1 locomotive provision should be noted:

• Because the design of the 800hp locomotive could not be completed to permit building in the timescale required, Type 2 (1000/1250hp) locomotives were substituted giving a total of fifty-two (in addition to the six 'Pilot Scheme' locomotives), ultimately D6300-57. The intention was that requirements for Type 1 and Type 2 locomotives within

- subsequent Area Schemes would be adjusted accordingly to reflect the development and introduction of the Swindon Type 1 diesel-hydraulic design.
- The 52 1000hp 'production' locomotives quoted were actually delivered with 1100hp capability.
- The supply of thirty-four 2200hp locomotives from NBL was subsequently reduced to thirty-three.
- Construction of the 116 main-line diesel-hydraulics together with the three shunting locomotives, combined with the condemnation of 246 steam locomotives, was approved at an estimated net outlay of £7,880, 576 (i.e. allowing for the scrap value of the steam locomotives).

- Once up-to-date quotations were obtained from the suppliers, it was found that the actual cost of the locomotives exceeded the original estimates in all three cases, necessitating further authorisations from the BTC; for further details see Section 2.1.1.

The order for the 52 Type 2s (subsequently D6306-57), was placed with NBL on 5 November 1957 under Swindon Lot No.440 and represented the largest single order for main-line diesels placed by BTC up to that time.

Details of the order as contained in the *NBL & Constituent Companies Engine Orders 1879-1961* ledgers are as follows:

Date of Quotation	8 April 1957
Date of Order	5 November 1957
NBL Order No.	L97
Construction	Queen's Park Works
BTC Contract No.	PRE/A/725/17
Order Details	Fifty-two (52) Diesel-Hydraulic Main-Line Locos. 1000bhp
	(*N.B. Drawing Office Register modified to 1100bhp*)
	Diesel Engine: NBL/MAN Type L12V18/21S (*where S = Supercharged*)
	Hydraulic Transmission: LT306r
Locomotive Weight	64 tons
Special Features	Provide for inter-changeability of NBL/MAN engines with Mekydro (*sic, Maybach*) engines and inter-changeability of Voith/NBL transmissions with Mekydro transmissions.
Delivery	Commence 5 March 1959 and continue at the rate of 3 locos per month.
NBL Progressive Nos.	27879-27930

D6308, 83D Plymouth Laira, 25 September 1960. (R.C. Riley [The Transport Library])

It should be noted that the BR/Swindon Type 1s, when actually built in 1964/65, were never allocated to the West of England to facilitate the transfer of NBL Type 2s elsewhere.

1.6 WR Area No.2 (Bristol) Scheme.

Two memoranda, one from the Western Area Board (5 September 1957) and one from the BTC Central Staff (6 September), moved onto Area Scheme No.2 and the 1959 Locomotive Building Programme.

Area No.2 was designed to link up with the West of England scheme and to extend the area of dieselisation over the whole of the Bristol motive power district (which included Bristol itself, running to points south of Gloucester, east of Swindon and west of Newbury) and including through services to and from London, Newton Abbot, South Wales and Gloucester. The scheme was scheduled for introduction in 1960.

Although the Area No.2 Scheme submission had not been fully developed, the memorandum sought authorisation for the construction of the required locomotives as part of the 1959 Building Programme to meet the required 1960 completion date. The *latest estimated* requirement was as follows (with the earlier February 1957 forecast provided in brackets for comparison):

	Horse-power			Total
	2000/2400	1000	600/800	
No. of Locos	90 (86)	54 (42)	56 (62)	200 (190)

Quite how these numbers dealt with the Area No.1 substitution of 24 800hp locomotives by the same number of 1000hp locomotives is unclear. In any case the memorandum recognised the continued non-availability of the 800hp type and that (presumably fifty-six) further 1000hp substitutions would be necessary. The Memorandum recommended that the 200 locomotives for the Bristol area should be composed of the two diesel-hydraulic designs already approved, contrary to Bond's earlier reticence and the comments made by the BTC.

The estimate for the number of locomotives required included a 25 per cent allowance for maintenance. The projected availability level of 85 per cent would generate surplus locomotives which could be set-off against the requirements for subsequent Area Schemes. Requirements continued to be based on un-modified steam timetables.

Notwithstanding the non-availability of the 800hp locomotives, the forecast locomotive costs within the submission were as follows:

	Each	Estimated Cost
90 Type 4 2200hp	£100,000	£9,000,000
54 Type 2 1000hp	£62,675	£3,384,450
56 Type 1 800hp	£56,410	£3,158,960
		£15,543,410

The W&EC meeting on 11 September 1957 (Minute 987/20) recommended provisional approval for the Scheme, subject to financial re-assessment against the recently developed uniform code for Scheme justification. In addition, the Chairman requested that the question of the transmission type to be adopted should be discussed by the Technical Development & Research Committee (TDRC) at their meeting on 13 September with a recommendation to be made to the BTC.

The TDRC meeting (Minute 508), attended by Bond and K.W.C. Grand (General Manager [WR]), agreed to recommend the continued use of hydraulic transmission to the BTC. The arguments put forward to continue with diesel-hydraulic locomotive construction were clearly sufficiently compelling to convince Bond but were not itemised in the Meeting minutes.

The BTC at their meeting on 19 September 1957 (Minute 10/406) gave provisional approval to the Area No.2 scheme enabling the requirement for 200 locomotives to be formally built into the 1959 Building Programme; BTC accepted the deployment of hydraulic transmission as recommended by the TDRC.

A Memorandum to the W&EC, dated 14 January 1958, provided revised locomotive building costs, with the Type 2s and Type 1s increased to £63,500 and £56,500 each respectively.

A new Area No.2 submission, aimed at securing full BTC approval of the Scheme, was presented by Grand on 19 November 1958. The defined locomotive requirements, however, had shifted substantially over the ten months since the previous submission (at least partially explaining the delay in placing actual orders), and included requirements for new 'Super' Type 4 and Type 3 designs. Grand's submission commented, 'It has been in mind that some variation of types would be necessary as the Region's plans developed … The Types mentioned above are proposed, in agreement with the Chief Mechanical Engineer (BTC), following studies by the Region's technical and operating officers.'

Thus, the 'Super'-Type 4 (2700hp) was added to the range to cover more demanding traffic requirements. With respect to the Type 3 1500/1700hp type:

The Region's studies have shown that the existing 1000hp design will have insufficient power for the intermediate range of work this group of locomotives will be regularly required to undertake. The 1500/1700hp unit will cover these duties adequately and be suitable for heavier seasonal workings on certain of the main routes.

As a consequence of these changes, the 1000hp power category (now defined as Type 1) was seen as evolving into something very different. 'This locomotive is intended for local work and will be of a simpler and cheaper design than the 1000hp (*and 1100hp*) type now being built.'
Locomotive requirements for Area No.2 were, therefore, re-specified as follows:

	'Super'-Type 4	Type 3	New Type 1	Total
	2700hp	1500/1700hp	1000hp	
'Pure' Area No.2	72	37	37	146
With Birmingham/ Bristol	12	11	–	23
Total	84	48	37	169

Once again hydraulic transmission was stipulated for all designs and the displacement of 300 steam locomotives was still envisaged. The gross outlay figures for the 'Pure' Area No.2 requirements were presented as follows:

	Each	Estimated Cost
72 Type 4 2700hp	£107,000	£7,704,000
37 Type 3 1500/1700hp	£80,000	£2,960,000
37 Type 1 1000hp	£75,000	£2,775,000
Total estimated cost:		£13,439,000

Apart from the re-design work surrounding the 1000hp locomotive, the Grand report also included the following comment:

It is recommended that arrangements for the building of the Type 1 locomotives should be deferred until the enquiries now in process into unremunerative passenger services and the development of a comprehensive freight concentration scheme have reached the stage at which the eventual requirement can be more clearly seen.

Although not explicitly stated, the November 1958 submission, by recommending the 'Super'-Type 4, the new Type 3 and re-engineered Type 1 designs, effectively drew the line under ordering any further NBL Type 2s.

By the W&EC Meeting on 16 December 1958 (Minute 1340/6), the locomotive requirements for the Area No.2 scheme had further reduced, as follows:

	'Super'-Type 4	Type 3	New Type 1	Total
	2700hp	1500/1700hp	1000hp	
'Pure' Area No.2	67	34	33	134
With Birmingham/ Bristol	12	11	–	23
Total	79	45	33	157

The Area Scheme decision was again deferred, pending further supporting financial information as required by the code for Scheme approvals; however, it was agreed that provisional approval would be requested from the BTC for the 'Super'-Type 4 and Type 3 locomotive requirements within the Building Programme for 1960/61 (now deferred from 1959). This was ratified by the BTC on 18 December (Meeting Minute 11/538).

A memorandum to the W&EC dated 1 January 1959 concerning the 1960/61 Building Programme, referenced the Area No.2 requirements and included all 157 locomotives, i.e. 33 Type 1 (£2,475,000), 45 Type 3 (£3,600,000), 59 Type 4 (£7,965,000) built by contractors and 20 Type 4 built by BR Workshops (£2,700,000): Total cost £16,740,000.

The W&EC Meeting on 6 January 1959 (Minute 1342/33) recommended the construction of the 157 hydraulic locomotives, subject to final approval of the Area No.2 scheme, although no specific mention was made regarding the continuing design delays surrounding the new Type 1 design. However, the BTC on 8 January 1959 (Meeting Minute 12/4) deferred their decision pending receipt of a satisfactory Area Scheme submission and a decision from the Technical function regarding the acceptability of the proposed 'Hymek' Type 3 diesel-hydraulic design.

Over the next few months fifty locomotives were authorised, despite the fact that an acceptable version of the Area No.2 Scheme had still not been submitted and authorised; these were:

- Five Type 4s (2200hp 'Warships') in lieu of five 'Super'-Type 4s (2700hp 'Westerns'), thereby reducing the Area No.2 forecast from 79 to 74, to fill a production gap at Swindon before commencement of the 2700hp locomotives could begin (W&EC (Minute 1423/20, 07/04/59), BTC (Minute 12/160(a), 23/04/59).
- Forty-five Type 3 Beyer, Peacock-built 'Hymeks' (W&EC [Minute 1435/11, 21/04/59], BTC [Minute 12/160(b), 23/04/59]), following the Technical Department's recommendation to use Type 3 diesel-hydraulic traction.

J.R. Hammond (the latest WR General Manager) submitted a further memorandum on 17 June 1959 to financially justify the Area No.2 Scheme. This latest submission was in the form of a composite Area No.1 & No.2 scheme which inevitably had ramifications with respect to overall locomotive requirements, as follows:

	'Super'-Type 4 2700hp	Type 4 2000/2200hp	Type 3 1700hp	New Type 1/2 800/1000hp	Total
Total requirement					
Area Nos.1 & 2	74	76	32	94	276
Authorised					
Area No.1	–	71	–	58 (Note 2)	129
Area No.2	–	5	–	–	5
Authority Required	74	–	32 (Note 1)	44 (Notes 2/3)	150

Notes:
1. Despite forty-five Type 3 'Hymeks' being authorised by the BTC, for the purposes of the Area Nos.1/2 justification, they were considered as unauthorised. Thirteen fewer Type 3 locomotives were required for the composite scheme than ordered from Beyer, Peacock (Hymek) Ltd. The thirteen 'spare' locomotives were, therefore, made available for future Area Schemes.
2. Eight of the 1000hp NBL locomotives already authorised were no longer required for Area No.1 and were, therefore, designated for absorption into the future Area No.3 Scheme.
3. Given the removal of eight NBL Type 2s from the Area No.1 authorised figure (reducing the 58 figure to 50), the difference between the combined number of Type 1 and Type 2 locomotives required and those authorised was forty-four (94 less 50).
4. With respect to the forty-four Type1s requiring authorisation, an unquantified mix of new 1000hp and 800hp designs were envisaged (both with a single cab). The memorandum included the following statements regarding these locomotives:

   Future requirements for 1000hp locomotives will be met by a unit of a simpler design than the existing type, i.e. with one cab to overcome difficulties which have arisen in carrying out shunting duties.

There will remain a proportion of short-distance low-mileage freight turns for which, in the interests of economy, the lightest and cheapest unit which will meet the requirements should be provided. The question of adopting such a locomotive (e.g. of 800hp and without steam heating boiler) is still under consideration and, meanwhile, it has been assumed, for scheme purposes, that approximately half of the lower-powered locomotives will be of the cheaper type.

The precise requirements of the (800/1000hp) units will be established within the next few months and it is recommended that covering authority be also sought for their provision, subject to agreement with the Commission's Technical Officers on the question of the smaller locomotive and the division of the order between the two types.

The comments quite clearly indicated no further proliferation of the NBL Type 2 design, but, contrary to the BTC objective of limiting variety of types, did envisage two new (albeit) cheaper designs to replace one existing type.
5. The 276 main-line locomotives, together with 31 shunting locomotives previously authorised, were planned to displace 614 locomotives (612 steam, one gas-turbine and one diesel).

At the third time of asking, the W&EC (Minute 1495/17, 7 July 1959) decided to recommend that the Commission approve both the composite Area No.1/2 Scheme and the construction of 74 Type 4 (2700hp) (D1000-73) locomotives as part of the 1961 Building Programme. On 16 July 1959 the BTC (Minute 12/286) authorised both items. The W&EC Committee noted that 'a further submission would be made in respect of the Types 1 and 2 (800/1000hp) locomotives when the precise requirements were known'.

There was no subsequent mention in the archives of the 'new' 1000hp design and it is assumed that the idea was quietly dropped after appraisal of the unremunerative passenger services and freight concentration initiatives, with concentration wholly on the 800hp (subsequently 650hp) design.

1.7 Diesel Fleet Standardisation.
In between the final sign-off of the combined Area No.1/2 Area Scheme in July 1959 and the first submission of the Area No.3 (Stage 1) Scheme in May 1960, a considerable amount of work was undertaken to standardise the BR locomotive fleet to as few types as possible.

In response to a BTC Board action regarding locomotive standardisation (Minute 12/253, 25 June 1959), a Memorandum to the BTC Technical Committee dated 8 January 1960, entitled 'Standardisation of Main-Line Diesel-Electric Locomotives', specifically addressed this issue. This was produced by J.F. Harrison and S.B. Warder (Chief Mechanical and Electrical Engineers respectively).

A very similar Memorandum was presented to the Technical Committee on 15 September 1960 entitled 'Standardisation of

Diesel-Hydraulic Locomotives', again produced by Harrison and Warder. This report made the comment that a degree of standardisation had already been achieved by limiting all recent orders to 'Super'-Type 4 and Type 3 locomotives.

Key elements of the second memorandum pertinent to the NBL Type 2s are given below:

58 Type 2 diesel-hydraulic locomotives were authorised in association with the WR Area No.1 scheme, but when the combined Area Nos.1 and 2 schemes were approved by the Commission (Minute 12/286 of 16/7/59), it was noted in the relevant W&EC Minute 1495/17 of 7/7/59, that a further submission would be made regarding the additional 44 Type 1 or Type 2 locomotives required when precise requirements were known. The matter has accordingly been investigated in detail on the WR, and the conclusions reached may be summarised as follows:

(1) The turns concerned for which these locomotives are required … are principally on freight trip duties and associated shunting, generally involving low mileage and non-continuous working, and as upwards of 400 locomotives in this power range will ultimately be required, it is necessary that the least expensive type of unit capable of meeting the main requirement be used.

(2) The existing Type 2 diesel-hydraulic locomotive is at a disadvantage for the shunting work involved in these turns, on account of the two-cab arrangement, and in any event is unnecessarily powerful, and … too costly for freight trip duties. The Type 1 diesel-electric locomotive of 900hp for which quotations are now received, costs a minimum of £50,612.

(3) The standard 350hp shunter has insufficient speed for main-line tripping, and neither this type nor the 500hp English Electric locomotive recently tried, have the power needed.

(4) It is accordingly proposed that the requirements should be met by an 0-6-0 locomotive of 650hp with a maximum speed of 40mph. It is estimated

that such a locomotive would cost approximately £35,000 thereby effecting a saving in outlay of the order of £10-12m. on the 400 required … compared to the Type 2 locomotives currently in use, and £6m. compared to the 900hp Type 1 diesel-electric locomotive.

(5) The proposed 650hp locomotive would be a freight trip unit, and would not be equipped for passenger train-heating. Local and branch line passenger work in the WR will be covered almost entirely by DMUs …

(6) As a result of these proposals, it is recommended that no further Type 2 diesel-hydraulic locomotives should be ordered and the standard range of diesel-hydraulic main-line locomotives should be limited to:
Type 4 2700hp, Type 3 1700hp, Type 1 650hp.

The authors of the Memorandum were in agreement with the WR proposals and recommended that the Technical Committee approve the adoption of the three specified standard types of diesel-hydraulic locomotives including the 650hp Type 1 for all WR Area Schemes. Minute 865 of the Technical Committee Meeting held on 23 September 1960 indicated formal agreement.

No formal subsequent acceptance by the BTC has been found in the archives and presumably occurred ex-Committee. It will be noted that no further mention was made of the 1000hp single-cab locomotive option.

1.8 WR Area No.3 (Stage 1) Scheme.
The Area No.3 (Stage 1) Scheme covered the provision of diesel traction on the principal through passenger, parcels and freight services, together with some secondary services, on the London-South Wales, London-Gloucester-Cheltenham, London-Shrewsbury-Chester and South Wales-Shrewsbury routes.

The scheme was outlined by J.R. Hammond in a memorandum dated 18 May 1960; the indicated locomotive requirements were:

	Type 4 2700hp	Type 3 1700hp	Type 2 1100hp	Type 1 hp not specified	Total
Total requirement	150	69	9	11 (Note 3)	239
Already authorised	–	63 (Note 1)	8 (Note 2)	–	71
Authorisation required	150	6	1	11	168

Notes:
1. Ninety-five Type 3 diesel-hydraulic locomotives had been authorised by the time of Hammond's memorandum, i.e. forty-five under BTC Minute 12/160(b), 23/04/59, as previously described, plus a further fifty under Minute 13/110(g), 17/03/60. Thirty-two of these were authorised under the Area Nos.1/2 submission.
2. With the progressive standardisation on the Type 1, 3 and 4 types it is perhaps surprising to see the Type 2 (1100hp) type still included in the list of requirements. However, eight D63xx locomotives surplus from the combined Area Nos.1/2 requirements had to be accounted for and were, therefore, included in the Area No.3 submission, leaving a net requirement of one to be authorised!

3. Regarding the Type 1, the Hammond memorandum stated: 'Design to be decided in conjunction with the Central Staff.' Note the word 'Design' is singular thereby discounting the simplified 1000hp locomotive idea, with concentration on the lower horsepower trip-freight locomotive.
4. Thirty-two spare locomotives (15.5 per cent) were included in the above numbers.
5. The 239 diesel locomotives were planned to replace 499 steam locomotives.

A memorandum to the W&EC from the BTC Central Staff dated 31 August 1960 supported Hammond's scheme and recommended both the scheme and the acquisition of 168 diesel-hydraulic locomotives, as follows:

No. of Locos.	Building Programme	Estimated Cast
108	1963	£11,121,500
60	1964	£6,801,220

Repeating history, on 12 October 1960 the W&EC (Minute 1875/10) deferred a decision with respect to Hammond's memorandum pending further development of the benefits case.

A new scheme proposal was presented by the WR General Manager on 16 November 1960 with a 'beefed-up' financial case. The requirement for 239 locomotives remained unchanged, but the requirement for one new Type 2 locomotive was modified to Type 1, thereby increasing the Type 1 requirement to twelve. By the time of this memorandum the Type 1 locomotives were specifically quoted as *660hp* machines (at a significantly lower price), suggesting that design work at Swindon for this cheaper and lower horsepower type was now underway.

Revised locomotive costs and annual mileages were as follows:

No.	Type	Each	Gross cost	Predicted Miles p.a.	Comments
150	2700hp	£119,000	£17,850,000	79,640	Subsequently £117,000
69	1700hp	£80,000	£5,520,000	52,207	
8	1100hp	£75,000	£600,000	26,969	
12	660hp	£36,000	£432,000	26,558	
239			£24,402,000		

On 7 February 1961, the W&EC approved the Area No.3 (Stage 1) Scheme; documentation covering final BTC authorisation has not been found in the archives.

Although eight of the NBL Type 2 1100hp diesel-hydraulics were nominally included in the Area No.3 submissions, at no time were any of this Type actually allocated to the South Wales area either on initial introduction or later in life, although some of the Bristol-allocated locomotives worked in the Gloucester area in later years.

The Type 1 subject had obviously received considerable attention, with the estimated cost of £36,000 each being considerably less than the previous estimates of £58,000 and £75,000 each for the Type 1 and Type 2 locomotives respectively submitted six months earlier.

To complete the story, the six outstanding diesel-hydraulic Type 3s were authorised by the BTC on 8 February 1962 (Minute 15/39), but all further WR Type 3 requirements were satisfied by English Electric 1750hp diesel-electrics. Ultimately, all 150 Type 4s were built as diesel-electrics (Brush Type 4s) following the decision to dispense with diesel-hydraulic traction on cost grounds in mid-1962. The forty-four Swindon-designed 650hp Type 1 locomotives included in the combined Area No.1/2 submission and the twelve in the Area No.3 (Stage 1) submission were authorised by the BTC/BRB for construction on 8 February 1962 (26 locomotives) and 14 March 1963 (30).

1.9 D6358-D6377?

The revision of Types required as described in Sections 1.6 and 1.7 effectively saw the discontinuation of diesel-hydraulic Type 2s and their substitution by very basic Type 1s or more powerful Type 3s. The requirement for any further Type 2s was, therefore, formally eliminated by early/mid-1960. However, during mid-1960, the possibility of a further twenty diesel-hydraulic Type 2s manifested itself as a mechanism to provide continuity of production at NBL during a period of extreme financial difficulties and an impending shortage of orders.

A letter from Sir Brian Robertson (Chairman, BTC) to the Rt Hon Ernest Marples MP (Minister of Transport) dated 11 May 1960 represents the earliest document found within the National Archives on the subject (although correspondence had actually started over two months earlier):

I am glad to know from your letter of 29 April that you would like to have a chat with me about the affairs of NBL. You asked me in your letter to expand a little on the point which I made in mine to you of 25 April, that further orders for locomotives might not be forthcoming on strictly commercial grounds, and I think what I have to say below will clarify the matter.

In order that there may be no misapprehensions I should first of all say that the orders we have so far given to NBL were placed on strictly commercial and competitive grounds for locomotives of which we have a need. One of the types, a diesel-electric locomotive of 1100hp (*D6100-57*), has not been very successful and we do not intend to order any more. There are two other main types; a diesel-hydraulic locomotive for the Western Region of 2200hp (*D833-65*) … The number of locomotives of this type already ordered from NBL and our own shops fully meets our needs for locomotives of this type for the Western Region. The other type is an 1100hp diesel-hydraulic locomotive for the Western Region (*D6300-57*). Our requirements of these locomotives amount to 58, all of which have been ordered and are in course of delivery.

NBL, together with other manufacturers, will shortly be asked to tender for further requirements of diesel-electric locomotives for delivery in 1962 (*and 1963*). But the only thing which will help NBL at the present time is a repeat order of a type which they already have in production.

… As stated above, the Western Region have made provision for all the 2200hp locomotives they could economically employ. Their future intention in regard to a lower powered locomotive (the 1100hp diesel-hydraulic referred to above) is to go for a modified design of rather lower horse-power. But if asked to do so, the Region feels that they could accept a further 20 locomotives of identical design to the 58 which NBL are already delivering to us. These locomotives would cost us more than the same number of locomotives to the proposed new design … and it is because of this that a further order to tide NBL over their immediate difficulties would be placed on other than strictly commercial grounds.

I should let you know that at Mr. Coughtrie's and Lord Reith's (*both NBL*) request my people have seen them again today and have indicated that if your approval is forthcoming, the Commission would be prepared to assist the employment problem in Scotland and incidentally NBL to the extent of placing a repeat order of 20 1100hp locomotives for the Western Region to be delivered during 1961. Beyond this I do not feel we could go. Our investment for locomotives during 1961 is already fully taken up and it would be necessary for us to be given special dispensation, to the extent of approximately £1.5m., to enable the proposed order to be placed with NBL.

I am informed that Mr. Coughtrie and Lord Reith were very appreciative of what my people were able to tell them today and they will be approaching the Board of Trade again in regard to this matter and you will no doubt be hearing from them very shortly.

A Meeting between the Ministry of Transport (E. Marples MP, Sir James Dunnett, D. Serpell) and the BTC (Sir Brian Robertson, A.B.B. Valentine, J. Ratter) was held on 19 May. Notes from the meeting are given below:

North British Locomotive Company.
Mr. Ratter said that officials of the Commission had visited this firm and were satisfied that it was much better run than formerly … However, the position was that the BTC would not for their own purposes wish to order at present from NBL any more of the types of locomotive which that Company had recently built for the BTC.

The Commission would be going out to tender for a further batch of locomotives, but they would be for delivery at the end of 1963, which would be too late to tide the company over its more immediate difficulties. Mr. Ratter said that if HMG (*Her Majesty's Government*) so desired the Commission could order 20 diesel-hydraulic locomotives from NBL for delivery in 1961 and could 'profitably' employ them on the Western Region. However, the cost would be about £1½million, and the BTC had no spare capital available within their programme for 1961. Mr. Ratter admitted that the cost would be, to a large extent, bringing forward locomotive expenditure which the Commission would otherwise make in, say, 1963. But the present NBL types would probably be 10-15% more expensive in capital cost than those which the Commission would be able to have in 1963 or 1964. On operating costs the difference would be slight, but there might be a small disadvantage since most of the use to which the NBL locomotives would be put could probably be discharged by an 800hp locomotive instead of 1100hp …

Subsequent to this meeting Marples corresponded with the Rt Hon Reginald Maudling MP (President of the Board of Trade) on 25 May 1960, responding to a letter from him dated 10 March (one of the earliest pieces of correspondence amongst politicians regarding the plight of NBL and potential assistance in the form of a short-term additional order). Marples commented positively on the efforts being made by NBL senior management to turn the company around, but also recognised that an urgent follow-on order for twenty Type 2 diesel-hydraulics would be essential for NBL's survival. Marples also described NBL's current and potential future locomotive order book situation with the BTC, paraphrasing the contents Sir Brian Robertson's earlier letter of 11 May. Marples continued:

Against this background what the Commission are prepared to do, subject to an important overriding condition, is as follows. Although the diesel-electric locomotives for which the Commission will shortly be inviting the industry as a whole to tender will probably be some 10% cheaper in capital cost and slightly cheaper in running cost than the 1100hp diesel-hydraulic locomotives which they have ordered from NBL, they are prepared to order another 20 locomotives of the same design as those which NBL are already delivering, provided their investment ceiling for the year 1961 can be raised by £1.5m. There would, of course, be a corresponding reduction in the number of new diesel-electric locomotives they would order from the industry in later years. The immediate benefit to NBL would therefore be to the longer-term disadvantage of the industry as a whole at a time when their orders from the BTC will be running out fast.

It seems to me that, in the circumstances, the BTC's condition is a perfectly fair one. I must, however, make it quite clear, in view of the intense pressure on the investment programme for transport as a whole, that this £1.5m. must be additional to whatever figure is agreed between my Department and the Treasury for transport investment in 1961…..Provided the Treasury can agree that the £1.5m. in question is in a special category and will clearly be added to whatever is agreed between our two Departments, I for my part would be prepared to agree that the BTC should go ahead with this additional order with NBL on the lines they propose. The justification for

this course must, of course, be the urgent need to keep NBL alive. This is a matter for you and the Chancellor and not for me …

A copy of this letter goes to the Chancellor.

A letter from Rt Hon Derick Heathcoat-Amory MP (Chancellor of the Exchequer) to Marples dated 7 June 1960 (copy to Reginald Maudling) added a more pragmatic dimension to the debate now being carried out at a very high level:

You sent me a copy of your letter of 25 May to Maudling about the North British Locomotive Co.

In his letter to you on 10 March, Maudling says that he would not seek to influence the Commission in its choice of contractors for locomotives, and that this must be made on commercial grounds. I agree with him …

I think it would be quite wrong, at a time when it is necessary to try to reduce planned public investment somewhat, to increase the BTC's investment programme for 1961/62 in the way which you propose, so that they may order locomotives earlier than they want them. I would also think it quite wrong that they should be urged to order locomotives of a type which is apparently not the most economic. We are at present engaged in trying to get the Commission to look at investment projects in accordance with whether or not they are paying propositions, and it is not the time to press them to do something contrary to their own best commercial judgement.

While, therefore, I recognise that the Commission have approached the problem with every desire to help, I do not think we ought to ask them to act in this way.

A further meeting involving the Treasury, the Board of Trade and the Ministry of Transport was held on 8 June 1960. Minutes from the meeting record the subject under discussion as being 'The North British Locomotive Company and the Locomotive Industry'. Present were:

Treasury: Sir Frank Lee, M. Stevenson
Board of Trade: Sir Richard Powell, A.D. Neale
Ministry of Transport: Sir James Dunnett, T.F. Bird

Two problems were discussed, firstly the short-term issue of further orders for NBL, and, the longer-term problem of the future of the British locomotive industry as a whole. The following points quoted from the Minutes concentrate on the former:

North British Locomotive Company.
(a)   The central issue was whether the BTC's locomotive requirements under the modernisation programme

were such that they would not be met unless NBL continued to manufacture locomotives. Sir James Dunnett confirmed that this was not so. All the Commission's needs … could be met by the rest of the industry (excluding NBL) throughout the rest of the period of peak demand (i.e. up to 1963/4).

(b) The BTC orders on which NBL were at present working would be completed by June 1961. The company had no other current orders. They were competing for a large Belgian export order which would, if secured, keep them going for some time; but the Board of Trade were less optimistic than the Company of their chances of securing this contract. Unless, therefore, the BTC could give the Company some kind of follow-on order this summer, the Company's chances of surviving were remote.

(c) Even if NBL were given a BTC contract and/ or secured the Belgian contract, they would still be faced, at its completion, with the problem of competing in an increasingly difficult market … Given the long-term over-capacity in the British locomotive industry as a whole, diversification of production offered NBL their only firm long-term hope of keeping going …

(d) The BTC contract in question consisted of 20 diesel-hydraulic locomotives which the Commission did not require until 1962 or 1963. Also, the locomotives the Commission really needed in those years would probably be some 10% cheaper in capital cost and slightly cheaper in running cost than the 1100hp diesel-hydraulic locomotives which had already been ordered from NBL. If, therefore, the Government agreed to the BTC's suggestion that they should be allowed to order another 20 locomotives of the same design as those which NBL were now making for them:

   (i) the Government would be agreeing to the BTC acting on grounds which were neither strictly commercial nor competitive: this would be contrary to the Commission's basic policy and their financial interests,

   (ii) such action would also be out of line with Government policy in the whole field of assistance to industry, in that it would be the first occasion on which an industry has been kept going by unnecessarily expensive orders placed in anticipation of need,

   (iii) given the long-term over-capacity of the British locomotive industry as a whole, the immediate effect to NBL of such an order would be to the longer term disadvantage of the industry as a whole.

(e) For all these reasons it was agreed that it would not be fitting for the Government to encourage and assist the Commission to place a further immediate order with NBL. If NBL had to be kept going for social reasons, then it might be necessary to consider direct Government assistance to the Company to facilitate diversification of production. Any such assistance would be made from BOTAC (*Board of Trade Advisory Committee*) funds, and would require justification and examination on the usual criteria.

(f) It was agreed that Sir Richard Powell should report the conclusions recorded in (e) above to the President (*of the Board of Trade*), and obtain his views. The President would then reply to the Minister of Transport's letter of 25 May and, assuming the line proposed was acceptable to both Ministers, the Ministry of Transport would then have to speak to the BTC. The Government's decision would also have to be communicated to NBL.

At this point the archive goes quiet. However, a document entitled *Background Paper re. NBL*, produced by E.C.V. Goad (Ministry of Transport) on 9 February 1961, described how the subject played out. This document is incomplete, but the following extracts are pertinent:

In March last the President of the Board of Trade brought to the (*Transport*) Minister's attention representations he had had from Mr. Coughtrie and Lord Reith of the Company (*NBL*) who wished to get orders from the BTC … The Minister passed these representations on to Sir Brian Robertson, and the BTC then … prematurely told NBL that they would help them by placing a repeat order for 20 diesel-hydraulic locomotives for 1961 delivery if they could get the Minister's approval. Sir Brian asked as a condition of this that the Minister should give the Commission a special allocation for investment purposes of £1½m. This premature approach by the BTC caused some embarrassment when, after discussion and correspondence, the matter eventually came before the Cabinet. On the 25 June, 1960, after previous discussion at the Economic Policy Committee … the Cabinet considered a paper by the President of the Board of Trade in which he suggested that he would not be justified in asking the Chancellor and the Minister to take exceptional measures to meet the Company's immediate problem. The Cabinet agreed … that the BTC should not be authorised to place a repeat order for locomotives with the Company.

NBL ultimately went into liquidation on 19 April 1962.

Chapter 2

FINANCIAL CONSIDERATIONS

2.1 'Excess' Costs

The initial estimated cost of the D6300-5 batch of locomotives put forward by the Works & Equipment Committee and authorised by the BTC in early 1955 was £50,000 each but once quotes had been received from NBL this figure increased to £53,000 although the increase was not officially authorised by the BTC until 1958.

The £53,000 quote for D6300-5 was subsequently used by the W&EC and authorised by the BTC two years later, in February 1957, for the D6306-57 batch; however, the subsequent quote received from NBL for D6306-57 at £63,175 each far exceeded their previous quote for D6300-5.

NBL's quote for D6300-5 proved to be severely understated and they looked to secure an ex-gratia payment to cover costs in excess of their £53,000 quotation.

Further discussion on these topics is provided below in chronological order.

2.1.1 'Excess' Cost (D6306-57).

A Memorandum to the Works & Equipment Committee dated 18 June 1957 entitled *1958 Locomotive Building Programme. Western Region Supplementary Programme. 1000hp Diesel-Hydraulic Locomotives* sets the scene and offered two recommendations:

> Included in the 1958 WR Supplementary Programme, authorised by BTC Minute No.10/81, are 52 1000hp diesel-hydraulic main-line locomotives to be obtained from NBL, at an estimated cost of £53,000 each. This estimated amount was based on the price quoted for the six identical locomotives which are currently under construction by NBL for the WR.
>
> However, it is clear from an up-to-date quotation received from the firm, that the estimated price per locomotive will be exceeded by approximately £10,175. This additional amount covers general price increases since the date of the original quotation, modifications which have been made to the original design to meet BR requirements, and provision for inter-changeability of diesel engine and transmission units.
>
> The total additional expenditure over the original estimated cost of £2,756,000 amounts to £529,100 (approx. 19%) though the WR General Manager after re-examining the West of England Area Scheme is satisfied that there will be no significant effect on the 'shot' financial improvement of £300,000 p.a. mentioned in the memorandum to the Works & Equipment Committee for the WR 1958 Supplementary Programme dated 20 February 1957.
>
> It is therefore recommended that:
>
> (a) authority be given for the total additional expenditure of £529,100 to be associated with the 1958 Locomotive Building Programme;
> (b) the revised tender from NBL should be accepted for the 52 1000hp diesel-hydraulic main-line locomotives and orders placed for these locomotives at a total price of £3,285,100.
>
> The WR General Manager is in agreement with these proposals.

At the W&EC meeting on 26 June 1957 (Minute 936/31), the Committee decided to put forward the two recommendations for authorisation by the BTC on the basis that 'there was no practicable alternative to purchasing the locomotives from NBL'. The BTC, however, were not so forgiving and at their meeting on 27 June 1957 (Meeting No.10/269) issued the instruction that 'NBL be informed that the Commission were unwilling to accept the price offered by the Company'.

Three months later a memorandum from the BTC General Staff was circulated to the W&EC; unfortunately, this document has not been unearthed. It is, however, referenced in the W&EC meeting minutes dated 11 September 1957 (Minute No.988/21) as follows:

D6329, Aller Junction, Undated. (David Dunn Collection)

Submitted, memorandum dated 6 September 1957 by General Staff. The Committee noted that every endeavour had been made to obtain a reduction in price but without success and, in the circumstances, agreed to recommend to the Commission that approval be given to an additional expenditure of £529,100 and that the revised tender from NBL, at a total price of £3,285,100, be accepted.

This recommendation was passed onto the BTC for authorisation and duly authorised on 19 September 1957 (Meeting Minute No.10/405).

It is clear that the W&EC should have obtained up-to-date quotes from NBL before submitting the 1958 Locomotive Building Programme for authorisation by the BTC and it was unreasonable for the BTC to effectively ask for a reduced quotation subsequent to the tendering process.

The price paid by BR for D6306-57 was the NBL quoted figure of £63,175, subject to any price variation adjustments. Technically this should not be considered to be an 'excess'

cost, rather slightly dubious administrative arrangements on the part of the BTC.

What is more interesting, however, is the price hike between D6300-5 (£53,000) and D6306-57 (£63,175) and at least part is probably associated with extremely competitive tendering for the 'Pilot-Scheme' batch by NBL in 1955.

According to Brian Reed (*Diesel-Hydraulic Locomotives of the Western Region*, 1974) the price quoted by NBL for the D6306-57 batch was £61,700 whereas the W&EC archives indicate £63,175. This difference is probably explainable by the fact that NBL quoted for a 'standard' locomotive, rather than incorporating the facility for engine/transmission inter-changeability, features which attracted an additional cost of £1,450 per locomotive (see Section 3.12 for further details). Reed suggests a final price of about £64,500 including price variation, which may also have included further modification costs (Reed mentions the installation of pre-heaters at an additional £475 per locomotive, for example).

NBL Drawing Office charges for D6300-5 totalled about £15,000. Despite the fact that D6306-57 were essentially intended to be a repeat of the first six, the additional drawing office charges still grossed out at over £6,000. Quite how these costs were dealt with between BR and NBL is not known.

2.1.2 'Excess' Cost (D6300-5).

BTC authorisation for the excess cost of the D6300-5 batch was a very small part of a submission made to the Works & Equipment Committee by the Western Area Board on 14 May 1958 regarding the additional expenditure of £1,586,950 associated with Area Scheme No.1 (West of England) locomotive requirements.

The 'big-ticket' item was £1,535,400 associated with the additional estimated expenditure for construction of the 2000/2200hp 'Warship' locomotives (built by both NBL and BR Swindon). A 'mere' £79,050 was attributable to the six 1000hp NBL 'Pilot Scheme' locomotives (i.e. £13,175 per locomotive). To keep the mathematics right, the total excess expenditure within the Western Area Board submission to the W&EC was partially offset by transferring an order for two shunting locomotives, worth £27,500, into a later Building Programme.

The excess £79,050 cost associated with D6300-5 was made up of:

- The difference between BR's assumed cost of £50,000 and the subsequent NBL quotation of £53,000 (i.e. £3,000), and,
- The difference between NBL's quotations for D6300-5 (£53,000) and D6306-57 (£63,175) (i.e. £10,175).

Authorisation for the £3,000 makes sense, but the additional £10,175 implies that NBL had approached the BTC for an uplifted price for D6300-5, aligned to the cost of D6306-57. However, no evidence of such an approach has been found in the archives.

A separate Memorandum from K.W.C. Grand, General Manager (WR) dated 14 May 1958 explained that 'the increase is in the main due to under-estimation of the cost of building the new type of power, including inadequate allowance for purchased components other than engines and transmissions; modifications to meet technical requirements; and the general increase in the level of prices.'

Grand's comments were largely associated with the considerable 'excess' costs associated with the 'Warship' locomotives and their revised physical construction demands. Quite how the £79,050 increase for the D6300-5 locomotives is justified is unclear, unless seen in the context of NBL trying to correct overly competitive pricing.

A Memorandum to the Works & Equipment and Supply Committees dated 5 June 1958 entitled *Locomotive Building & Condemnation Programmes: Western Region Area No.1 Scheme* broadly repeated Grand's earlier memorandum and concluded with a recommendation to the W&EC to approve the additional costs.

The W&EC, at their meeting on 25 June 1958 (Minute No.1217/22), decided to approve the additional costs and sought authorisation from the BTC. The Committee noted that 'there is no question of re-opening the case for and against diesel-hydraulic locomotives as opposed to diesel-electric locomotives in respect of Area No.1.'

A BTC meeting was held on 26 June 1958 but there is no reference in the minutes to the authorisation of the additional costs. It appears, however, that the BTC did not pay anywhere near the estimated cost of £63,175 for D6300-5, with a figure of £53,000 being much closer to the mark albeit subject to the usual price variations over the period between contract placement and locomotive delivery. Brian Reed indicates a final price of the order of £55,000.

2.2 NBL Ex-Gratia Payment Request (D6300-5).

As with a number of other archive topics there are gaps in available correspondence on this somewhat murky subject; however, sufficient material is available to achieve an insight into the financial discussions taking place during late-1961 and early-1962 regarding NBL attempts to secure additional money to cover the design and construction costs of D6300-5. That NBL ultimately failed in this attempt was another 'nail in the coffin' with respect to the survival of the company.

The basis of NBL's claim for an ex-gratia payment was made using the 'price variation' clause associated with quotes accepted at the time of order placement. Price variations allowed for inflation (covering wages, raw material costs, etc) between the time of order placement and the time of the contracted locomotive delivery date. In the case of the D6300-5 contract, NBL tried to apply the 'price variation' clause to the actual (later) delivery date contesting that the delivery delays were caused by BR rather than NBL.

The contracted delivery date for D6300-5 was 'To begin in 18 months from date of order at the rate of 2 locomotives per month' i.e. mid-May to mid-July 1957. The actual Swindon delivery dates achieved were D6300-2 (December 1958) and D6303-5 (May, June and August 1959 respectively).

Under normal circumstances, late orders were dealt with separately via a 'liquidated damages' clause within the contract.

A letter from R.J. Kirkman (Administration Controller, NBL) to an unspecified person within the BTC dated 19 September 1961 picks up the story:

<u>Five 2000hp and six 1000hp DH Locomotives.</u>
We refer to recent correspondence with the Accountant, Western Region, on the deduction of £19,509.10s.11d in relation to the 2000hp locomotive contract and the deduction of £19,574.9s.8d in relation to the 1000hp locomotive contract. From their letter of 30 August 1961 we understand that all correspondence has been sent to you and that the instruction to make these deductions emanated from your headquarters.

Our views were expressed in a letter dated 2 November 1959 addressed to Mr. Webb, Regional Accountant, WR, wherein we stated that these two contracts were clearly of a developmental nature as the locomotives were prototypes. In view of this contractual delivery dates could not possibly be used to calculate price variation claims.

The continual modification discussions which took place with your engineers before and during production affected these delivery dates and if reference is made to your engineers they will agree with this statement. Apart from the knowledge of your engineers, it is undoubtedly a fact that these two contracts were the first main-line diesel locomotives of BR. The prototype design is also recognised by the fact that the order was for very small quantities …

Mr. E.S. Cox in his lecture *British Railways' Experience with Diesel and Electric Traction* given in March 1961 on behalf of UKRAS says:

'In the beginning, in the first 174 <u>prototype</u> main-line diesels which were ordered in 1955, hydraulic transmissions were ordered for the Western Region, and electric for the others, with some idea that merit might be established as a guide to future policy (our underlining of the word 'prototype').

The office of the Chief Mechanical and Electrical Engineer of the WR will vouch for the fact that the drawings for these prototype locomotives were delayed because many discussions and much correspondence had to take place with them, BTC and stylists. At least three different designs were prepared for the 1000hp locomotive … Discussions between BR and this company began in January 1955 and continued throughout that year at roughly two-monthly intervals until July 1956. The notes taken at these meetings confirm the numerous changes in design …

There were innumerable separate discussions on styling and we had to prepare a full-size mock-up of the cab and controls.

Having already expressed our dissatisfaction to the Treasurer in our letter of 31 July 1961 and in

view of the foregoing we would ask you to rescind your previous instruction and have payment of the £39,084.0s.7d effected.

It appears that T. Coughtrie (Chairman, NBL) subsequently escalated matters, and, as a consequence, S.C. Robbins (Chief Contracts Officer, BTC) wrote the following letter to Coughtrie on 28 December 1961:

<u>5 2000hp and 6 1000hp Diesel-Hydraulic Locomotives.</u>
I refer to your letter of the 18 December, 1961, and to earlier correspondence and discussions regarding the price variation claims relating to the above contracts …

When we last discussed the matter I pointed out the basis on which your claims had been prepared was contrary to the terms of the contracts but promised to consider the matter further. I have now ascertained the facts and there do not appear to be any grounds which would justify an ex-gratia payment.

In earlier correspondence the Company suggested a concession could be made because of the prototype nature of the orders. While this is a valid argument for relieving the company of liability for damages arising from the delay in delivery, it does not seem reasonable to expect the Commission to pay a higher price because the Company misjudged the time required for designing and producing the locomotives. Our technical supervision seems to have been in line with normal procedure, and in this connection I have been advised by the Region that they are unaware of any circumstances which would have justified an extension of the contract period, if such an application had been made at the time. A number of similar contracts were placed with other suppliers at about the same time and in most cases the deliveries were late, but price variation claims were prepared and paid in accordance with the terms of the contracts …

I very much regret that I feel unable to recommend to the Commission that a further concession should be made.

Coughtrie responded to Robbins on 2 February 1962:

<u>5 2000hp and 6 1000hp Diesel-Hydraulic Locomotives.</u>
I refer … to your letter of 28 December.

The essence of the matter is, of course, the fact that because of the prototype nature of these orders and the time involved in discussing with the Commission's Staff the details of design, the contractual date should have been adjusted by agreement at the time. I regard this as a purely technical matter which, had the application been made, would have been readily conceded by your engineers and contract department. It does not, therefore, seem to me unreasonable that the Commission should pay a higher price …

You will recall that I mentioned this matter to Dr. Beeching … and I would be grateful if I could have your assurance that the matter has been referred to him before a final decision is made. I do feel strongly that we have a very reasonable claim on the Commission for this modest sum.

The BTC Chief Contracts Officer sent a memorandum to the Supply Committee on 12 February 1962 and repeated much of the content of his letter to Coughtrie on 28 December 1961; this memorandum contained a few additional details, notably that:

- the WR accountants had failed to notice the £39,000 'overcharge' and because of this 'oversight, these claims were paid by the Region as submitted'. When the mistake was discovered, the overpayment was deducted from payments due under other contracts.
- 'deliveries ranged from 12 to 28 months late', and,
- 'the contracts mentioned are among those for which the Commission decided to abandon claims for damage for late delivery, on the grounds that on balance it would have been contrary to the Commission's interest to pursue them'. The ex-gratia claim by NBL was considerably less than NBL's total liability for liquidated damages resulting from late delivery.

The Memorandum was discussed at the BTC Supply Committee Meeting on 15 February 1962 and the NBL ex-gratia claim clearly moved onto delays caused by design and styling issues rather than engineering and technical. Minute 1062 recorded:

North British Locomotive Co. Ltd.
The Chief Contracts Officer was asked to obtain further information from the Region in regard to the contention of the Company that the requirements of the stylists had contributed to the delay in delivery, to enable further consideration to be given to the matter at the next meeting.

A further Memorandum from the Chief Contracts Officer to the Supply Committee was produced on 26 February 1962:

North British Locomotive Co. Ltd.
1. With reference to Committee Minute 1062, the Design Officer [G.E. Williams] was invited to comment on the Company's contention that the requirements of the stylists contributed significantly to the delay in delivery of the initial batches of diesel-hydraulic locomotives. He has replied as follows:

The locomotives … were, in common with others ordered under the Pilot Scheme, developed before the Design Panel was set up. There was, however, an arrangement between all concerned that proper attention should be given to questions of appearance and amenity and Mr. Barman arranged for consultant designers to collaborate with the Headquarters and Regional Engineering staff and with those contractors concerned.

NBL had, however, already accepted the responsibility for 'styling' their own locomotives and had by that time already appointed their own design consultant, Mr. J. McCrum. The responsibility for all aspects of the design … were, therefore, the Company's, but it was quite natural that we should be asked to report from time to time on progress and development.

In their letter of the 2 February, the Company states that 'there were innumerable separate discussions on styling and we had to prepare a full-size mock-up of the cab and controls.' There is nothing unusual about either of these two activities. Undoubtedly there would need to be discussions with their own designers during the development of the prototype locomotives and the construction of a cab mock-up is essential in the case of a new locomotive in order to produce a real basis for the necessary discussions on cab amenity with Union representatives.

Under the circumstances, they cannot expect the Commission to accept an extra charge for work which is normal to the proper development of any product, the financial implications of which must have been taken into account at the time.

2. I am still of the opinion the circumstances do not justify an ex-gratia payment and particularly so as this would involve treating NBL more generously than the other contractors who received orders under the Pilot Scheme referred to by the Design Officer.

The Supply Committee Meeting Minute No. 1074 of 2 March 1962 recorded that an ex-gratia payment to NBL to reflect the impact of design and styling factors on final delivery times could not be justified.

As already stated, it appears that BR actually paid £53,000 for each of the 'Pilot-Scheme' locomotives plus price variations applicable between the order placement date and the contracted delivery date.

2.3 NBL Liquidation

Following a prolonged period of financial difficulties, NBL went into liquidation on 19 April 1962. Complete locomotives contracts outstanding on this date were:

- Two of thirty-three Type 4 'Warship' locomotives (D864/5). D864 was expected to be delivered imminently and D865 by end-May 1962, and,
- Seventeen of fifty-two Type 2 locomotives (D6341-57), three of which were expected imminently. The Liquidators proposed to complete the contract, with delivery by end-August 1962.

BR's initial expectation was that delivery of the locomotives would trigger payment in accordance with the conditions of contract, after deducting 'liquidated damages' for delays in completion. This deduction was contested by the Liquidators, but it is unclear from the available archives how this issue was resolved.

A Memorandum to the Supply Committee dated 26 June 1962 reported that eleven of the seventeen outstanding Type 2s and both of the Type 4s had been delivered to the Western Region. The Memorandum went on to comment that:

Whilst the liquidators are making every effort to continue deliveries … they have not formally adopted the contracts. Before doing so they wish to commute the liability under the conditions of contract to rectify defects of workmanship and material for twelve months after acceptance of the locomotives … They have in mind firstly the undetermined amount which may be involved which precludes an interim dividend, and, secondly the need to continue the liquidation until after the end of the 'guarantee' period. The liability arises on the equivalent of 9 Type 4 and 21 Type 2 locomotives …

As a result of negotiation with the liquidators a tentative settlement has been reached whereby on the payment by NBL of £65,000 for the locomotives … the Commission would relieve the liquidators of the liability. The overall figure of £65,000 for both types of locomotives is equivalent to £2,167 per locomotive. Past experience indicates that a settlement on this basis would provide a reserve more than adequate to meet the extra cost of maintenance likely to be incurred by the Commission. The Chief Mechanical Engineer concurs and the Committee's approval of the proposed settlement is requested.

The Supply Committee approved the proposed settlement at their Meeting on 28 June 1962 (Minute 1127), thereby effectively reducing the ex-Works price paid for D6337-57 to £61,008.

2.4 D63xx Diesel-Hydraulic v. D61xx Diesel-Electric Price Comparisons

	Contract Price	Contract Date	Actual Price Paid (per Brian Reed)
D6300-05	£53,000	16/11/55	~£55,000 (inc. price variations)
D6306-57	£63,175	05/11/57	~£64,500 (D6306-31)/ ~£64,750 (D6332-57) (inc. price variations and up-grade modifications)
D6100-09	£62,400	16/11/55	~£65,000 (inc. price variations)
D6110-37	£66,800	01/05/57	~£68,200 (inc. price variations)
D6138-57	£73,850	14/07/58	?

Notes:
1. D6300-5: 18 per cent lower than D6100-9, maybe, in part, in the hope of securing further orders (a 'loss-leader').
2. D6306-57: A more realistic 8 per cent lower than D6110-37.

Chapter 3

TECHNICAL ASPECTS

3.1 Preamble

Much of the technical information regarding the D63xx locomotives produced in railway journals in the early days related to the production locomotives (D6306-57). It is possible that this bias was deliberate on BR's part to ensure the release of information appertaining to their most modern equipment. Whilst this is understandable, it does make the whole process of understanding the key differences between the 'Pilot Scheme' and the production locomotives more difficult. Major differences were described (e.g., engine, transmission, cooling system up-grades) to illustrate technological advancement but some of the more subtle variations were less well publicised (e.g., cab and general equipment layout changes, control system changes, weight-saving initiatives, alternative braking and train-heating arrangements, etc).

Every effort has been made to tease out as many of the differences as possible, but I believe that some differences still remain to be explicitly identified.

3.2 Locomotive Classifications

Classification System	D6300-5	D6306-57
WR	6300	6306
BR (1955)	D10/2	D11/5
BR (1962)	10/4A	11/4A
BR (1968/73 TOPS)	22	22

The first two numerals of the 1955 and 1962 systems indicated the locomotive's horsepower in hundreds. The second numerical part of the 1955 system differentiated the various locomotive types within the defined horsepower rating, whereas in the 1962 system the suffix number specifically defined the manufacturer of the locomotive with '4' the allotted number for NBL; it was necessary to use a final suffix 'A' for the D63xxs to allow differentiation from the D6100-57 locomotives.

3.3 Leading Particulars.

D6300-5

Engine: One NBL/MAN L12V18/21A, 12-cylinder, 4-stroke, 180mm (7.087in) bore, 210mm (8.268in) stroke.

Maximum continuous rated output: 1,000hp at 1,445rpm.

Transmission: Voith/NBL L306r.

Control system: BTH (electro-pneumatic).

Multiple-working code (introduced 1961): 'Orange Square' (up to three locomotives, compatibility with D600-4 and other D6300-5 only).

Performance (based on BR Diagrams):

Maximum Tractive Effort: 41,920lb at 27.6% adhesion.

Continuous Tractive Effort: 23,900b at 10.4mph with 927hp input to the transmission.

Braking: Air for locomotive and vacuum for train giving brake force of 78.18% of locomotive weight in working order.

Minimum Curve Negotiable: 4.5 chains (min. radius curve without gauge widening at dead slow speed).

Bogie Wheelbase: 8ft 6in.

Total Wheelbase: 31ft 6in.

Bogie Centres: 23ft 0in.

Wheel Diameter: 3ft 7in.

Width overall: 8ft 8in.

Height overall: 12ft 10in.

Length overall: 46ft 8½in.

Weight (in working order): 67t 16cwt.

Axle Weights (in working order): A-end bogie: 16t 18cwt, B-end bogie: 17t 0cwt.

Weight of Diesel Engine (inc. bedplate): 4.25t.

Fuel Tank Capacity (engine & boiler): 450gal.

Cooling Water Capacity: 135gal.

Boiler Water Capacity: 500gal.

Train-Heating Equipment: Spanner Swirlyflo (steaming capacity 1,000lb/hr).

Wheel Arrangement: B-B.

Maximum Permitted Speed: 75mph.

Route Availability: 4, or, 'Yellow Circle' (maximum 16t axle-loading). See Notes below.

D6306-25 (where different from above)

Engine: One NBL/MAN L12V18/21BS, 12-cylinder, 4-stroke.

Maximum continuous rated output: 1,100hp at 1,530rpm.

Transmission: Voith/NBL LT306r.

Control system: Brown-Boveri (all-electric).

Multiple-working code (introduced 1961): 'White Diamond' (up to three locomotives, but compatibility with D803-70 and other D6306-57 only).

Performance (based on BR Diagrams):

Maximum Tractive Effort: 40,000lb at 27.6% adhesion.

Continuous Tractive Effort: 30,000lb at 8mph with 1,036hp input to the transmission.

Braking: Air for locomotive and vacuum for train giving brake force of 74.18% of locomotive weight in working order.

Weight (in working order): 64t 14cwt.

Axle Weights (in working order):

A-end bogie: 16t 5cwt, B-end bogie: 16t 2cwt.

Train-Heating Equipment: Clayton RO-100 (steaming capacity 1,000lb/hr [1,035lb/hr per DLRC]).

Route Availability: 4, or, 'Yellow Circle' (maximum 16t axle-loading). See notes below.

D6326-57 (where different from above):

Performance (based on BR Diagrams):

Maximum Tractive Effort: 40,180lb at 27.6% adhesion.

Continuous Tractive Effort: 30,000lb at 8mph.

Braking: Air for locomotive and vacuum for train giving brake force of 73.84% of locomotive weight in working order.

Weight (in working order): 65t 0cwt.

Axle Weights (in working order):

A-end bogie: 16t 6cwt, B-end bogie: 16t 4cwt.

Train-Heating Equipment: Stone-Vapor OK4610 (steaming capacity 1,000lb/hr).

Data Panel Information (1968) (D6306-57)

Class	22
Weight tons	68
Brake Force tons	29
RA	4
Max Speed mph	75

Notes:

1. Weight

D6300-05

The pre-construction NBL Drawing Office estimated weight for the 'Pilot Scheme' locomotives was 64t, giving a 16t axle-loading.

When completed D6300 weighed 61.4t 'dry', increasing to 67.2t with the full complement of fuel, oil, water, etc. When all modifications had been made and ATC equipment fitted, the 'dry' weight was 62.3t and the fully laden weight 68t.

The approximate weight summary was: mechanical portion 39.5t; engine and associated equipment 11.25t; transmission 8.8t; electrical equipment 2.75t. Within the mechanical portion, the bogies (including wheels, axles, axle drives and brake gear) accounted for 25.2t, the mainframe 7.5t, and the superstructure 4.5t.

A letter from NBL to BTC CM&EE Department, Swindon, dated 27 November 1957 regarding the weight of the D6300-5 batch commented that:

"The latest detailed examination of the total weight of the above locomotive indicates that the axle-load will be 17tons instead of the 16tons specified. The weight increase is partly due to increases in weights of bought-in equipment and to casting weights which have been underestimated.

"In order to avoid delay in completion of the locomotives by large scale revision of parts already completed or in course of manufacture, we should be glad to know if you would accept the increases in axle-load as stated."

BR's immediate response has not been found in the archives but the excess weight was ultimately accepted (see also following Section).

D6306-57

The estimated weight for the production batch was 65t, a calculation which proved to be accurate. Each locomotive in the D6306-25 batch weighed 60.2t 'dry' and 64.7t fully laden; for D6326-57 locomotives weighed an additional 0.3t, reflecting the heavier Stone-Vapor boiler.

Quite what caused the 1968 Data Panel weight figure to be increased to 68 tons for this batch is unknown.

2. Route Availability

The WR route availability colour-code system allowed for locomotives with 'Blue Circle' and 'Yellow Circle' restrictions access to lines with a 17.6t and 16t maximum axle weight respectively.

Given that the weight of all of the various sub-series was above 64t (in full working order) and, therefore, over 16t axle-load, then all should technically have been allocated the 'Blue Circle' code. However, photographic evidence shows that, in reality, D6306-57 were all allocated the 'Yellow Circle' code as indeed were the D6300-5 series, at least in later life. Good quality colour shots of D6300-5 in their early days are somewhat hard to come by and I have only seen two showing the 'Blue Circle' coding on the cab side, as follows:

- D6300, May 1965 (MLI197 [p59]), but previously illustrated in as-built condition with 'Yellow Circle' (p42).
- D6302, Undated (1962) (*Diesel Hydraulics: A Colour Perspective*, 2021 [p53]).

Trains Illustrated magazine (May 1959) states, 'It is reported that these locomotives (D6300-5) have been placed in the WR yellow route restriction category, which should give them as wide a route availability as a 45xx 2-6-2 tank.'

However, Hugh Dady in his D63xx class introduction in MLI197 comments that 'Route availability determined by axle-loading was shown as 'Blue Circle' for the "Pilot" machines, "Yellow Circle" for the majority of the production run, but with some locomotives of the final batch "Blue Circle".'

No photographic evidence has been seen of any locomotive in the final, slightly heavier, D6326-57 batch with anything other than 'Yellow Circle'.

It may be that either the NBL Type 2s were given special dispensation, the WR relaxing the definition of the various colour codes at some point either reflecting the abolition of steam (and their associated additional 'hammer-blow' forces to the track), or following Region-wide civil engineering upgrading.

According to Hugh Dady (via e-mail), 'There were several debates at the time as to whether axle-loading should be based on the weight of a loco empty or with a full (or even half) load of fuel/water/oil.'

Mark Parsons (also via e-mail) suggests that the 16.25t axle-loading for the D6306-57 batch was 'much closer to yellow than blue and thus it would have been ignored.' Given that the WR had no lighter alternative diesel-hydraulic motive power available (until the Class 14s arrived) this may very well have been the case.

3. Multiple-Working

In 1962 the 'Orange Square' multiple-unit coupling code was prescribed for D6300-5 and D600-4; similarly, the 'White Diamond' code for D6306-57 and D803-70. It was intended that these codes be painted on the buffer beams although no photographic evidence of this has been found, with the exception of the eight locomotives painted in the BFY(v2) livery during 1970/71 (see Volume 2).

4. Speed

Despite the D6300s having a top designed speed of 75mph, they rarely, if ever, achieved that figure, even when working in tandem or multiple with D600 or D800 locomotives; the West Country lines and services were hardly suitable for such speeds!

Garry Morris in his article 'D63xx' in *Traction* magazine (No.206) stated that: 'Originally designed for 90mph, their over-speed relay was recalibrated to 80mph, reflecting their changing role to secondary duties off the main line.' Morris also lists D6326 as being 'The first locomotive to be recalibrated to 80mph max speed'.

These comments are incorrect. All locomotives were designed and operated with a maximum speed of 75mph. An internal NBL memo dated 30 October 1959 stated that the original overspeed relay was set to trip at 90mph, but that BR Swindon had issued an instruction on 22 September to re-set these relays to trip at 80mph. At the time of the memo D6306-25 had already been fitted with the original relays set to trip at 90mph and the memo stated that BR would carry out the necessary modifications on these locomotives. The remaining thirty-two locomotives (D6326-57) were fitted with relays set to trip at 80mph by NBL.

5. Tractive Effort

The Maximum Tractive Effort entry on the Diesel Locomotive Record Card for D6320 gives 40,090lb at 27.6 per cent adhesion, the average of the figures given for D6306-25 and D6326-57 on the BR Main-Line Locomotive Diagrams (see pages 24–25). Coincidental or deliberate?

3.4 Diagrams

Diagram DH/2100/1. D6300-5 Side-Elevation. NBL/MAN engine rated at 1,000hp, NBL/Voith L306r transmission and Spanner Swirlyflo train-heating boiler. Note the incorrect reference to the BS version of the NBL/MAN engine rather than L12 V18/21A. The Swindon CM&EE stipulated the use of 'A-end' and 'B-end' (as opposed to 'No.1' and 'No.2') in a letter to NBL dated 11 February 1958. (BR Main-Line Diesel Locomotive Diagrams, 1961)

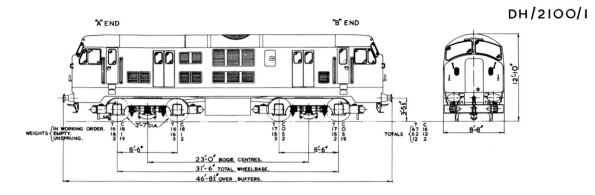

1000 H.P. N.B.L. TYPE 2 B-B DIESEL HYDRAULIC LOCOMOTIVE.

Diagram DH/2100/2. D6306-25 Side-Elevation. NBL/MAN engine rated at 1,100hp, NBL/Voith LT306r transmission and Clayton train-heating boiler. The diagrams used for all three versions of the NBL Type 2s were identical and did not illustrate the subtle changes consequent from the design upgrades; thus Diagram DH/2100/2 did not include the modified body-side radiator grille arrangement. The change to the boiler exhaust port resultant from the deployment of the Clayton boiler was also not incorporated in the Diagram; in fact, all three diagrams failed to include the boiler exhaust port at all! (BR Main-Line Diesel Locomotive Diagrams, 1961)

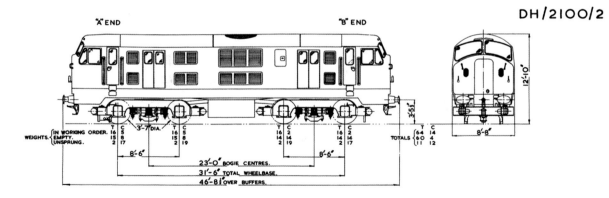

1100 H.P. N.B.L. TYPE 2 B-B DIESEL HYDRAULIC LOCOMOTIVE.

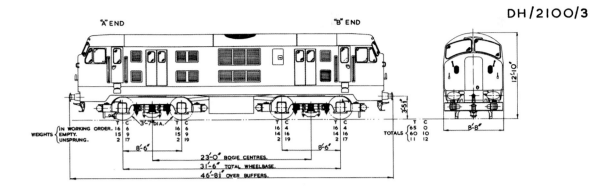

DH/2100/3

"A" END   "B" END

	T	C	
WEIGHTS	IN WORKING ORDER.	16	6
	EMPTY.	15	9
	UNSPRUNG.	2	17

3'-7" DIA.

8'-6"

23'-0" BOGIE CENTRES.
31'-6" TOTAL WHEELBASE.
46'-8¼" OVER BUFFERS.

TOTALS

12'-0"

3'-5¾"

8'-8"

ENGINE.	No. MAKE & TYPE.	ONE. N.B.L.-M.A.N. L.I2 V 18/21 B.S.	SPEED.	MAX. PERMITTED SERVICE SPEED.	75 M.P.H.
	No. OF CYLS. & CYCLE.	12 CYLS. 4 STROKE.	CURVE.	MIN. RAD. CURVE	WITHOUT GAUGE WIDENING: 4½ CHAINS.
	MAX. CONT. RATED OUTPUT.	1100 H.P. AT 1530 R.P.M.			AT DEAD SLOW SPEED: 4½ CHAINS.
TRANSMISSION.	TYPE & OTHER PARTICULARS.	VOITH-NORTH BRITISH LT.306r.			
PERFORMANCE	MAX. TRACTIVE EFFORT.	40180 LB. AT 27.6% ADHESION.	TRAIN HEATING EQUIPMENT.	BOILER MAKE & TYPE.	STONE-VAPOR OK.4610.
	CONT. TRACTIVE EFFORT.	30000 LB. AT 8 M.P.H.		STEAMING CAPACITY.	1000 LB./HOUR.
BRAKING.	TYPE	FOR LOCO. AIR.	TANK CAPACITIES.	ENGINE FUEL	450 GALLS.
		FOR TRAIN. VACUUM.		BOILER FUEL	
	BRAKE FORCE.	% OF LOCO. WEIGHT IN WORKING ORDER. 73.84%.		BOILER WATER.	500 GALLS.

Diagram DH/2100/3. D6326-57 Side-Elevation. NBL/MAN engine rated at 1,100hp, NBL/Voith LT306r transmission and Stone-Vapor train-heating boiler. Again, the original 'Pilot Scheme' radiator grille was incorrectly illustrated, and, no boiler exhaust port included. These diagrams were published prior to commencement of the use of head-code boxes. (BR Main-Line Diesel Locomotive Diagrams, 1961)

A-end   B-end

D6325   D6325

12'-10" OVER PANELS

3'-5¾"

8'-6"   3'-7" DIA.   8'-6"

23'-0" BOGIE PIVOT CRS.
46'-8¼" OVER BUFFERS.

8'-8" OVER PANELS

SCALE. FT
0 1 2 3 4 5 6 7 8 9 10

1. N.B.L./M.A.N. ENGINE.	6. TURBO.CHARGER.	11. COOLING WATER FAN.		16. WATER TANK FILLER.	21. FLEXIBLE GANGWAY.
2. N.B.L./VOITH HYD. TRANS.N.	7. ENGINE AIR DUCT.	12. RADIATORS.	DIESEL-HYDRAULIC	17. FUEL TANK.	22. COMPRESSOR.
3. CARDEN SHAFT DRIVE.	8. DYNOSTARTER.	13. CONTROL CUBICLE.	TYPE 2 LOCOMOTIVE.	18. CONTROL DESK.	23. EXHAUSTERS.
4. PRIMARY GEARBOX.	9. SERCK. FAN PUMP.	14. TRAIN HEATING BOILER.		19. DRIVER'S SEAT.	
5. SECONDARY GEARBOX.	10. SERCK FAN MOTOR.	15. WATER TANK.		20. ASSISTANT'S SEAT.	

D6306-25 Side-, Top- and End-Elevations and Internal Layout Diagram. Modified body-side radiator grille illustrated. No boiler exhaust port shown on top elevation. Item 13 ('Control Cubicle') is labelled twice against each of the cab bulkheads; this is incorrect - item 13 at the B-end bulkhead is the battery rack. (BR Main Line Locomotive Layout Diagrams, Undated)

D6300-5 Equipment layout. Engine positioned slightly off-centre in relation to the longitudinal centre line. Radiator bank and fan also slightly off-centre to allow a walkway passage along one side. Both sets of external body-side doors in opposing positions.

D6306-57 Equipment layout. Engine re-positioned exactly along the longitudinal centre line of the locomotive. Radiator bank and fan still slightly off-centre in relation to the longitudinal centre line. A-end external bodyside doors in off-set positions to facilitate improved access to the engine. Bodyside grille positioning not shown.
Key: 1. Control cubicle, 2. Diesel engine, 3. Water tank, 4. Hydraulic transmission, 5. Radiator, 6. Fuel tank, 7. Heating Boiler, 8. Compressor, 9. Air intake filters, 10. Exhausters, 11. Dynastarter.
Item 1 is labelled twice against each of the cab bulkheads; this is incorrect - item 1 at the B-end bulkhead is the battery rack.

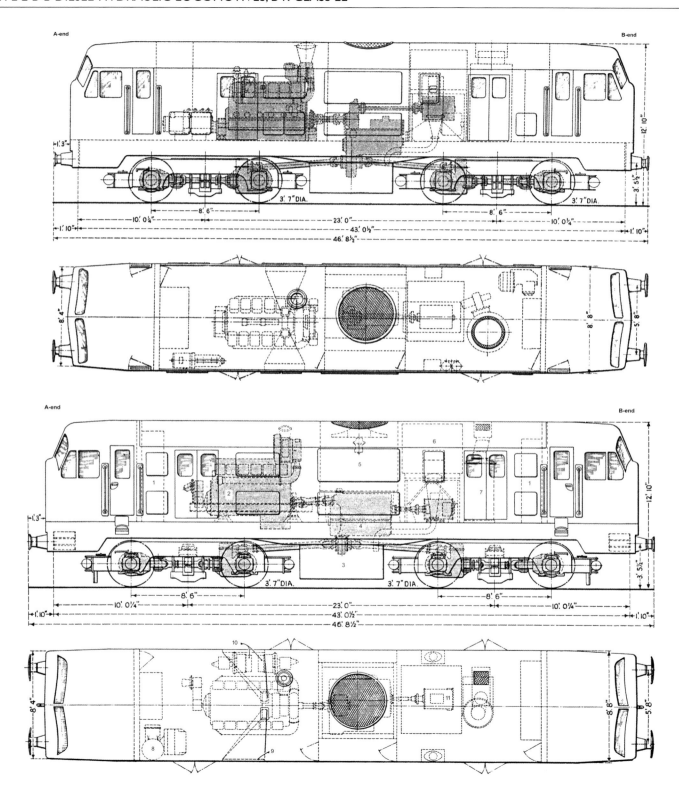

3.5 Summary of Major Components

Component	Supplier/Type	D6300-5	D6306-25	D6326-57
Engine	MAN L12V18/21A	x		
	MAN L12V18/21B		x	x
Transmission	Voith L306r	x		
	Voith LT306r		x	x
Control System	BTH (electro-pneumatic)	x		
	Brown Boveri (all-electric)		x	x
Boiler	Spanner Mk.1	x		
	Clayton		x	
	Stone Vapor			x
Brake Gear	Westinghouse	x		
	Oerlikon/Davies & Metcalfe		x	x
Compressors	Westinghouse	x	x	x
Exhausters	Westinghouse	x		
	Reavell		x	x
Dynastarters	Electric Construction Co.	x	x	x
Pre-Heater	Vapor Watchman		x	x

Notes:
1. Source: BR (document undated).
2. The subject of pre-heaters is dealt with in more detail in Section 3.15.

3.6 Mainframe

The mainframe of the 'Pilot Scheme' locomotives was very similar to that used in D600-4, with heavy steel sections (15x6in. girders) riveted and welded together to produce the traditional heavy-duty frame favoured by the BTC. The frame was formed of two longitudinals, box-frame cross-stretchers and tapering drop-ends, the latter mating up with cast steel drag-boxes to resist damage under normal end-loading conditions. The use of a single transmission unit in the D6300s necessitated the provision of an aperture in the centre of the frame, rather than the system of driving through hollow bogie pivots as used in D600-4.

The mainframe of the production locomotives was made of main longitudinal members with cross-stretchers all fabricated from steel plates, a change which, along with the lighter LT306r transmission, enabled a substantial weight reduction.

3.7 Superstructure and Equipment Layout.

Given the inherent strength of the mainframe, there was no requirement for load-bearing members in the superstructure. The use of aluminium to form the lightweight superstructure was largely aimed at off-setting the heavy mainframe in

achieving the objective of 64t all-up weight. In addition, part of NBL's logic behind the use of aluminium in the D63xxs was to permit the manufacture of components similar to those specified for D600-4 so as to generate larger orders with suppliers at more economical rates.

The cabs were supplied as completed aluminium units from Lightalloys Ltd of Glasgow, although some of the design and casting work was carried out at their North Acton facility in London. Each of the two driving cabs was a single sub-assembly of several castings welded together using the argon process, jig-mounted for final assembly. Corrosion of the steel/aluminium joints at the mainframe interfaces was prevented by the use of a zinc-chromate primer. Cab handrails were stainless steel. Light alloy hinged doors were fitted in the cab noses to give gangway passage from one locomotive to another when coupled together.

The side structure and roof were formed from Kynal sections and aluminium sheeting. Two sets of double-doors , with droplight windows, were provided on each side of the locomotive to give access to the engine and boiler.

External details were generally similar to D600-4 with louvred body-side grilles, polished aluminium window

Driver's desk and control pedestal (D6300-5). This photograph actually illustrates the cab desk arrangements of a D600 locomotive which were broadly similar to D6300-5. In a letter dated 19 May, 1959, the BR CM&EE Department, Swindon, requested that NBL look into the question of duplicating the power and brake controls on D6300-57 and presumably NBL supplied the requisite drawings and costings.

BR Swindon subsequently sent a letter to NBL dated 9 December 1959 stating that "….the final considered opinion of the question of duplication of controls in locomotives fitted with double cabs from the WR Running & Maintenance Officer (is) that the expense involved in such provision is not warranted". The matter was closed. (Project Class 22 Society)

surrounds, combined air-horn and air-intake grilles (much more of which later!) and end marker lights beneath head-code discs.

The locomotive ends were designated A and B, with the A-end cab being nearest to the engine. From A- to B-end the internal equipment layout can be summarised as follows:

- A-end cab.
- Control cubicle and compressor, against cab bulkhead.
- NBL/MAN engine and exhausters.
- Voith transmission, with radiator and roof fan above.
- Dynastarter, plus a 450 gal. fuel tank (positioned in the roof space above and slightly offset to enable a walkway down one side of the locomotive).
- Train-heating boiler.
- Battery rack, against cab bulkhead.
- B-end cab.

A 500gal. water tank was slung between the bogies.

Some of the subtle differences between the D6300-5 and D6306-57 batches (i.e. equipment disposition, cardan shaft arrangements (variously connecting the engine, transmission, dynastarter and final drives) and the location of the bodyside-doors) are illustrated on page 26.

In general terms, the layout of the equipment was dictated by the location of the hydraulic transmission, the output flanges of which were positioned symmetrically about the locomotive longitudinal and centre lines.

3.8 Driving Cab

The internal cab design of D6300-5 reflected the apparent lack of any formal detailed agreements between the BTC and Unions and as a result, NBL developed their own arrangements, with the resulting layout of the driver's controls described in various quarters as being somewhat idiosyncratic and overly-simplistic.

On the left-hand side of the nose-end gangway doors was a desk containing the driver's main gauges (speedometer, vacuum brake gauge, brake cylinder pressure gauge and main reservoir pressure gauge); one warning light only was provided to signal any fault on the locomotive (or locomotives in multiple). On the right of the gangway doors were the lighting controls and control equipment for the train-heating boiler.

Brake controls for the locomotive and train were situated on a shelf to the driver's left whilst a pedestal to his right, between him and the gangway doors, contained various warning lights, the engine start/stop controls, the power control lever and the forward/reverse lever. The direction selection lever was positioned below the power controller and had five positions (FOR [forward], EO [engine only], OFF, EO, REV [reverse]).

Gangway connection equipment was supplied by A.G. Wild & Co. Ltd, Sheffield . Given the virtual absence of a nose end, entrance to the flexible gangway connecting two locomotives working in multiple was effected directly from the cab. This enabled the secondman to access the train-heating boiler in the rear locomotive when working in multiple on passenger services.

'Deadman' controls were provided in the form of a floor pedal on the left-hand (driving) side of the cab and by a push button on the right-hand side. WR ATC (automatic train control) equipment was installed at Swindon from new on D6306-57 as part of the commissioning process but was fitted retrospectively on D6300-5.

The cabs included a warm air cab heating system with air brought from external apertures on the cab front end and heated by the engine coolant circuit. Trico-Folberth windscreen wipers were provided, together with warm air demisting of the windscreens with warm air taken from the cab heating system.

Fitted to the cab bulkhead were the handbrake, fire-extinguisher, emergency alarm bell, food locker, hot-plate and the control for operating the foam extinguishers over the engine and train-heating boiler.

The cabs were kitted out in a manner similar to D600-4, with extensive use of plastic laminate panels. Glass fibre insulation was provided in the bulk-heads, cab sides, roof and under-floor areas for heat and noise insulation.

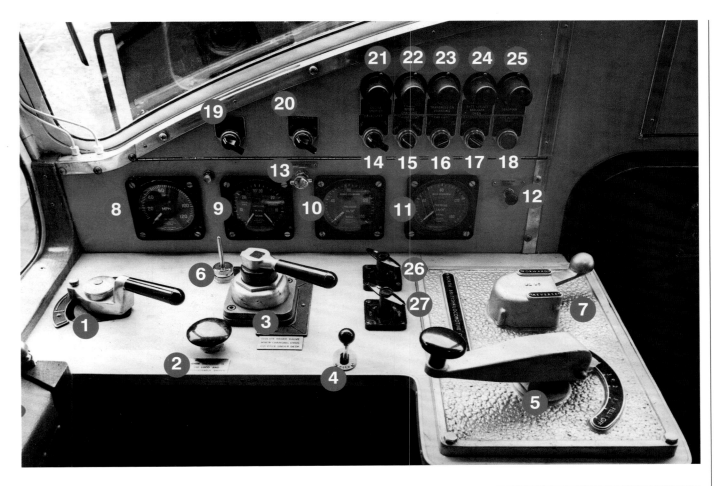

Driver's control desk (D6306-57).
Key: 1. Train brake valve (air/vacuum), 2. Second loco hold-over button, 3. Locomotive straight air brake valve, 4. Valve for 'Desilux' air horns, 5. Power controller, 6. Sand valve, 7. Forward/reverse direction selector, 8. Speedometer, 9. Vacuum brake gauge, 10. Brake cylinder gauge, 11. Main reservoir pipe gauge, 12. Heater air control, 13. Windscreen wiper control, 14. Exhauster on/off switch, 15. Gauge light dimmer switch, 16. Cab light switch, 17. Heater/de-mist switch, 18. Fire alarm test button, 19. Power on/off switch, 20. Compressor on/off switch, 21. Engine stopped warning light, 22. Engine speed changing light, 23. Transmission changing light, 24. Battery breaker open light, 25. Deadman warning light. 26/27. Engine start/stop switch. (Colin Marsden Collection)

NBL/MAN L12V18/21B Engine. The L12V18/21 model descriptor highlighted the following attributes: 'L' for Locomotive, '12' for the number of cylinders, 'V' indicating a V- or Vee-form engine, and '18/21' specifying the cylinder bore and piston stroke dimensions in centimetres.
Model variants:

- L12V 18/21S   NBL alternate designation of the MAN L12V18/21A 1,000hp turbo-charged engine.
- L12V 18/21B   NBL designation for the up-graded normally-aspirated engine.
- L12V 18/21BS   NBL designation for the up-graded turbo-charged engines (illustrated).

'High-Speed Diesel-Electric Train Sets' referred to the 'Blue Pullman' units. (NBL Publicity Material)

N.B.L.-M.A.N. Type L12V 18/21 BS Diesel Engine as being supplied to British Railways for Main Line Diesel-Hydraulic and Diesel-Electric Loco-motives and Inter-city High Speed Diesel-Electric Train Sets. This series of engine has been developed for the specific requirements of Diesel Rail Traction and High Speed Marine Craft. The engine is a 12-cylinder Vee form unit with 6 cylinders per bank operating on the 4-stroke cycle using the pre-combustion chamber principle. The crankcase is fabricated from steel pressings and mild steel castings. The maximum rated speed is 1,600 r.p.m. and the present power output is 1,100 b.h.p. at 1,500 r.p.m. The engine weighs approximately 4·25 tons, including water and oil.

L12V 18/21B SERIES 680/1,100 B.H.P.

Whilst cab instrumentation was somewhat minimalist, additional instruments were provided on a panel within the engine compartment, including a Smith's engine speed indicator, engine coolant thermometer, oil pressure gauge, transmission fluid thermometer, and various fault indicator lights.

A complete re-design of the driver's controls on D6306-57 was undertaken to bring them more into line with the standards evolving on the BR/Derby Type 2 diesel-electric locomotives. The pedestal was removed and the engine start/stop switches, the direction selector and the power controller were all re-positioned on the desk directly in front of the driver along with the brake valves.

3.9 NBL/MAN L12V 18/21 Engine

NBL was aware that MAN were seeking an outlet in the UK and this led to engine production being inaugurated at their Atlas works in Glasgow. The engines for D6300-57, were the conventional form four-stroke MAN L12V18/21 units built by NBL in order to meet the delivery terms imposed by the BTC with respect to country of manufacture. The Glasgow-built engines made use of British ancillary components to minimise dependence on imported parts; substitute equipment included dynastarters from ECC rather than Brown-Boveri, CAV fuel injectors instead of Bosch and Napier turbochargers in lieu of MAN.

D6300-5 were fitted with the NBL/MAN L12V18/21A engine variant which, with turbocharging, was set to 1,000bhp at 1,445rpm. The model name L12V18/21S was sometimes used by NBL, the S-suffix standing for supercharged (or turbocharged) in place of the German A for Aufladung (meaning supercharged!). This change caused much confusion with spare parts inventory listings in later years, particularly after NBL went into liquidation.

In simple terms, a turbocharger was a gas-turbine coupled directly to a centrifugal air compressor, in which the turbine was driven by engine exhaust gas before going to atmosphere. The compressor forced more air into the cylinders and increased the power of the engine.

The engine was cradled in a sub-frame mounted on semi-resilient pads to minimise vibration and was positioned over the A-end bogie. On D6300-5 the whole assembly was slightly offset from the locomotive's longitudinal centre-line with the output end of the engine facing away from the nearest A-end cab.

The L12V18/21A engine crankcase and cylinder blocks were of mild steel with seven cast steel transversals welded up as one piece, with an angle of 60° between the two cylinder banks in V-form, together with flat stiffeners across the top of the V.

A one piece chrome-molybdenum alloy steel gear-driven camshaft, in the neck of the V, was used to actuate all forty-eight valves (two inlet and two exhaust valves for each of the twelve separate pre-combustion chamber cylinder heads); all valves were of the same diameter and their double springs had heat treated surfaces and were galvanised.

Two six-ram CAV fuel injection pumps were mounted in tandem above the V in the early engines and driven off one end of the single camshaft.

The cast-iron cylinder liners were of the wet-type and were clamped at the top by the individual cast-iron cylinder heads and were sealed at the lower end by a sliding joint.

Pistons were one-piece castings in aluminium alloy, each having four compression rings (of which the top ring was chrome-plated to extend life) and two oil control rings, the latter intended to prevent excess crankcase oil passing into the combustion chambers and thus burnt off. There was no provision for oil to be directed against the underside of the piston as a precaution against overheating.

Connecting rods were plain, two being arranged side-by-side on each crankpin, which meant that opposite cylinders were slightly staggered. The rods were drilled for pressure lubrication of the gudgeon pins.

The hardened alloy steel crankshaft was carried in seven copper-lead steel-backed bearings. A vibration damper was fitted at the free end of the shaft.

The engine weight in dry condition was approximately 4.25tons.

During 1956 and 1957, MAN mounted a concerted effort to increase the output of its engines, with the improved L12V18/21A engine designated L12V18/21B. D6306-57 received the up-graded L12B18/21BS model which, with turbocharging, was set to 1,100bhp at 1530rpm.

NBL production was revised to incorporate the various improvements which included:

- stronger forged aluminium-alloy pistons, replacing the cast type,
- chrome-plated top piston rings,
- re-designed connecting rods,
- big ends split diagonally, with serrated matching faces in place of the old plain-faced joint,
- single-piece exhaust manifolds for each cylinder, replacing the previous two-piece manifolds, with branches tuned for optimum turbocharger performance by the insertion of a helix to keep the exhaust pulses separate until each reached the turbocharger branch,
- re-sited fuel injection pumps,
- revised crankshaft with larger diameter crankpin journals (increased from 118mm to 125mm) and a sleeve-spring vibration damper at the free end of the crankshaft, both

measures to help offset torsional vibration at higher crankshaft speeds.

Engine weight was increased to approximately 4.5tons but still lacked piston cooling. British-made ancillary equipment was retained on the new engines.

In addition, NBL incorporated electric priming pumps controlled by the starting circuit to improve engine oil circulation during start-up. Activated by the operation of the driver's starting switch, the pump supplied lubricating oil at 25psi until the engine reached a steady idling speed, at which point its own inbuilt mechanical pumps became effective, causing a pressure-sensitive switch to isolate the electric pump.

The revised L12V18/21BS model was given the railway rating of 1100bhp at 1530rpm following experience with the modified engines and a Deutshe Bahn 80-hr continuous test run at that output. The equivalent brake mean pressure (bmp) in the cylinders at 1100bhp and 1500rpm was 146lb/in², a figure which was considered to be very high for a conventional engine without piston cooling; this may have been the origin of many of the troubles encountered with the upgraded engine and comments suggesting that the engine had been developed beyond its intrinsic capability.

The L12V18/21BS engines in D6306-57 were re-positioned centrally about the longitudinal centre-line.

3.10 Power Control Systems and Multiple-Working.

D6300-5 featured British Thomson-Houston electro-pneumatic power control whereas D6306-57 incorporated Brown Boveri all-electric control. Both variants featured notched control (as did D600-4 and all D800 variants).

The control system employed on D6300-5 used a seven notch power handle controlled by the driver (i.e. idle, plus six power notches or pre-determined engine speed notches) which energised electro-pneumatic valves. The engine was fitted with a form of pneumatic 'stepper motor' converting the air supply from the electro-pneumatic valves into mechanical movement to provide the input speed demand to the governor.

The multiple-unit (MU) control system was electrical using cables via an MU jumper which in turn actuated the electro-pneumatic valves on the 'slave' locomotive to effect engine speed control. Given the complexity of the electro-pneumatic arrangement, the air supply was not shared between locomotives and MU control was 'communicated' electrically. The electro-pneumatic control in D6300-5 (coded 'Orange Square') enabled multiple operational compatibility with D600-4 and other D6300-5 locomotives only.

The electro-pneumatic control system was interlocked to prevent the reversal of the transmission except when the locomotive was stationary, and to prevent the selection of any engine power setting above minimum when the reversing lever was in the 'Engine Only' position. Another safeguard isolated the controls of the unoccupied cab as well as those of any locomotive coupled in multiple.

The production locos (D6306-57) had a different control arrangement and offered eight notches (Idle, plus seven speed notches) which actuated electro-magnetic relays to effect engine speed control via an Ardleigh 302/IG/3 engine governor. Multiple-unit operation between locomotives was electrical via MU jumpers (coded 'White Diamond'), actuating the electro-magnetic relays on the 'slave' locomotive. Multiple-unit compatibility was achievable between D6306-57 and D803-70 only.

The notch settings for the D6306-57 and D833-65 fleets were set as follows:

	D6306-57	D833-65	Comments
Notch 0	650rpm	600rpm	Idle, torque converter empty.
Notch 1	600rpm	600rpm	No increase in speed demand, torque convertor 'fill' valve energized.
Notch 2	900rpm	950rpm	
Notch 3	1025rpm	1140rpm	
Notch 4	1150rpm	1270rpm	
Notch 5	1275rpm	1370rpm	
Notch 6	1400rpm	1460rpm	
Notch 7	1530rpm	1530rpm	

Notes:
1. 'Fill': Transmission filled with oil but without additional power being provided by the engine. Wheels started to turn on release of the locomotive/train brakes.
2. Note the speed differences between the D6306-57 and D833-65 class, most likely to reduce 'tugging' by the Type 2 when working in multiple with a Type 4 as a result of their lower effective gearing and speed range.
3. Engine speed setting differences between the two classes may also have been to avoid any vibration periods.
4. Speeds reported for each class also varied slightly between various official documents.

3.11 NBL/Voith Hydraulic Transmission.

Two different models of Voith transmission were installed on the diesel-hydraulic Type 2s. The 'Pilot Scheme' locomotives (D6300-5) received the L306r model, made by NBL in Glasgow. Sixteen transmission units were provided for the D600-4 and D6300-5 fleets with three spares.

The L306r transmission had an input capacity of 927hp at 1445rpm engine speed which suited the MAN 1000bhp engine. The engine drove the L306r triple-converter transmission via a short horizontal cardan shaft through step-up gears located above the input end of the main transmission casing. The transmission block projected downwards through the floor into a space between the two water tanks which fed the train-heating boiler. The L306r model had the output directly below the input, and the short output shaft had two flanges to take cardan shafts going forward and backward to the inner axle on each bogie, from where separate shafts relayed drive to the outer axles. D6300-5 had an extra external shaft taken from the input step-up gears to the dynastarter.

All cardan shafts were of German *Gelenkwellenbau* (GWB) design, licence-built by Hardy-Spicer, while axle-drives were manufactured by David Brown.

In D6300-5 the transmission block rested on trunnion and sandwich mountings.

The production batch (D6306-57) had the LT306r version, which was both more compact and lighter than the L306r; the power input for this machine was set at 1036hp at 1530rpm; two power output routings were deployed, first to the axles (as above) and secondly to drive the dynastarter via an extension of the primary shaft of the transmission.

In D6306-57 the different model led to the transmission input centre line being higher than the engine crankshaft centre line; as a consequence the primary cardan shaft was longer and set at an upward angle instead of being horizontal as on D6300-5.

The step-up gears in D6306-57 were within the main transmission block, as compared to the bolted on cast-iron casing on top of the block for D6300-5.

In D6306-57 the transmission block was mounted on Metalastik feet.

One hundred and eighteen transmission units were provided for the D833-65 and D6306-57 fleets with twelve spares.

Both the L306r and LT306r models had three torque-converters each of different sizes, oil capacities and blade formations to suit operating requirements. The starting or low-speed 'high torque' converter was the largest and conversely the high speed 'low torque' converter the smallest. Changeover from one torque converter to another took place at approximately 23 and 45mph in D6300-5, and 26 and 52mph in D6306-57. Converters tended to change down at a slightly higher line speeds. There was no interruption of power during the converter changing process.

NBL/Voith L306r Transmission (D6300-5). The letter 'L' in the L306r model descriptor referred to its Locomotive application, the digit '3' to the number of torque-converters, '0' to the number of fluid couplings, '6' to the maker's power category and 'r' to the fact that the reversing gear was included within the transmission block. The input flange/shaft from the engine into the step-up gears was at the top and the output flange/shaft to the final drive at the bottom of the transmission block.
(NBL Publicity Material)

L306r TRANSMISSION

VOITH/NORTH BRITISH fully automatic hydraulic transmissions are manufactured in sizes ranging from 75 to over 1,000 b.h.p. in individual units. The transmissions can be used in a wide field of applications as well as in rail traction work. The illustration shows the Type L306r which has a maximum input power of 1,036 h.p.

All transmissions incorporate various arrangements of fluid circuits. The basic Voith principle is that the most suitable arrangement of drive is selected by filling one circuit with transmission fluid and leaving the others empty. This operation is entirely automatic under the influence of the transmission governor. The locomotive driver is concerned only with the operation of the engine throttle. There is no mechanical connection between the diesel engine and the road wheels. In all cases a Torque Converter is used for starting and low speed duty.

Comparative torque-converter speed change points:

Loco. Nos.	Type	First/Second Converter	Second/Third Converter
D600-4	L306r	28/31mph	52/55mph
D6300-5	L306r	22/25mph	42/45mph
D6306-57	LT306r	26/29mph	51/53.5mph
D833-65	LT306r	39.5/43mph	75/79mph

Gear reductions in the final drive after the hydraulic portion were necessarily different in the 'Pilot-Scheme' and production locomotives to maintain the required traction characteristics. The higher rated speed of the L12V18/21B engines, combined with a different step-up ratio in the LT306r transmission and the revised torque-converter change-over times required that the output shaft gear ratios be increased by a factor of 30 per cent in order to preserve the same 75mph top speed in the third converter stage with the engine running at maximum power. Thus, the ratio was 3.43:1 in D6300-5 and 4.45:1 in D6306-57.

Production of some of the LT306r transmissions took place at the Queen's Park works of NBL, although various sources suggest that between ten and twenty-two units were supplied by Voith (Heidenheim), or as kits of parts provided by Voith for assembly by NBL in Glasgow. Such, I guess, was the deliberate fog surrounding the manufacture of equipment in Germany so soon after the Second World War.

To prevent damage to a transmission by putting a locomotive into reverse whilst moving forward, an air operated Standstill Detector device was fitted over the secondary shaft which detected whether this shaft was rotating. If it was, this device supplied an air feed to a locking piston which engaged with the operating mechanism to the reverser, preventing it from operating.

3.12 Engine/Transmission Interchangeability

An archive document signed by K.W.C. Grand (WR General Manager) made specific reference to engine and transmission interchangeability. Although undated and without a list of recipients, this document was in all probability sent to the Works & Equipment Committee during mid-February 1957; the document was marked Item 14' indicating that it was a supporting document for a W&EC agenda item for a meeting held on 27 February 1957 (see Section 1.5). The content of the document was as follows:

Locomotive Building and Condemnation Programmes, 1958 (Supplementary). Provision of Main-Line Diesel Locomotives.

It is necessary … that early arrangements be made for production and, subject to the Commission's approval of the programme, it is recommended, following consultation with the Chief Mechanical Engineer, that:

1. 30 of the 2000hp locomotives be built at Swindon and incorporate Maybach engines and Mekydro transmissions;
2. the balance of 34 (*subsequently* 33) be built by NBL to the Swindon design incorporating MAN engines and Voith transmissions;
3. the 52 1000hp locomotives … be built by NBL to the same design as the six already on order from them, incorporating MAN engines and Voith transmissions; and,
4. the specification should provide for the complete inter-changeability of engines and transmissions in all 2000hp and 1000hp locomotives.

The fourth point is pertinent here in that, for the first time in print that I have found, there was an explicit requirement for interchangeability, a concept copied from the Deutsche Bahn. Whilst this point was not specifically recorded in the subsequent W&EC and BTC meeting minutes (848/14 [27 February 1957] and 10/81 [28 February] respectively), the interchangeability requirement was progressed across the proposed fleet of locomotives for the combined Area No.1/2 Scheme (ultimately D6306-57 and D833-65 [MAN engines, Voith transmissions] and D803-32, and, ultimately, D866-70 [Maybach engines, Mekydro transmissions]).

Following authorisation of the fifty-two diesel-hydraulic Type 2s in February 1957, NBL tendered for the contract in the following month. According to Brian Reed (*Diesel-Hydraulic Locomotives of the Western Region*, 1974), NBL did not tender for this contract on the basis of interchangeable equipment, quoting engine interchangeability (£500 per locomotive) and transmission interchangeability (£975) as extras. These features were subsequently sanctioned by the BTC at an aggregate cost of £76,700.

The capability for equipment interchangeability was potentially advantageous both operationally (improved locomotive availability) and financially (lower engine/transmission inventory levels). Conceptually, the idea was simple, but the reality proved to be much more complicated. Engine and transmission inter-changeability required the following factors to be addressed:

- the geometry of the locomotive to be capable of physically accommodating equipment of differing sizes and weights within prevailing operating restrictions (e.g. loading gauge, axle-loading, etc.),
- the development of a suitable universal sub-frame to carry differing engine types,
- the provision of differing cardan shaft layouts and dimensions to cover the various equipment permutations,
- flexible provision of engine/transmission servicing arrangements (e.g. fuel/oil supply, coolant pipework, etc),
- electrical control re-calibration between locomotive types (notch control and associated engine rpm, torque-converter changeover points, etc.).

It is suspected that the £76,700 worth of extras sanctioned by the BTC for the D6306-57 batch related to the first two points only, with the other three left to be addressed later once operational demands for installing alternate engines or transmissions presented themselves.

Using the modern vernacular, straightforward 'plug-and-play' across alternative engines and transmissions was not as easily achievable as first thought and, to maintain reasonable Works shopping turn-round times, the widespread application of the concept was never fully implemented across the WR. Specifically, the potential opportunity to outshop D6306-57 with Maybach or Mekydro equipment was never taken, even when spares shortages sidelined MAN/Voith D833-65 or D6306-57 locomotives for extended periods. However, relatively straightforward inter-changeability between the D6300-5 and D600-4 fleets, and, between the D6306-57 and D833-65 fleets was achieved, although the differing traction characteristics of the two fleets still necessitated some electrical control re-calibration.

3.13 Dynastarter

All of the diesel-hydraulic Type 2s incorporated a dynastarter, the name recognising the double function of acting as a dynamo (electrical current generator) or as a motor (current user). When operating as a dynamo, current was supplied to the electrically driven auxiliaries, lighting and control systems and for battery charging. When acting as a motor it was used for engine starting with current drawn from batteries.

On D6300-5 the dynastarter, mounted on a welded steel carrier secured to the floor, was driven by a long cardan shaft from the rear side of the 2:1 step-up gear box mounted on top of the transmission; originally this was to have been 35kW capacity but was altered to 50kW before the first locomotive was delivered.

In D6306-57 the dynastarter was bolted directly to the floor and driven by a short cardan shaft from the rear end of the primary transmission shaft (with a 2.375:1 step-up). It was

originally intended to accommodate both Voith and Mekydro units in the NBL Type 2s which led to the dynastarter being relocated to the locomotive floor; this avoided the use of the steel carrier used on D6300-5, a feature which proved excessively resonant in service.

3.14 Cooling Equipment

The space above the transmission in the middle of the locomotive formed the cooling compartment.

In D6300-5 the basic principle was for air to be sucked in by a roof-mounted fan past radiator banks located near the locomotive side walls and then expelled upwards through the roof. The fan was driven by a 32hp electric motor and a Drayton temperature regulator at the engine exit controlled the water temperature, so that the greater the engine load, and the higher the water temperature, the faster the fan speed. By this means, whatever the engine load up to its maximum, the cooling water temperature was set within a narrow 'thermostatic' range.

In the first six locomotives each radiator bank was covered by a triple set of fixed louvres in the upper body-side, below which was a further triple set of smaller ventilation louvres.

The decision was taken in 1958 to equip D6306-57 with Behr-Serck cooling equipment mirroring the Swindon-built D803-32 'Warship' fleet. The main feature of the Behr system was the replacement of the electric fan motor by a hydrostatic unit under automatic control. This, in conjunction with the use of hydraulically-operated radiator shutters controlling the flow of air over the radiator elements, made the cooling process more precise.

When the engine was started and idled, the pump circulation of the water through the radiator was sufficient to keep the temperature within bounds without the fan running. When the driver's control handle was moved to the first power notch the fan began to move and the shutters began to open. Thereafter, as power was increased, the fan speed increased and the shutters opened wider. Usually the thermostatic control was set to begin operation around 78/80°C, to bring the engine back to idling if water temperature rose beyond 88/90°C, and to cut out the thermostatic action if the water exit temperature fell to 75°C. In normal working, the fan speed and quantity of air passed were constantly varying due to changing engine load from variations in gradient and track speed.

Ultimately, the system was under thermostatic control and should coolant temperature rise or fall beyond predetermined limits, the normal relationship between engine speed and cooling airflow would be overridden. The original arrangement shut off the engine completely once coolant temperature rose above a pre-set level; however, based on operational experience, this was subsequently modified by merely returning the unit to idling, allowing the coolant to be circulated through the radiators and back to the engine's water jacket. This prevented the possibility of latent heat trapped within a stationary engine, raising coolant temperatures to levels where damage might result.

On D6306-57, the bodyside radiator grilles were replaced by a single large square aperture without the ventilating louvres below. As before, air was expelled through the roof but without any subsidiary air flow through the engine room. The shutters also fulfilled the function of helping to prevent freezing-up during winter night lay-overs.

The Behr system enabled complete cooling units to be lowered into or lifted out of the locomotive as one unit.

Engine lubricating oil and transmission oil were also cooled via the water circuit heat exchangers.

3.15 Engine Pre-Heating.
Diesel engine wear is most severe during start-up due to the higher viscosity of the lubricating oil, increasing the possibility that the priming part of the start-up cycle might not adequately lubricate the bearing surfaces. Fuel dilution of the lubricating oil is another significant issue. During cranking unburnt fuel enters the cylinders, and there will be incomplete combustion until the engine has warmed; this can dilute the lubricating oil on the cylinder liner walls and diminish the lubrication of the contact with the piston liners. Engine pre-heating helps to reduce the adverse impact of these issues. MAN recommended the use of pre-heaters on their engines although usage was not considered to be mandatory.

An undated document in the NRM Archive entitled 'Summary of Components' for the diesel-hydraulic fleet explicitly lists the fitment of Vapor Watchman pre-heating equipment to D6306-57 but not D6300-5 (see page 27).

In general terms, pre-heating was achieved via an independent device such as the oil-fired Vapor Watchman boiler. However, D6300-5 were alternatively fitted with a heat exchanger arrangement incorporated into the engine cooling circuit with its own electrically-powered circulating pump. The heat exchanger drew its heat from steam generated by the Spanner train-heating boiler operated directly from the locomotive batteries.

The position regarding D6306-57 is much less clear. According to Brian Reed, 'Installation of (*an independent*) pre-heater was agreed at a later stage, November 1959, at a cost of … £475 per locomotive.' Whether this should be interpreted as an agreement regarding price or for actual installation is open to question.

One school of thought is that, following satisfactory experience with cold-starting on D6300-5, pre-heating was not specified for D6306-57 thereby saving considerable cost. J.K. Lewis (*The Western's Hydraulics*) disagrees with this, suggesting 'the installation of a marine-style oil-fired engine pre-heater

which, not being specified by the BTC until late 1959, was fitted to earlier ('*production*') locomotives retrospectively.'

D6306/7 entered traffic during October 1959 with no further locomotives that year; a glut of introductions to traffic followed during January 1960 (i.e. D6308-15). Of these, D6308-10 averaged 87 days in Swindon Works for commissioning work prior to introduction, and for D6311-4 an average of 21 days. These extended periods in Works might, *stress* might, suggest pre-introductory modifications beyond pure commissioning work, perhaps including pre-heater fitment, with D6308-14 being fitted at Swindon using equipment supplied by NBL. If fitted, D6306/7 would have received the pre-heating equipment retrospectively.

The key questions are: were any of the D6306-57 batch actually fitted with Vapor-Watchmam pre-heaters, and, if so, how many?

Evidence for the fitment of an independent pre-heater:

- BR33003/84 Driver's Handbook (June 1961) i.e. reference to a pre-heater switch in the 'Controls in Engine Compartment' section.
- The Swindon Works 'Blue File' for D6313 which documented that the Vapor Watchman control panel was removed and re-fitted to facilitate a boiler change during its March/April 1960 visit; also noted was the fitting of an extension to the Vapor Watchman exhaust during April/May 1960. (N.B. 'Blue Files' for other locomotives make no reference to pre-heaters, although the number of files available to peruse is admittedly limited.)
- *Modern Locomotives Illustrated* No.197 (p44): D6306-57 were described as being 'provided with a small oil-fired heater inserted in a by-pass of the engine water system so that the water could be pre-heated to prevent any dead cold start.'
- Locomotives in the D6326-57 batch (fitted with Stone-Vapor steam generators) had two boiler compartment roof grilles. It has been suggested, but not confirmed, that the smaller oblong grille was associated with the Vapor-Watchman pre-heater (see Volume 2). A significant number had these apertures plated over later in life.

Evidence suggesting that pre-heaters were not fitted, or, not fitted fleet-wide, include:

- Lack of any reference to such equipment in several BR operations documents e.g. General Arrangement Sectional Drawings, Equipment Schedules (other than a control switch), Diesel Maintenance Course Manuals (see page 36), and, Driver's Fault Guides.
- No obvious physical external evidence of a separate pre-heater exhaust flue on D6306-25 (although venting via the boiler flue, or, under the frame might have been a possibility).

D6306-57 Cooling Circuit (as built). CH = Cab Heater (two per cab). NBL wanted to avoid using electric heating for cab heating and windscreen demisting. Sourcing heat from the train heating boiler would not be satisfactory when these locomotives were working freight trains or running light and during the summer months. The alternative to the provision of electric heating was to utilise the waste heat from the engine cooling system with appropriate fan and ducting. The fan could be used for cooling the cab in hot weather. Hot water cab heaters were subsequently replaced by electric heaters.

No mention of a pre-heater circuit. (BR Diesel Maintenance Course notes; Mark Parson's Collection)

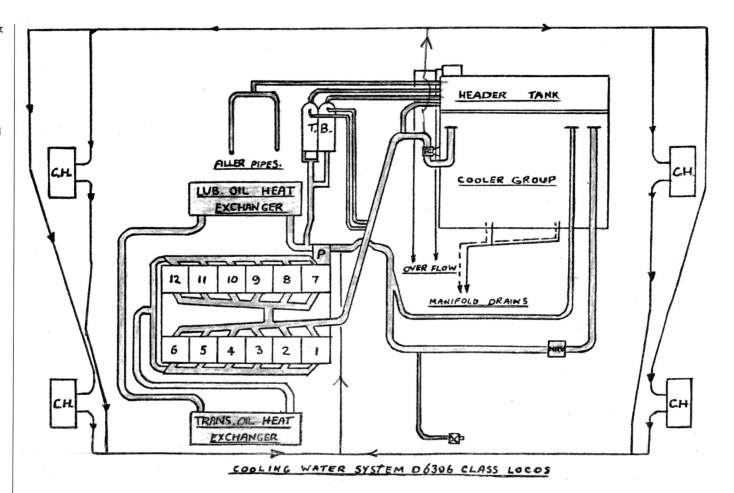

COOLING WATER SYSTEM D6306 CLASS LOCOS

- Mark Parsons (Swindon Works fitter in the mid-1970s) comments that he cannot recall ever hearing about pre-heaters being fitted to the D63xxs, a comment repeated by colleagues employed at Newton Abbot and Laira depots during the mid-1960s and early-1970s.
- D833-65, ordered at the same time as D6306-57 and introduced from July 1960, were not fitted with pre-heaters (which *might* imply that D63xx locomotives were similarly not fitted, or, that only locomotives numbered below D6326 (or lower) were pre-heater fitted.

The apparent fitment of D6313 with pre-heater equipment, and the subsequent lack of observations of such equipment being fitted by Mark Parsons' colleagues at Newton Abbot and Laira might suggest the removal of this equipment from locomotives initially fitted with this equipment by 1965. However, Swindon Works modification listings for D6306-57 make no reference to the retrospective removal of pre-heaters.

Mark strongly suspects that very few, if indeed any, D63xx locomotives were fitted with pre-heaters, arguing that any fitted would still have them installed, even if isolated, by the time withdrawals commenced in 1968, but he has not seen or heard of any locomotives so fitted after 1965. Mark wonders whether the BR33003/84 and 'Blue File' references to the pre-heater control switch and panel actually relates to an 'original' control panel specified prior to any plan of fitting pre-heaters being dropped.

Any further information on this subject would be much appreciated and will be included in Volume 2.

3.16 Compressor

Air from the single Westinghouse compressor on D6300-5 was used for the locomotive brakes, sanding, windscreen wipers, and for the electro-pneumatic control system, and, similarly for D6306-57 except for the control system which was all-electric.

3.17 Exhausters

The single Westinghouse exhauster in D6300-5 and the two Reavall exhausters in D6306-57 were used for the vacuum train brakes.

3.18 Bogies

The bogies fitted to D6300-57 were specifically described as B-B, as opposed to Bo-Bo. The following definitions explain the difference:

- **B-B:** Two bogie locomotives each with two axles with one master drive connected through to each axle through shafts (e.g. diesel-hydraulic locomotives with primary and secondary gearboxes connected via cardan shafts).
- **Bo-Bo:** Two bogie locomotives each with two axles with separate drives for each axle (e.g. diesel-electric locomotives with independent traction motors on each axle).

The bogies were the two-axle equivalents of the three-axle type used under D600-4. They were built up out of heavy box sections constructed mainly using $^7/_{16}$in. steel plates, with cross stretchers and headstocks riveted to the frame.

The superimposed weight of around 42.5t was supported on two cup-shaped flat-faced side bearers on each bogie, carried on a bolster with swing links and double full elliptical springs on each side. No weight was taken through the bogie pivot which only dealt with pivoting, traction, braking and transverse forces.

D6300-31 were built with Timken roller-bearing axle boxes and D6332-57 with the SKF type. All had manganese steel thrust surfaces and were supported by compensating beams and coil springs. One bogie on each locomotive was fitted

with a Smith's axle-mounted mileage-counter and Smith-Stone speedometer generator.

Dynamically balanced spoked wheels of 43in diameter were used.

The final drive units were of the spiral-bevel and helical gear variety similar to D600-4, albeit with a different reduction ratio to compensate for the Type 2's lower designed speed.

Eight sandboxes were fitted.

Although the bogie structure was essentially the same for the whole class, various details were different to sufficient degree that bogies between the D6300-5 and D6306-57 batches were not readily inter-changeable and differentiated serial numbers were allocated (see bogie-plate photographs above). Differing elements included final drive gear ratios, brake cylinder diameters and brake rigging configuration.

3.19 Brakes

Westinghouse straight air brakes were specified for D6300-5, interlocked with train vacuum brakes for normal use but capable of independent operation. The two brake systems were interconnected so that whilst application of the locomotive's straight air brake by the driver was always independent of the train vacuum brake, service operation of the latter would incur a corresponding application of the locomotive's own brakes via a proportional valve.

Clasp rigging applied two brake blocks to each wheel through four lightweight Comprestal 8in x 8in cylinders per bogie giving a brake force of 45t. The cylinders were charged by a single Westinghouse compressor located adjacent to the control cubicle on A-end cab bulkhead; one motor-driven

Bogie Plates. Bogie numbers 6300/1 to 6300/118 were originally allocated. However, in a letter from the BR CM&EE Department, Swindon, to NBL dated 17 February 1960 regarding bogie-numbering, BR stated that:

> "…..it has now been decided that locomotives D6306-D6357 shall be treated as a distinct class for bogie numbering, and this involves a revision to the numbers allocated to the bogies. Thus instead of the numbers being 6300/15-118 they should now be 6306/1-104 inclusive, and I trust you will be able to modify the plates you are making accordingly."

Thus bogies 6300/1-6300/12 were allocated to D6300-5, with two spares (6300/13 and 6300/14). Bogies 6306/1-104 were allocated to D6306-57 with four additional spares (presumably 6306/105-8).

The surprisingly high number (29) of the '6300' plate illustrated suggests a '6306' bogie being converted for use with a '6300' locomotive, either as an additional spare or following serious derailment damage to an existing '6300' bogie."
(Alan Whincup)

Bogie, D6329. Mileage-counter on nearest axle box cover. Two sandboxes. (RCTS)

exhauster, also Westinghouse, was floor-mounted beside the engine to service the train vacuum brakes.

D6306-57 had Oerlikon straight air brakes (license-built by Davies & Metcalfe) and for the train vacuum brakes two Reavell exhausters were provided. Four larger Comprestal 8in x 8¾in cylinders were used giving an increased brake force of 50t resulting from both the revised cylinder capacity and modified brake rigging leverage.

The D6300-5 batch had a pair of buffer-beam mounted air pipes slightly below and 'inboard' of the buffers i.e. four in total at each end, whereas the D6306-57 batch had a single air pipe slightly below and 'inboard' of each buffer i.e. two in total at each end. The two additional 'inner' brake pipes on D6300-5, somewhat unusually, connected 'master' and 'slave' locomotives to effect a straight air-brake application in the latter when working in multiple. D600-4 were similarly fitted with four pipes at each end, and represented a further multiple unit compatibility limitation. Normally with most other types of MU control fitted during this era, the straight air-brake only worked on the controlling locomotive.

The two 'outer' pipes, also evident on D6306-57, were the normal main air reservoir interconnections.

3.20 Train-Heating Boiler.

Spanner Mark 1a train-heating boilers were installed in D6300-5, Clayton RO-100 type (manufactured under licence by English Electric/Robert Stephenson & Hawthorn) in D6306-25, and Stone-Watchman Vapor OK4610 (supplied by J. Stone & Co. Deptford) in D6326-57. All boilers were rated at 1000lb/hr steaming capacity.

Clayton and Stone-Vapor boilers could operate with the engine turned off, additional battery capacity being provided to suit, for which the BTC paid extra. Subsequently, it is believed that the WR limited electrical supply from the batteries to one hour only. In later years many locomotives had their boilers isolated because of infrequent use on passenger duties and even in London their use on empty stock duties saw a decreasing requirement to heat trains, a job increasingly carried out by the train locomotive.

Diesel Locomotive Record Card for D6320.

Chapter 4

APPEARANCE DESIGN AND STYLING

D604, Swindon Works, circa 1959. The similarities between the NBL Type 2 and Type 4 products are evident; the longer nose-ends on the Type 4s, however, resulted in a more satisfactory appearance. (Rail-Online)

D6119, Strathyre, circa 1966. NBL's diesel-electric Type 2 equivalent. In my view, the greater length of the D61xxs resulted in a better proportioned locomotive compared with the D63xx fleet; the use of Commonwealth bogies further enhanced their visual attractiveness.

(N. Forrest [Transport Treasury])

With their common NBL roots, shared use of major components and input from the same design consultant (Joseph P. McCrum, head of the Department of Industrial Design, Glasgow School of Art), it was inevitable that there were strong appearance design similarities between the NBL Type 2s (both diesel-electric and diesel-hydraulic) and the Type 4 D600s.

Whilst there is a considerable amount of archive material available covering the Type 4s, there is considerably less on the Type 2 diesel-electrics and less still on the diesel-hydraulics. Misha Black (Design Research Unit) provided over-arching support to the BTC in matters concerning locomotive design and, following a visit to NBL in Glasgow in July 1958 made the following comment regarding the D61xxs, a comment equally applicable to the D63xxs:

It will be remembered that these 1000hp locomotives have a cab which is identical to the large type built by NBL. The same aluminium castings have been used but the nose of the cab has been cut off, resulting in an almost flat front…..The appearance of this locomotive is thus slightly odd but may, in fact, appear very acceptable to those who are not aware of how the design was developed."

Brian Haresnape (*BR Fleet Survey: 2 Western Region Diesel-Hydraulics*, 1982) had a less complimentary view:

"…..The (*design work on D600-4*) produced a quite pleasant nose-end shape despite the need to accommodate the gangway doors. Far less satisfactory was the front end of the smaller NBL B-Bs, which utilised many of the same components but simply had the nose, so to speak, 'cut-off'. And that is exactly how they looked!"

J.K. Lewis (*The Western's Hydraulics*, 1997) provided a broader perspective:

"…..the degree to which the finished Type 2 was to copy the larger locomotive would reflect the pressures imposed on NBL by the locomotives' ultra-competitive pricing. In order to allow at least some measure of profit in the finished result, economies had needed to be made wherever possible, including drawing office and production costs, and it showed…..

"In the Type 4s, the resulting assembly had been one of the most attractive used on any diesel locomotive to date; on the D6300s the same cab frame but with the nose end truncated to a mere six inches or so gave an overly-arcuate impression when seen from ahead and a most unattractive spectacle of tight curves and sharp edges when viewed in profile.....Livery arrangements were not sufficient to disguise the basic inelegance of the design."

In my personal opinion the design of the NBL Type 2 diesel-electrics was far superior to their diesel-hydraulic counterparts due to the greater length of the D61xxs (51ft 6in, compared with 46ft 8½in), helped further by their proportionately longer wheelbase (37ft 0in versus 31ft 6in). The bogie wheelbase was the same for both locomotives at 8ft 6in, although the lighter-weight look of the Commonwealth design on the D61xxs appeared more proportionate to the body dimensions. The net effect of these key dimensions was that the D6300s looked very 'stubby'.

D6307, Plymouth, September 1969. A 'stubby' locomotive, diminutised even by the lowly 16t mineral wagon.
(Rex Conway [Rail-Online])

Chapter 5

DELIVERY AND ACCEPTANCE TESTING

5.1 NBL Order Delivery Promises

Loco. Nos.	Delivery Promises
D600-4	First locomotive 15 months from date of order (*16/11/55*) continuing at one locomotive per month (February 1957 to June/July 1957).
D6300-5	To begin 18 months from date of order (*16/11/55*) at the rate of two locomotives per month (May 1957 to July/August 1957). Original delivery promise for first locomotive: July 1957.
D6100-9	First locomotive 15 April 1959 and last locomotive 15 September 1959.
D6110-37	Ordered 01/05/57. To start in 21 months and continue at rate of 3/4 locomotives per month (February 1959 to October/November 1959).
D6138-57	Ordered 14/07/58. No delivery details specified (November 1959 to April/May 1960, assuming continuous production after D6137 and same rate of 3/4 locomotives per month).
D6306-57	Ordered 05/11/57. Commence 5 March 1959 and three locomotives per month (March 1959 to September 1960). Original delivery promise for first locomotive: February 1959.
D833-65	18/21 months from date of order (*03/07/58 per letter of intent*). Commence at two locomotives per month rising to three per month during contract (February/May 1960 to June 1961).

Notes:
1. Blue text: NBL promise commentary converted into specific dates.
2. Red text: BTC progress documents (published from 1958) indicated Original Promise dates i.e. D6300 (July 1957) and D6306 (February 1959).

5.2 NBL Actual Deliveries (1958-62)

Delivery of D6300/1 was expected in May 1957, with the remainder following at the rate of two per month. In the event three years elapsed between the placement of the order for D6300-5 in November 1955 and the delivery of D6300 in December 1958, against the promised 18 months.

Delays to the delivery of D6306-57 were exacerbated by the long period between receipt of the NBL tender by the BTC in April 1957 and the eventual placement of the order seven months later in November. The promised delivery was commencement in February/March 1959 and then three locomotives per month indicating order completion by August/September 1960.

As things turned out, the delivery of D6306 was six months late, and, after the delivery of D6333 in August 1960, further deliveries were essentially suspended for nineteen months until March 1962, with only D6334-6 delivered and accepted during this period. Deliveries resumed in late-March 1962 with D6357 finally being delivered to the WR in November 1962.

The delay to the commencement of the production locomotives was due to a number of factors, including the stresses and strains of building up to the combined production of the D61xx and D63xx fleets, the work on reducing the weight of D6306-57 to achieve something close to a 16t axle-load (e.g. frame construction modifications,

NBL Deliveries (1958-62).

Month	D600-4	D8400-9	D6100-57	D6300-57	E3036-45	D833-65
01/58	D600					
02/58						
03/58	D601					
04/58						
05/58						
06/58		D8400/1				
07/58		D8402/3				
08/58		D8404				
09/58	D602	D8405-9				
10/58						
11/58	D603					
12/58	D604		D6100-2	D6300-2		
01/59						
02/59			D6104			
03/59			D6105-7			
04/59			D6108/9			
05/59			D6103/10-4	D6303		
06/69			D6115-9	D6304		
07/59			D6120			
08/59			D6121	D6305		
09/59			D6122-5	D6306/7		
10/59			D6126-30	D6308-10		
11/59			D6131-3			
12/59			D6134-7	D6311-4		
01/60				D6315		
02/60			D6138-40	D6316-8		
03/60			D6141-3	D6319-22	E3036	
04/60			D6144-6	D6323	E3037	
05/60			D6147-9	D6324-6		
06/60			D6150-2	D6327-31	E3038	
07/60			D6153/4	D6332/3	E3039	D833/4
08/60			D6155		E3040	D835
09/60			D6156		E3041	D836
10/60					E3042	D838
11/60				D6334/5	E3043	D837/9
12/60			D6157		E3044	D841/2
01/61						D843
02/61						D840
03/61					E3045	D844
04/61						D845-8
05/61						D849
06/61						D850
07/61				D6336		D851/2
08/61						D853

Month	D600-4	D8400-9	D6100-57	D6300-57	E3036-45	D833-65
09/61						D854
10/61						D855
11/61						D856
12/61						D857/8
01/62						D859/60
02/62						D861
03/62				D6337/8		D862
04/62				D6339/40		D863
05/62				D6341-5		D864
06/62				D6346-51		D865
07/62				D6352/3		
08/62				D6354/5		
09/62				D6356		
10/62						
11/62				D6357		
12/62						

Notes:
1. D600-4, D8400-9, D6100-57, D6300-35 and E3036-45 delivery dates are based on NBL Invoice Dates (as distinct from BR acceptance dates). In the absence of NBL archive data, D6336-57, D833-65 deliveries are based on BR acceptance dates.
2. It took virtually four years in total to build D6300-57.

etc) and the introduction and accommodation of the new LT306r transmission.

The disproportionately heavy delivery delays to D6334-57 were as a direct consequence of difficulties experienced with setting up the NBL production line for the Swindon-designed bodyshells for the D833-65 order, combined with delays in supplies of key components from external suppliers. As a consequence of these problems, the BTC was forced into choosing between D833-65 or D6334-57 and the decision was made to prioritise the former. Further delays to the diesel-hydraulic Type 2s resulted from ongoing design modifications, some made after experience with the first few locomotives in traffic and others as a result of up-grades requested by the BTC (e.g. snow plough brackets, brake accelerating devices, etc.), although not all modifications were applied to every locomotive.

Perhaps surprisingly, the placing of NBL into administration had no adverse impact on deliveries of the Type 2s once the D833-65 order had been cleared, indicating the urgency which the liquidators placed on resolving outstanding financial liabilities.

5.3 Delivery Routing
The routing for the NBL Type 2s from Glasgow to Swindon Works for acceptance trials was: Glasgow-Carlisle (presumably via Kilmarnock)-Preston-Crewe-Nantwich-Market Drayton-Wellington-Wolverhampton-Birmingham Snow Hill-Leamington-Banbury-Didcot-Swindon (with a recess at Oxley TMD en route).

An interview with John Blyth formed the basis of an article, 'Blyth Spirit!', in *Classic Diesels & Electrics* (No.9). Blyth worked in the Research Section of the Operating Manager's Office at Paddington from 1955 to 1963 and was heavily involved with the introduction and operation of the diesel-hydraulics; his comments regarding the release and delivery of the D63xx locomotives from NBL make interesting reading:

Blyth on the D6300s.
Inspector Joe Field, ex-Newport District, by then at HQ, was a quiet-spoken man, but he would get really worked up when he had had a bad time at Glasgow collecting a couple of these things.

Arriving on the appointed day to give them, he hoped, a quick once over to see that everything worked, he would find that assembly was incomplete, the paint, even in the cabs, was still wet (having been slapped on quickly that morning!) and many things wanting adjusting such as the suspension, to give some approximation of the right axle-load. Often he had to wait an extra day, occasionally two.

5.4 Commissioning and Acceptance Testing.
All locomotives were subject to acceptance testing at Swindon; work carried out included:

- Locomotive functional testing and NBL defect rectification.
- WR ATC equipment installation.
- Gangway equipment installation (up to D6331; fitted by NBL thereafter).
- Locomotive weighing and axle-weight adjustments.
- Height adjustments.

5.5 Running-In
Before entering traffic at Plymouth Laira, new D6300 locomotives were run-in from 82C Swindon, often with two in tandem to reduce track occupation, on various passenger, parcels and freight services. It is understood that the highest power setting on their controllers were locked-out during this initial running-in period.

Details of some of the services operated from Swindon are listed below using extracts from 1959/60 *Trains Illustrated* magazines:

D6300-2, arrived at Swindon in January [1959] … the new diesels were noted on trials as twin-units between Swindon and Gloucester during January. (March 1959)

The NBL … diesel-hydraulic units made their London debut early in February [1959] when D6301/2 were operating between Swindon and London on the up Wootton Bassett milk and the 8.30 parcels to Cardiff; on 21 February the pair were noted on a recent 'Warship' duty, the 7.50a.m. Taunton-Paddington and down afternoon parcels. (April 1959)

D6301/2 worked from Swindon to Plymouth with the 4.15p.m. ex-Paddington on March 8 [1959]. Soon afterwards, D6302 returned to Swindon, but D6300/1 began consistent multiple-unit working between Penzance and Plymouth on the 1.20p.m. Penzance-Paddington and 11.10 Swansea-Penzance. (May 1959)

D6306/7 worked up to Paddington with the 7.5a.m. from Cheltenham on October 7, 9, 12, 14, 16 [1959], returning to Swindon with the Kensington-Whitland milk empties; on October 13 the pair were seen on the 7.50a.m. Taunton-Paddington and 2.20p.m. parcels down from Paddington. (December 1959)

In January [1960] pairs of NBL 1,000hp diesel-hydraulic locomotives were working multiple unit on the 7.50a.m. Taunton-Paddington and an afternoon down parcels back to Swindon; On January 7, 8 and 9 D6308/11 were

D6309, Preston, 13 October 1959. Boiler water refilling access door open. (Arnold Battson [Transport Treasury])

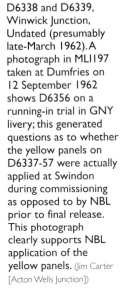

D6338 and D6339, Winwick Junction, Undated (presumably late-March 1962). A photograph in MLI197 taken at Dumfries on 12 September 1962 shows D6356 on a running-in trial in GNY livery; this generated questions as to whether the yellow panels on D6337-57 were actually applied at Swindon during commissioning as opposed to by NBL prior to final release. This photograph clearly supports NBL application of the yellow panels. (Jim Carter [Acton Wells Junction])

thus employed, on January 13 D6309/13 and on January 18 D6312/8 (*sic D6308/12*), but on the last occasion D6308 developed a fault and the parcels working left for Swindon behind 'Hall' 4962; D6314/5 appeared on this turn on January 26. (March 1960)

5.6 Liquidated Damages for Late Deliveries and Poor Workmanship.

During 1961, and possibly into 1962, the BTC considered and commenced claims against NBL for liquidated damages resulting from late deliveries and poor workmanship, a process which also involved the Ministry of Transport and the Board of Trade. Unfortunately, information in the archives is somewhat disjointed due to its incomplete nature and commercial sensitivity. The size of the damages potentially claimed by the BTC was somewhat vague although an overall figure of £300,000 was quoted. The following documents provide an interesting insight nonetheless:

Internal Memorandum to BTC Supply Committee, 24/02/61.
North British Locomotive Co. Ltd.

1. The North British Locomotive Co. Ltd. ['the Company'] have had 12 contracts, valued at approximately £15m for a total of 239 diesel locomotives … There have been delays in delivery on all of the 10 contracts completed, and on the 2 outstanding contracts, the largest, deliveries are also much behind schedule. Many of the locomotives delivered have been unsatisfactory technically and have had to be modified. Quite apart from this, the delays on the contracts completed have involved the Commission in losses. The contracts still to be completed are for 52 Type 2 and 33 Type 4 diesel-hydraulic locomotives, and if as seems certain the delays will have involved the Commission in losses on these too; the Company's contractual liability for liquidated damages could exceed £1m. The major part would arise on the contracts still running, but it is necessary to give some indication now of our intentions on the earlier contracts.

2. In their 1959 Accounts the Company set aside £150,000 against such liabilities, and in the annual report the Chairman mentioned that … charges could be a great deal more.

3. In recent years the Company has incurred substantial trading losses and they are now financially weak and their future prospects uncertain. If we claim our maximum entitlement they might be forced into liquidation. It might be contrary to our own interest to allow this to happen. Firstly, because there are secured bank loans and loan capital which would rank first and we might receive only a small dividend; and secondly, because they have a separate contract for 74 sets of Voith/NBL transmission equipments required for ['*Western*'] locomotives being manufactured in Railway Workshops. This contract is not due for completion until October 1962, and on the basis of present planning it seems likely that further requirements for similar equipment will arise. The loan capital includes a Treasury grant of £1¾m granted in 1959 to assist the Company in their difficulties …

4. There are other locomotive manufacturers who have failed to fulfil delivery promises, but the shortcomings of NBL have been the most serious … It would be undesirable and unfair to claim damages every time a delivery promise is broken, but, on the other hand, if contractors let us down badly and the Commission is involved in serious losses, it would be wrong to release them from all liability. If we did so we would certainly be criticised.

5. … I recommend that we should pursue the claim against NBL, with a view to compromising if possible for a worthwhile cash payment.
Signed: S.C. Robbins (Chief Contracts Officer).

Supply Committee Meeting, 03/03/61.
Min.908. North British Locomotive Co. Ltd.
A confidential memorandum dated 24 February 1961 was submitted by the Chief Contracts Officer reporting upon the position of NBL and their contractual liability in respect of losses incurred by the Commission as a result of late delivery.

D6318, Swindon Works (AE Shop), 27 March 1960.
(Norman Preedy [Kidderminster Railway Museum])

In the course of the discussions which ensued, Mr. Hanks (*BTC*) mentioned that, in addition to the matters referred to by Mr. Robbins, the Western Region had under consideration a claim against the Company for expenditure incurred in rectifying faults in the locomotives.

The Committee agreed that as a matter of principle the Commission should pursue their claims against NBL. They instructed the Chief Contracts Officer to approach the Management of the Company informally after he had consulted the General Manager of the WR about claims arising under the maintenance clause of the contracts, and to report further to the Committee in due course.

Background Paper re. NBL. produced by E.C.V. Goad (Ministry of Transport), 16/05/61.
Subject: Potential Government intervention re. BTC's £300,000 claim for damages against NBL for late delivery.

N.B. First page missing, so starting from Page 2:

1. … the President of the Board of Trade, who has copied his letter to the Chancellor and the Secretary of State for Scotland, suggests that the Minister should put a paper to EPC [Economic Policy Committee] raising the question whether the Government would be justified in intervening with the Commission in a claim which the Commission are contemplating against NBL for damages of £300,000.
2. NBL have been a thorn in our flesh since at least March 1960. They have on several occasions moved the Board of Trade and the Secretary of State for Scotland to approach the Minister [of Transport] suggesting that they should be specially favoured in getting orders from the Commission for locomotives and should be allowed to revise tenders already submitted to the Commission. These suggestions have been before the EPC and the Cabinet on several occasions, on each of which it has been decided that no special action should be taken to assist NBL, even though they are: (i) in receipt of Government assistance via the Board of Trade; and, (ii) located in Scotland which has a higher unemployment rate than the rest of Great Britain.
3. The general grounds on which past approaches have been resisted have been that the placing of orders is a matter for the Commission's commercial judgement and they must be expected to act as any commercial undertaking would. These arguments apply *a fortiori* to intervention in a matter which is purely contractual between the Commission and their suppliers.
4. In addition, however, in this latest approach by the President of the Board of Trade there is the point that if the Board of Trade are so keen to see NBL

D6348 and D6349, Swindon Works (A Shop Yard), June 1962. (Rail-Online)

D6356, Swindon Works (A Shop Yard), 25 September 1962. (N.W. Skinner [David Dunn Collection])

D6306 and D6307, Swindon, 9 October 1959. (N.W. Skinner [David Dunn Collection])

survive because they have a future apart from making locomotives, the Board of Trade presumably have funds at their disposal, from which they have already assisted the company, which could be used again to tide them over any difficulties which might be caused by the Commission securing damages from the Company. This is the honest way of propping the Company up. It is quite dishonest and could cause quite an outcry if it became known that the Commission were being persuaded by the Government to forego damages which, because of the Commission's financial position, would fall upon the taxpayer.

Supply Committee Meeting, 02/06/61.
Min.950. North British Locomotive Co. Ltd.
With reference to Minute 908, the Committee noted the letter dated 29 May 1961 (*not seen*), which had been sent by the Chief Contracts Officer to NBL, copies of which had been circulated for information.

Memorandum to BTC, 08/09/61.
Locomotives and Rolling Stock: Recovery of Damages Arising from Delays in Delivery.
The Commission's General Conditions of Contract for Locomotives and Rolling Stock provide for the payment to the Commission of liquidated damages at the rate of one half per cent of the contract unit price per week, but subject to a maximum of 15%, if the Contractor fails to make delivery at the proper time and, in consequence, the Commission suffers loss. The Contractor is entitled to ask for an extension of time for completion if during the performance of the contract it appears that delay is likely to arise because of industrial disputes or other causes outside the Contractor's control.

It is not our practice to claim damages every time a delivery promise is broken. To do so would be unreasonable and might prejudice our relationship with industry generally. Delays can arise from a variety of causes and each case is considered on its merits. Claims are pursued only if the Contractor's shortcomings are serious and have involved the Commission in substantial loss.

At the present time fairly substantial claims are being pursued against NBL who have been persistently late, in some cases more than a year late, with deliveries on a number of contracts for locomotives …
The Supply Committee considered the Commission should be informed of the position. Supplementary information as to the approximate sums involved can be given orally at the Commission meeting."
Signed: A.B.B. Valentine
(Chairman, Supply Committee).

BTC Meeting, 14/09/61.
Minute 14/316. Locomotive and Rolling Stock Contracts: Delay in Delivery.
The Commission considered a Memorandum from the Chairman of the Supply Committee dated 8 September 1961, reporting the position with regard to claims by the Commission against Contractors for delay in delivery of locomotives and rolling stock. The Chief Contracts Officer attended for this item.

The Chairman outlined what had transpired following a request he had received to discuss the position with the Chairman of NBL, whom he was meeting shortly, in regard to the claims against that Company. He had made it clear that the purpose of the meeting was to discuss any proposals for ameliorating the difficulties of the firm, but not to consider modifications of the Chairman's claims. The Commission agreed that the Chairman should negotiate with the Chairman of NBL on the lines he indicated. There was, however, the possibility that pursuit of the claim against NBL would cause the Company to fail, leading to unfavourable publicity and little financial gain to the Commission.

An internal memorandum from the Chief Contracts Officer to the Supply Committee, dated 12 February 1962, with respect to the D6300-5 contract, stated that it was "among those for which the Commission decided to abandon claims for damages for late delivery, on the grounds that on balance it would have been contrary to the Commission's interest to pursue them". Whether the same applied to D6306-57 is not known but highly likely given BTC's full awareness of NBL's parlous financial state.

Chapter 6

ALLOCATIONS

6.1 Data Presentation.

A full allocation history of the D63xx locomotives is provided over the next few pages. To ensure comprehensive listings and to maximise period-ending accuracy, numerous commercial and society sources were researched and compared.

All information is presented as week-ending periods for consistency, despite the fact that during the 1965/66 period many sources listed re-allocations using week-commencing periods (presumably following Rolling Stock Library contemporary reporting practice). However, given that 1 week commencing 13/09/65 (Monday), for example, can only accurately be converted to 2 week ending 25/09/65 (Saturday), both dates are provided in such instances to ensure maximum accuracy.

Abbreviations used are as follows:

Depots:
81A: Old Oak Common (London), **81D:** Reading.
81F: Oxford.
82A: Bristol Bath Road, **82C:** Swindon.

83A: Newton Abbot.
83D: Plymouth Laira (to 08/09/63).
84A: Plymouth Laira (from 09/09/63).
85A: Worcester.

Storage:
st: Store.
st(u/r) or **(u/s):** Stored 'Unrepaired' or 'Unserviceable' (seemingly used interchangeably). Almost invariably only one description was used in any given weekly period, the only exception being 2we 08/05/71 where D6309/12/5/8/20/3/7/54 were shown 'store u/r', whilst D6340 was shown 'store u/s'. Many locomotives were stored without qualification.

Other:
NYA: Not yet allocated (before entering traffic).
wc: Week-commencing.
we: Week-ending.

6.2 Allocation History

Loco. No.	Stock Changes	
	xwe (All dates Saturdays)	Precise Dates
D6300	4we 27/12/58-NYA	
	4we 24/01/59-82C	12/01/59
	4we 21/02/59-83D	xx/02/59
	4we 28/09/63-84A	09/09/63
	1we 11/05/68-st (84A)	
	1we 01/06/68-Wdn (ex-st (84A))	26/05/68
D6301	"4we 24/01/59-NYA, then 82C"	
	4we 21/02/59-83D	19/02/59
	4we 28/09/63-84A	09/09/63
	2we 13/05/67-st (84A)	08/05/67
	3we 15/07/67-84A	26/06/67
	1we 11/11/67-st (84A)	09/11/67
	1we 30/12/67-Wdn (ex-st (84A))	30/12/67

Loco. No.	Stock Changes	
	xwe (All dates Saturdays)	Precise Dates
D6302	4we 24/01/59-NYA, then 82C	
	4we 21/02/59-83D	19/02/59
	4we 28/09/63-84A	09/09/63
	1we 11/05/68-st (84A)	
	1we 01/06/68-Wdn (ex-st (84A))	26/05/68
D6303	4we 16/05/69-NYA	
	4we 13/06/59-83D	22/05/59
	4we 28/09/63-84A	09/09/63
	1we 11/05/68-st (84A)	
	1we 01/06/68-Wdn (ex-st (84A))	26/05/68
D6304	4we 11/07/59-83D	23/06/59
	4we 28/09/63-84A	09/09/63
	1we 11/05/68-st (84A)	
	1we 01/06/68-Wdn (ex-st (84A))	26/05/68

Loco. No.	Stock Changes	
	xwe (All dates Saturdays)	Precise Dates
D6305	4we 30/01/60-83D	11/01/60
	4we 28/09/63-84A	09/09/63
	1we 11/05/68-st (84A)	
	1we 01/06/68-Wdn (ex-st (84A))	26/05/68
D6306	4we 03/10/59-NYA	
	4we 31/10/59-83D	12/10/59
	4we 28/09/63-84A	09/09/63
	1we 21/12/68-Wdn (ex-84A)	21/12/68
D6307	4we 03/10/59-NYA	
	4we 31/10/59-83D	12/10/59
	4we 28/09/63-84A	09/09/63
	1we 27/03/71-Wdn (ex-84A)	27/03/71
D6308	4we 30/01/60-83D	07/01/60
	4we 28/09/63-84A	09/09/63
	1we 14/06/69-st(u/s) (84A)	xx/06/69
	1we 14/03/70-Swindon Works	09/03/70
	1we 06/06/70-82A	05/06/70
	2we 08/05/71-84A	xx/05/71
	1we 14/08/71-st (84A)	11/08/71
	1we 11/09/71-Wdn (ex-st (84A))	11/09/71
D6309	4we 30/01/60-83D	12/01/60
	4we 28/09/63-84A	09/09/63
	2we 08/05/71-st(u/r) (84A/Exeter)	02/05/71
	1we 22/05/71-Wdn (ex-st (84A))	22/05/71
D6310	4we 30/01/60-83D	05/01/60
	4we 28/09/63-84A	09/09/63
	3we 15/07/67-83A	xx/06/67
	1we 05/07/69-82A	xx/06/69
	1we 27/03/71-Wdn (ex-82A)	27/03/71
D6311	4we 30/01/60-83D	07/01/60
	4we 28/09/63-84A	09/09/63
	1we 17/06/67-83A	xx/06/67
	2we 16/09/67-82A	xx/09/67
	1we 06/01/68-84A	xx/01/68
	1we 14/09/68-st(u/r) (84A)	xx/09/68
	1we 28/09/68-Wdn (ex-st (84A))	23/09/68
D6312	4we 30/01/60-83D	14/01/60
	4we 28/09/63-84A	09/09/63
	3we 18/02/67-83A	xx/02/67
	2we 16/09/67-82A	xx/09/67
	6we 02/12/67-84A	xx/11/67
	2we 08/05/71-st(u/r) (84A/Exeter)	02/05/71
	1we 22/05/71-Wdn (ex-st (84A))	22/05/71
D6313	4we 30/01/60-83D	12/01/60
	4we 28/09/63-84A	09/09/63

Loco. No.	Stock Changes	
	xwe (All dates Saturdays)	Precise Dates
D6313	2we 11/02/67-83A	xx/01/67
	3we 25/02/67-82A	xx/02/67
	2we 13/05/67-83A	xx/05/67
	2we 16/09/67-82A	xx/09/67
	1we 11/05/68-84A	xx/05/68
	1we 15/06/68-st(u/r) (84A)	xx/06/68
	1we 03/08/68-Wdn (ex-st (84A))	03/08/68
D6314	4we 30/01/60-83D	25/01/60
	4we 28/09/63-84A	09/09/63
	3we 19/11/66-83A	xx/11/66
	2we 11/03/67-84A	xx/01/67
	1we 19/04/69-st(u/s) (84A)	18/04/69
	1we 26/04/69-Wdn (ex-st (84A))	26/04/69
D6315	4we 30/01/60-83D	25/01/60
	4we 28/09/63-84A	09/09/63
	3we 19/11/66-83A	xx/11/66
	2we 16/09/67-82A	xx/09/67
	1we 11/05/68-84A	xx/05/68
	2we 08/05/71-st(u/r) (84A/Exeter)	02/05/71
	1we 22/05/71-Wdn (ex-st (84A))	22/05/71
D6316	4we 26/03/60-83D	01/03/60
	4we 28/09/63-84A	09/09/63
	2we 15/10/66-83A (1wc 04/10/66)	xx/10/66
	2we 16/09/67-82A	xx/09/67
	1we 23/03/68-st (85A)	xx/03/68
	1we 06/04/68-Wdn (ex-st (85A))	31/03/68
D6317	4we 26/03/60-83D	01/03/60
	4we 28/09/63-84A	09/09/63
	2we 20/08/66-83A (1wc 09/08/66)	xx/08/66
	2we 16/09/67-82A	xx/09/67
	1we 11/05/68-84A	xx/05/68
	1we 07/09/68-st(u/r) (84A)	xx/09/68
	1we 28/09/68-Wdn (ex-st (84A))	23/09/68
D6318	4we 26/03/60-83D	14/03/60
	4we 28/09/63-84A	09/09/63
	2we 20/08/66-83A (1wc 09/08/66)	xx/08/66
	2we 16/09/67-82A	xx/09/67
	1we 11/05/68-84A	xx/05/68
	2we 08/05/71-st(u/r) (84A)	02/05/71
	1we 22/05/71-Wdn (ex-st (84A))	22/05/71
D6319	4we 23/04/60-83D	11/04/60
	4we 28/09/63-84A	09/09/63
	2we 20/08/66-83A (1wc 09/08/66)	xx/08/66
	2we 16/09/67-82A	xx/09/67
	1we 10/08/68-st(u/s) (85A)	

Loco. No.	Stock Changes	
	xwe (All dates Saturdays)	Precise Dates
D6319	1we 17/08/68-84A	xx/08/68
	1we 27/03/71-Wdn (ex-84A)	27/03/71
	1we 08/05/71-84A	02/05/71
	1we 04/09/71-st(u/r) (84A)	02/09/71
	1we 11/09/71-Wdn (ex-st (84A))	11/09/71
D6320	4we 26/03/60-83D	23/03/60
	4we 28/09/63-84A	09/09/63
	2we 30/04/66-83A (1wc 18/04/66)	xx/04/66
	3we 15/07/67-82A	xx/06/67
	2we 08/05/71-st(u/r) (82A)	02/05/71
	1we 22/05/71-Wdn (ex-st (82A))	22/05/71
D6321	4we 23/04/60-83D	07/04/60
	4we 28/09/63-84A	09/09/63
	2we 30/04/66-83A (1wc 18/04/66)	xx/04/66
	4we 24/06/67-82A	xx/06/67
	1we 15/06/68-st(u/r) (85A)	xx/06/68
	1we 03/08/68-Wdn (ex-st (85A))	03/08/68
D6322	4we 23/04/60-83D	07/04/60
	4we 28/09/63-84A	09/09/63
	1we 18/09/65-83A	xx/08/65
	3we 20/05/67-82A	xx/05/67
	4we 24/06/67-84A	xx/06/67
	1we 09/10/71-Wdn (ex-84A)	03/10/71
D6323	4we 23/04/60-NYA	
	4we 21/05/60-83D	25/04/60
	4we 28/09/63-84A	09/09/63
	1we 18/09/65-83A	xx/08/65
	3we 18/02/67-82A	
	3we 25/02/67-83A	
	3we 20/05/67-82A	xx/05/67
	1we 14/09/68-84A	xx/09/68
	2we 08/05/71-st(u/r) (84A)	02/05/71
	1we 22/05/71-Wdn (ex-st (84A))	22/05/71
D6324	4we 18/06/60-83D	01/06/60
	4we 28/09/63-84A	09/09/63
	1we 21/01/67-82A	xx/01/67
	1we 10/08/68-st (85A)	xx/08/68
	1we 14/09/68-Wdn (ex-st (85A))	14/09/68
D6325	4we 18/06/60-83D	14/06/60
	4we 28/09/63-84A	09/09/63
	1we 18/09/65-83A	xx/09/65
	3we 21/01/67-82A	xx/12/66
	1we 28/09/68-st(u/r) (85A)	xx/09/68
	1we 05/10/68-Wdn (ex-st (85A))	05/10/68
D6326	4we 21/05/60-83D	16/05/60

Loco. No.	Stock Changes	
	xwe (All dates Saturdays)	Precise Dates
D6326	4we 28/01/61-83A	xx/01/61
	4we 24/03/62-83D	xx/03/62
	4we 28/09/63-84A	09/09/63
	4we 28/09/63-81A	xx/09/63
	1we 03/04/71-84A	xx/03/71
	1we 02/10/71-st(u/r) (84A)	30/09/71
	1we 09/10/71-Wdn (ex-st (84A))	03/10/71
D6327	4we 18/06/60-NYA	
	4we 16/07/60-83D	30/06/60
	4we 28/01/61-83A	xx/01/61
	5we 25/07/64-84A	xx/07/64
	1we 10/07/65-83A	xx/07/65
	2we 18/12/65-81A (1wc 06/12/65)	xx/12/65
	1we 07/02/70-82A	xx/02/70
	2we 08/05/71-st(u/r) (82A)	02/05/71
	1we 22/05/71-Wdn (ex-st (82A))	22/05/71
D6328	4we 18/06/60-83D	18/06/60
	4we 28/01/61-83A	xx/01/61
	5we 27/07/64-84A	xx/07/64
	1we 10/07/65-83A	xx/07/65
	2we 18/12/65-81A (1wc 06/12/65)	xx/12/65
	1we 02/01/71-82A	xx/12/70
	2we 08/05/71-84A	xx/05/71
	2we 17/07/71-st (84A)	08/07/71
	2we 17/07/71-Wdn (ex-st (84A))	17/07/71
D6329	4we 18/06/60-83D	18/06/60
	4we 28/01/61-83A	xx/01/61
	2we 18/12/65-81A (1wc 06/12/65)	xx/12/65
	2we 18/12/65-83A (1wc 13/12/65)	xx/12/65
	3we 21/01/67-82A	xx/01/67
	2we 16/09/67-83A	xx/09/67
	1we 05/10/68-82A	xx/10/68
	1we 02/11/68-st(u/r) (85A)	27/10/68
	1we 30/11/68-Wdn (ex-st (85A))	30/11/68
D6330	4we 16/07/60-NYA	
	4we 13/08/60-83D	23/07/60
	4we 28/01/61-83A	xx/01/61
	2we 25/12/65-81A (1wc 13/12/65)	xx/12/65
	1we 15/01/66-83A	xx/01/66
	2we 19/11/66-82A	xx/11/66
	2we 16/09/67-83A	xx/09/67
	2we 20/07/68-84A	xx/07/68
	1we 14/09/68-st(u/r) (84A)	xx/09/68
	1we 28/09/68-Wdn (ex-st (84A))	23/09/68
	1we 13/09/69-84A	08/09/69

Loco. No.	Stock Changes	
	xwe (All dates Saturdays)	Precise Dates
D6330	1we 10/01/70-83A	xx/01/70
	2we 08/05/71-84A	xx/05/71
	1we 09/10/71-Wdn (ex-84A)	03/10/71
D6331	4we 16/07/60-NYA	
	4we 13/08/60-83D	26/07/60
	4we 28/01/61-83A	xx/01/61
	2we 19/11/66-82A	xx/11/66
	2we 16/09/67-83A	xx/09/67
	1we 14/12/68-82A	xx/12/68
	1we 03/04/71-Wdn (ex-82A)	27/03/71
D6332	4we 16/07/60-NYA	
	4we 13/08/60-83D	28/07/60
	4we 25/02/61-83A	xx/02/61
	1we 15/01/66-81A	xx/01/66
	1we 24/04/71-st(u/s) (81A)	20/04/71
	1we 22/05/71-Wdn (ex-st (81A))	22/05/71
D6333	4we 13/08/60-83D	03/08/60
	4we 25/02/61-83A	xx/02/61
	2we 15/10/66-82A (1wc 04/10/66)	xx/10/66
	2we 16/09/67-83A	xx/09/67
	2we 08/05/71-84A	xx/05/71
	1we 18/12/71-st (84A)	18/12/71
	1we 01/01/72-Wdn (ex-st (84A))	01/01/72
D6334	4we 03/12/60-83D	01/12/60
	4we 15/07/61-83A	xx/07/61
	2we 15/10/66-82A (1wc 04/10/66)	xx/10/66
	2we 16/09/67-83A	xx/09/67
	2we 08/05/71-84A	xx/05/71
	1we 09/10/71-Wdn (ex-84A)	03/10/71
D6335	4we 25/02/61-83D	22/02/61
	4we 15/07/61-83A	xx/07/61
	6we 10/10/64-81A	xx/09/64
	1we 10/08/68-st(u/s) (81A)	xx/08/68
	1we 14/09/68-Wdn (ex-st (81A))	14/09/68
D6336	4we 15/07/61-83A	03/07/61
	2we 20/08/66-82A (1wc 09/08/66)	xx/08/66
	2we 20/05/67-st (82A)	08/05/67
	3we 15/07/67-82A	26/06/67
	2we 16/09/67-83A	xx/09/67
	2we 20/07/68-84A	xx/07/68
	1we 09/11/68-81A	xx/11/68
	2we 08/05/71-84A	xx/05/71
	1we 09/10/71-Wdn (ex-84A)	03/10/71
	1we 23/10/71-84A	21/10/71
	1we 18/12/71-st (84A)	18/12/71

Loco. No.	Stock Changes	
	xwe (All dates Saturdays)	Precise Dates
D6336	1we 01/01/72-Wdn (ex-st (84A))	01/01/72
D6337	4we 24/03/62-83A	13/03/62
	2we 30/07/66-82A (1wc 19/07/66)	xx/07/66
	2we 16/09/67-83A	xx/09/67
	1we 10/01/70-84A	xx/01/70
	1we 23/10/71-Wdn (ex-84A)	21/10/71
D6338	4we 24/03/62-NYA	
	4we 21/04/62-83D	29/03/62
	4we 14/07/62-83A	xx/07/62
	2we 20/08/66-82A (1wc 09/08/66)	xx/08/66
	2we 20/05/67-st (82A)	08/05/67
	3we 15/07/67-82A	26/06/67
	1we 15/06/68-83A	xx/06/68
	1we 29/08/70-82A	24/08/70
	1we 24/10/70-83A	xx/10/70
	1we 08/05/71-84A	xx/05/71
	1we 18/12/71-st (84A)	18/12/71
	1we 01/01/72-Wdn (ex-st (84A))	01/01/72
D6339	4we 21/04/62-83D	02/04/62
	4we 14/07/62-83A	xx/07/62
	4we 06/10/62-83D	xx/10/62
	4we 28/09/63-84A	09/09/63
	1we 14/11/64-83A	xx/11/64
	1we 08/05/71-84A	xx/05/71
	1we 09/10/71-Wdn (ex-84A)	03/10/71
	1we 30/10/71-84A	25/10/71
	1we 18/12/71-st (84A)	18/12/71
	1we 01/01/72-Wdn (ex-st (84A))	01/01/72
D6340	4we 21/04/62-83D	03/04/62
	4we 14/07/62-83A	xx/07/62
	4we 28/09/63-84A	09/09/63
	1we 10/07/65-83A	xx/07/65
	2we 30/04/66-81A (1wc 18/04/66)	xx/04/66
	2we 04/03/67-82A (on loan)	xx/02/67
	3we 13/05/67-82A (permanent)	xx/05/67
	2we 19/08/67-81A	xx/08/67
	2we 08/05/71-84A	xx/05/71
	5we 08/05/71-st(u/s) (84A)	04/05/71
	1we 22/05/71-Wdn (ex-st (84A))	22/05/71
D6341	4we 19/05/62-83D	12/05/62
	4we 28/09/63-84A	09/09/63
	1we 05/06/65-83A	xx/05/65
	2we 30/04/66-81A (1wc 18/04/66)	xx/04/66
	3we 13/05/67-82A	xx/05/67
	2we 20/05/67-st (81A)	08/05/67

Loco. No.	Stock Changes	
	xwe (All dates Saturdays)	Precise Dates
D6341	3we 15/07/67-82A	26/06/67
	2we 19/08/67-81A	xx/08/67
	1we 10/08/68-st (81A)	
	1we 17/08/68-81A	
	1we 02/11/68-st(u/r) (81A)	xx/11/68
	1we 30/11/68-Wdn (ex-st (81A))	30/11/68
D6342	4we 19/05/62-83D	11/05/62
	4we 11/08/62-83A	xx/08/62
	4we 06/10/62-83D	xx/10/62
	4we 28/09/63-84A	09/09/63
	1we 05/06/65-83A	xx/05/65
	1we 30/10/65-81A	xx/10/65
	4we 24/06/67-82A	xx/06/67
	2we 20/04/68-81A	
	1we 04/05/68-82A	
	1we 21/12/68-Wdn (ex-82A)	21/12/68
D6343	4we 19/05/62-83D	10/05/62
	4we 11/08/62-83A	xx/08/62
	4we 06/10/62-83D	xx/10/62
	4we 28/09/63-84A	09/09/63
	3we 13/06/64-81A	xx/05/64
	2we 08/05/71-84A	xx/05/71
	1we 09/10/71-Wdn (ex-84A)	03/10/71
D6344	4we 19/05/62-83D	18/05/62
	4we 11/08/62-83A	xx/08/62
	4we 06/10/62-83D	xx/10/62
	4we 28/09/63-84A	09/09/63
	1we 05/06/65-83A	xx/05/65
	1we 30/10/65-81A	xx/10/65
	1we 10/08/68-st(u/s) (81A)	xx/08/68
	1we 14/09/68-Wdn (ex-st (81A))	14/09/68
D6345	4we 19/05/62-83D	19/05/62
	4we 11/08/62-83A	xx/08/62
	4we 06/10/62-83D	xx/10/62
	4we 28/09/63-84A	09/09/63
	1we 05/06/65-83A	xx/05/65
	1we 30/10/65-81A	xx/10/65
	1we 17/08/68-st(u/s) (81A)	xx/08/68
	1we 14/09/68-Wdn (ex-st (81A))	14/09/68
D6346	4we 16/06/62-83D	08/06/62
	4we 28/09/63-84A	09/09/63
	1we 05/06/65-83A	xx/05/65
	1we 30/10/65-81A	xx/10/65
	1we 02/11/68-st (81A)	xx/10/68
	1we 09/11/68-81A	

Loco. No.	Stock Changes	
	xwe (All dates Saturdays)	Precise Dates
D6346	1we 25/01/69-st(u/r) (81A)	xx/01/69
	1we 26/04/69-Wdn (ex-st (81A))	26/04/69
D6347	4we 16/06/62-82A	02/06/62
	2we 17/11/62-83D	xx/11/62
	4we 28/09/63-84A	09/09/63
	1we 05/06/65-83A	xx/05/65
	2we 25/09/65-81D (1wc 13/09/65)	
	2we 02/10/65-81A	
	1we 23/03/68-st (81A)	
	1we 06/04/68-Wdn (ex-st (81A))	31/03/68
D6348	4we 16/06/62-83D	14/06/62
	4we 28/09/63-84A	09/09/63
	1we 05/06/65-83A	xx/05/65
	2we 25/09/65-81D (1wc 13/09/65)	
	2we 02/10/65-81A	
	1we 10/02/68-83A	xx/02/68
	1we 15/06/68-84A	xx/06/68
	1we 21/09/68-81A	xx/09/68
	1we 19/04/69-84A	xx/04/69
	1we 10/05/69-st (84A)	05/05/69
	1we 14/06/69-82A	xx/06/69
	1we 07/02/70-st (82A)	
	1we 07/03/70-82A	xx/03/70
	2we 08/05/71-84A	xx/05/71
	2we 17/07/71-st (84A)	13/07/71
	1we 24/07/71-Wdn (ex-st (84A))	24/07/71
D6349	4we 16/06/62-83D	14/06/62
	2we 17/11/62-82A	xx/11/62
	5we 04/04/64-84A	xx/03/64
	1we 05/06/65-83A	xx/05/65
	2we 25/09/65-81D (1wc 13/09/65)	
	2we 02/10/65-81A	
	1we 20/01/68-84A	xx/01/68
	1we 30/03/68-81A	xx/03/68
	2we 20/04/68-82A	xx/04/68
	1we 10/08/68-84A	
	1we 17/08/68-st(u/s) (84A)	
	1we 14/09/68-Wdn (ex-st (84A))	14/09/68
D6350	4we 14/07/62-83D	27/06/62
	2we 17/11/62-82A	xx/11/62
	5we 04/04/64-84A	xx/03/64
	1we 05/06/65-83A	xx/05/65
	2we 25/09/65-81D (1wc 130965)	
	2we 02/10/65-81A	
	1we 10/08/68-st (81A)	xx/08/68

Loco. No.	Stock Changes		Loco. No.	Stock Changes	
	xwe (All dates Saturdays)	Precise Dates		xwe (All dates Saturdays)	Precise Dates
D6350	1we 14/09/68-Wdn (ex-st (81A))	14/09/68	D6354	1we 11/01/69-83A	xx/01/69
D6351	4we 14/07/62-83D	27/06/62		1we 05/07/69-82A	xx/06/69
	4we 06/10/62-82A	xx/10/62		2we 08/05/71-st(u/r) (82A)	02/05/71
	3we 19/09/64-81A	xx/09/64		1we 22/05/71-Wdn (ex-st (82A))	22/05/71
	1we 09/11/68-st(u/r) (81A)		D6355	4we 08/09/62-82A	24/08/62
	1we 30/11/68-Wdn (ex-st (81A))	30/11/68		2we 31/10/64-81A	xx/10/64
D6352	4we 14/07/62-83D	12/07/62		1we 10/08/68-st(u/s) (81A)	xx/08/68
	4we 06/10/62-82A	xx/10/62		1we 14/09/68-Wdn (ex-st (81A))	14/09/68
	3we 19/09/64-81A	xx/09/64	D6356	4we 06/10/62-82A	27/09/62
	1we 14/06/69-st (???)			2we 31/10/64-81A	xx/10/64
	1we 14/06/69-82A	xx/06/69		1we 10/05/69-84A	xx/05/69
	1we 29/08/70-83A	xx/08/70		1we 14/06/69-st (???)	
	1we 24/10/70-82A	xx/10/70		1we 14/06/69-84A	
	1we 08/05/71-Wdn (ex-82A)	02/05/71		1we 13/09/69-st(u/r) (84A)	xx/09/69
D6353	4we 14/07/62-83D	12/07/62		1we 06/12/69-Swindon Works	04/12/69
	4we 06/10/62-82A	xx/10/62		1we 07/02/70-81A	xx/02/70
	1we 14/11/64-81A	xx/11/64		2we 08/05/71-84A	xx/05/71
	1we 07/09/68-st(u/r) (81F)	xx/09/68		1we 09/10/71-Wdn (ex-84A)	03/10/71
	1we 28/09/68-Wdn (ex-st (81F))	23/09/68	D6357	2we 17/11/62-82A	13/11/62
D6354	4we 11/08/62-82A	02/08/62		3we 19/09/64-81A	xx/09/64
	4we 28/09/63-84A	09/09/63		1we 14/12/68-st (81D)	
	3we 19/09/64-81A	xx/09/64		1we 21/12/68-Wdn (ex-st (81D))	21/12/68

Notes:

1. Supporting information:

D6308/28/36/43/8/56	Arrived at 84A Plymouth Laira on 02/05/71.
D6327	*Trains Illustrated*, December 1963: 'A second unit of the class, D6327, has reached the London area.' *Trains Illustrated*, February 1964: 'Laira's NBL Type 2, D6327, did not spend long in the London area for it had returned to local duties in the Plymouth Division by the end of November …' N.B. No official reporting of this transfer published in any commercial or society magazine.
D6335	Noted at Paddington 31/08/64.
D6340	Shown in most publications as re-allocated to 82A in 02/67 and 05/67 without any intervening transfer. The Birmingham Locomotive Club (BLC) reported the 02/67 allocation as 'on loan'; it is presumed, therefore, that the 05/67 re-allocation made the 82A move 'permanent'.
D6347-50	To 81D Reading 09/65, then 81A. Only LCGB/BLC reported the 81D transfer.
D6349	To 84A 08/68 immediately prior to withdrawal; only reported as such by LCGB/BLC.
D6352/6	Very brief storage period during we14/06/69; only recorded by BLC.

2. Periods at depots: 84A: 02/59-01/72; 83A: 01/61-05/71; 82A: 06/62-11/64 and 07/66-05/71 and 81A: 09/63-05/71. The gap in the allocation of D63xx locomotives at 82A was covered by the D95xx Type 1s (07/64-08/67).

3. D6300-7/9 were only ever allocated to 83D/84A Plymouth Laira (excluding any short initial periods at 82C Swindon).

4. D6355 and D6357 were the only locomotives never allocated to 84A.

5. D6301 was the first withdrawal and D6333/6/8/9 were the final withdrawals in 01/72.

6. Four locomotives were withdrawn and subsequently reinstated i.e. D6330 in 1969 and D6319/36/9 in 1971. In addition, two locomotives were stored long-term and subsequently reinstated i.e. D6308/56 both in 1970.

7. Twenty-six different Class 22s were allocated to 81A; all were in the D6326-57 batch fitted with Stone-Vapor train-heating boilers.

8. All remaining Class 22s were concentrated at 84A from May 1971. The July 1971 edition of the *Railway Observer* remarked, 'Old Oak Common's Class 22s were duly transferred to Laira at the start of the new timetable. With the exception of one (*D6340*) which worked west on the 14.38 Paddington-Bristol parcels on 30 April, all travelled light via Bristol on 2 May.'

In total eleven Class 22s were transferred to 84A in May 1971 i.e. D6308/28/48 (ex-82A), D6330/3/4/8 (ex-83A) and D6336/40/3/56 (ex-81A).

To balance up the Laira fleet, D6309/12/5/8/23 (already allocated to 84A) and D6340 (newly arrived from 81A) were stored, and D6352 withdrawn. With eleven re-allocated to 84A (including D6340), six existing 84A locomotives stored (including D6340) and one withdrawn, the net Laira Class 22 allocation was temporarily increased by four.

Three other locomotives not allocated to 84A in May 1971 (D6320/7/54 [82A]) were placed into store at Gloucester (85B) or 82A without re-allocation to 84A, together with D6332 (81A) withdrawn at Old Oak Common.

9. A number of locomotives continued working after official storage or withdrawal; see Section 8 for details.

10. Whilst not wishing to be critical of other publications, some re-allocation information published is so grossly incorrect as to require highlighting to avoid any further repetition (the Sources & References section (see Volume 2) identifies the publications in question abbreviated below):

D6308   AHBRDE5: Shown as stored (82A) in 06/69 even though previously allocated to 84A. Sightings indicate initial storage at 84A.

D6328/48   AHBRDE5: Both shown as stored 05/71 and withdrawn 08/71. Incorrect.

D6331   AHBRDE5: Shown as stored 12/68 and withdrawn 03/71. Grossly incorrect!
C22: The withdrawal date of 27/03/71 is questioned and 02/05/71 is proposed instead presumably because it <u>allegedly</u> hauled other D63xxs to 84A on 02/05/71, catching fire en route. However, all other sources explicitly record 27/03/71 as the withdrawal date for D6331, indicating that the move on 02/05/71 may have been an example of WR locomotive usage post-withdrawal.

D6333   AHBRDE5: Shown as stored 08/68, withdrawn 09/68 and reinstated 05/71. Grossly incorrect! Perpetuated by C22.

D6334   AHBRDE5: Shown as stored 12/68 and reinstated 05/71. Grossly incorrect!
C22: No re-allocations shown after 09/67.

D6340   AHBRDE5: Shown as stored c11/68 and reinstated 05/71.
C22: Records '08/67: 81A Old Oak Common; (Spent period in store at OOC); 05/71: 84A Laira.' Both grossly incorrect!

6.3 WR Use of Depots and Workshops

The deployment of lightweight quick-running engines and hydraulic transmissions resulted in a substantially different maintenance and servicing philosophy on the WR compared with other regions. Component replacement was undertaken at the major depots with Swindon Works carrying out repairs to removed components together with Classified and Unclassified locomotive body repairs. 10-ton cranes at the depots were sufficient to handle all major items of equipment, unlike diesel-electric where the heavy slow-running engines and the generators required significantly higher capacity equipment. The WR approach kept locomotives away from works for long periods and assisted improved locomotive availability. The downside was greater volumes of component stocks and periodic accounting initiatives to reduce inventories did cause some locomotives to stand idle awaiting repaired components on occasions.

In the early days, before the major depots were brought fully on-stream, Swindon dealt with engine and transmission changing, plus locomotives requiring accident repairs and

81A Old Oak Common

D6343, 81A Old Oak Common, 3 October 1970. (Anthony Sayer)

design modifications. Once fully commissioned, Plymouth Laira and Cardiff Canton undertook the component replacement work on most hydraulic locomotives, installing equipment re-fettled at Swindon, with Laira being the major centre for the D63xxs. Laira was completed in 1961, followed by Cardiff Canton in 1964.

Below these two major centres were smaller depots which undertook lighter maintenance, inspection and servicing, including Newton Abbot, Bristol Bath Road and Old Oak Common (London). Old Oak Common (fully opened in 1965) undertook some major maintenance on their D63xxs, thereby avoiding long-distance transfers to Laira.

82A Bristol Bath Road.

D6318, D1057 and D0280 *Falcon*, 82A Bristol Bath Road, 24 April 1968.

(Jim Binnie)

84A Plymouth Laira

D6315, 84A Plymouth Laira, 29 August 1969.

(Fred Castor)

Chapter 7

OVERHAUL AND REPAIRS

7.1 Swindon Works Overview

The Swindon Works 'A' Shop and 'A' Shop Extension were developed over a period of about twenty-four years from concept to completion. The main 'A' Shop extension facilities were composed of 'AW' Wheel Shop, 'AE' Erecting Shop, 'AV' Boiler Shop and 'AM' Machine Shop. The first area fully opened for the purpose intended was the 'AW' Shop in March 1920, followed by the 'AE' and 'AM' Shops, and finally the 'AV' Shop in August 1923.

The 'AE' Erecting Shop covered an area of 480x240ft, roughly fifty per cent of the 'A' shop extension. The Shop consisted of two bays of twenty pits each, either side of a 42ft-wide 80t traverser. Each of the forty repair pits were 95ft long and were served by two 100t overhead cranes to each bay, four in total. These cranes could lift the heaviest locomotives of the day and were able to carry them above others in adjacent pits up or down the shop.

Access to the 'AE' Shop locomotive pits was either via the 42ft traverser, or, one of the four 100t cranes. As far as the diesel-hydraulic locomotives were concerned, the D63xx and 'Hymek' (D7000-100) locomotives could use either route, but

D6310, Swindon Works (AE Shop), 19 September 1965. Undergoing Classified body repair, including fitment of headcode boxes and other front-end modifications. Residual evidence of GSY livery carried prior to entry into the Works (with discs). (David Dunn Collection)

the 'Warships' (D600-4, D800-70) and the 'Westerns' (D1000-73) could only use the 100t Crane route due to their wheelbase exceeding 42ft. The heaviest diesel-hydraulics, the "Warships" (D600-4) and "Westerns", once relieved of fuel, water, oil, sand etc, weighed less than 100 tons.

In 1962, Swindon Works became part of the BR Workshops Division and from 1970 part of British Rail Engineering Ltd (BREL), a wholly-owned subsidiary of the BRB. That latter re-organisation allowed BREL commercial activity beyond purely BR requirements. More fundamentally, it engendered an arms-length relationship between BREL and BR with the ultimate aim at driving profitability.

Whilst the vast bulk of the diesel-hydraulic component repair work was undertaken by Swindon, in the early days a few MAN engine repairs, beyond immediate warranty requirements, were undertaken by NBL in Glasgow; however, NBL was reluctant to undertake such work because the BTC insisted on a six-month guarantee when engines were returned, a demand which effectively required NBL to turn out virtually new engines.

7.2 Swindon Works Visits

Listed below are known visits of the D63xxs to Swindon Works based on visit sightings, photographic evidence and known paint date information. The value of this information will become abundantly clear in Volume 2, most notably in determining dates and sequencing of detail differences and livery changes.

Swindon Works Visits.

Date	Works Sightings (excluding commissioning)
15/03/59	AE Shop: D6302
03/05/59	Nil
07/06/59	AE Shop: D6301
28/06/59	Nil

Date	Works Sightings (excluding commissioning)
26/07/59	Nil
06+27/09/59	Nil
01/11/59	Nil
08/11/59	82C (Stock Shed): D6301

D6329, Swindon Works (AE Shop), 6 March 1966.
(Author's Collection)

Date	Works Sightings (excluding commissioning)
13/12/59	82C (Stock Shed): D6301
19/12/59	Nil
31/12/59	82C (Stock Shed): D6301
07/02/60	82C (Stock Shed): D6301
28/02/60	Works Yard: D6303
27/03/60 Ph	AE Shop: D6318
01/05/60	Weigh Shop: D6313, 82C (Stock Shed): D6301
15/05/60	AE Shop: D6302
19/06/60	AE Shop: D6302/17/20, 82C (Stock Shed): D6301
24/07/60	AE Shop: D6302/20/6
18/08/60	AE Shop: D6324, Works Yard: D6313, Location (?): D6330 (minor adjustments)
24/08/60 Ph	Works Yard: D6302/25/30
04/09/60 Ph	A Shop Yard: D6330
11/09/60	AE Shop: D6300/2, Works Yard: D6304/15/9/23, 82C: D6322
18/09/60 Ph	AE Shop: D6333, A Shop Yard: D6304
09/10/60	AE Shop: D6301/2, Works Yard: D6300, Timber Yard: D6318, 82C: D6322/31
16/10/60	AE Shop: D6301/8/10, Works Yard: D6300/9/18/32, 82C (Stock Shed): D6322
06/11/60	AE Shop: D6301/8/33, Works Yard: D6302, 82C: D6309/18/31/2
13/11/60	AE Shop: D6301/3/22, Works Yard: D6308
05/12/60	AE Shop: D6303/19/31, Works Yard: D6301/12/21
29/01/61	AE Shop: D6301/3/5/9/10
05/02/61	AE Shop: D6303/5/9/10
14/02/61 Ph	Works Yard: D6302
19/02/61	AE Shop: D6301/3/5
26/03/61	AE Shop: D6303, Works Yard: D6321, 82C: D6313 (ex-Works)
16/04/61	D6303
06/05/61 Ph	A Shop Yard: D6303
28/05/61	AE Shop: D6305/9, 82C (Stock Shed Yard): D6319/21
14/06/61 Ph	A Shop Yard: D6302
25/06/61	Works Yard: D6309/21, 82C (Stock Shed Yard): D6305/19
19/07/61	AE Shop: D6308/19/21, 82C (Stock Shed): D6303
23/07/61	AE Shop: D6306/11/9
26/07/61 Ph	A Shop Yard: D6319
30/07/61	AE Shop: D6301/3/6/19/28, Works Yard: D6311
20/08/61	AE Shop: D6303/8/29
17/09/61	AE Shop: D6306/8/21, 82C (Stock Shed Yard): D6303
24/09/61	AE Shop: D6321, Wks Yd: D6306, Timber Yd: D6308, 82C (Stock Shed Yd): D6303
05/11/61	AE Shop: D6301/3/20, Works Yard: D6325
12/11/61	AE Shop: D6320, Works Yard: D6303
03/12/61	AE Shop: D6306/34

Date	Works Sightings (excluding commissioning)
17/12/61 Ph	D6305/34
07/01/62	AE Shop: D6315/23, Weigh Shop: D6334
04/02/62	AE Shop: D6315/23/34
04/03/62	AE Shop: D6315/23
06/05/62	Nil
27/05/62	AE Shop: Nil
17/06/62	82C (Stock Shed): D6302
24/06/62	AE Shop: Nil, 82C (Stock Shed): D6302
01/07/62	AE Shop: D6302
12/08/62	AE Shop: D6346, Timber Yard: D6316/40/1, Works Yard: D6336
19/08/62	AE Shop: D6346 (fire damage), Timber Yard: D6316/40/1, Works Yard: D6336
26/08/62 Ph	A Shop Yard: D6336, Timber Yard: D6316 (plus at least one more)
09/09/62	AE Shop: D6316/46, Timber Yard: D6340/1, Works Yard: D6335
16/09/62 Ph	Timber Yard: D6340/1, Works Yard: D6316
23/09/62 Ph	Timber Yard: D6340/1
30/09/62	AE Shop: Nil, Timber Yard: D6340/1
21/10/62	AE Shop: D6346, Timber Yard: D6340/1
04/11/62	AE Shop: D6341/6/57, Timber Yard: D6340
18/11/62	Nil
09/12/62	AE Shop: D6321
27/01/63	Nil
10/02/63	AE Shop: D6321
17/03/63	AE Shop: D6311, Works Yard: D6352
24/03/63	AE Shop: D6311
21/04/63	D6311
28/04/63	D6300/11
12/05/63	AE Shop: D6311
09/06/63	AE Shop: D6303/11
08/07/63	Nil
28/07/63	AE Shop: D6305/28
18+21/08/63	AE Shop: D6305
15+29/09/63	Nil
27/10/63	Nil
10+18/11/63	Nil
01+15+22/12/63	AE Shop: D6328
19+26+28/01/64	AE Shop: D6328
23/02/64	AE Shop: D6304
01+22/03/64	AE Shop: D6304
01+12/04/64	AE Shop: D6304
26/04/64	Nil
10/05/64	Nil
20+21/06/64	Nil
26/07/64	AE Shop: D6346
16/08/64	Nil

Date	Works Sightings (excluding commissioning)
06/09/64	D6335/57 (incomplete list)
13/09/64	AE Shop: D6357, Works Yard: D6335
20/09/64	AE Shop: D6335/52
27/09/64	AE Shop: D6335/52, Weigh Shop: D6357
11/10/64	AE Shop: D6335/52/6
18/10/64	AE Shop: D6335/56, Works Yard: D6330/55
25/10/64	D6330/55/6
04/11/64	D6307/30/55/6
08/11/64	AE Shop: D6307/30/55/6
22/11/64	AE Shop: D6307/30/51, Works Yard: D6326/56
29/11/64	AE Shop: D6307/26/30/51
13/12/64	D6307/30 (incomplete list)
20/12/64	Nil (incomplete list)
17/01/65	D6307/26/30/8/53
24/01/65	AE Shop: D6307/26/30/8/51
31/01/65	D6306/7/30/54
14/02/65	Works Yard: D6326/30
07/03/65 Ph	AE Shop: D6354
14/03/65	AE Shop: D6306/54
28/03/65	AE Shop: D6317
03/04/65	AE Shop: D6317/40
10/04/65	D6317/43
09/05/65	AE Shop: D6310/7
30/05/65	AE Shop: D6310/7, Works Yard: D6357
06/06/65	D6310/7 (incomplete list)
20/06/65	AE Shop: D6310/7
15/07/65	AE Shop: D6310/9
08/08/65	AE Shop: D6310/9
19+26/09/65	AE Shop: D6304/10/9
03/10/65	AE Shop: D6304/10/9/34/5
10/10/65	AE Shop: D6304/10/9/35
05/12/65	AE Shop: D6304/10/5/9/31/5, Weigh House: D6326/56
12/12/65	AE Shop: D6304/15/26/9/31/56
19/01/66 PD	D6315
23/01/66	AE Shop: D6309/15/26/30/1/56
06/03/66 Ph	AE Shop: D6329 (repainted)
13/03/66	AE Shop: D6309/12/29/44, New Loco Reception/ Despatch Shed: D6308
13/04/66	D6308/12/6/29
17/04/66 Ph	AE Shop: D6308 (GNY)/29 (repainted), Weigh Shop: D6348 (repainted)
24/04/66	D6308/12/6/29/32
07/05/66	D6306/11/3/6/51
05/06/66	AE Shop: D6308/11-3/6/51, Works Yard: D6328
26/06/66	D6308/11/3/51
31/08/66	D6305/21/2/48 (D6323 possibly mis-recorded as D6322)

Date	Works Sightings (excluding commissioning)
04/09/66	AE Shop: D6305/21/48, Works Yard: D6323
11/09/66	D6323 "had left the Works" (BLS)
14/09/66	D6305/21/48/52
19/09/66 Ph	AE Shop: D6305
02/10/66	D6305/20/4/48/52/3
22/10/66	D6300/5/20/4/53
13/11/66	D6300/5/14/20
04/12/66	AE Shop: D6300/5/14
28/12/66 Ph	AE Shop: D6300
13/02/67 Ph	AE Shop: D6322 (accident damage)
26/02/67 PD	D6327
12/03/67	D6303/18/22
31/03/67 PD	D6318
02/04/67	AE Shop: D6318/22/4/5
05/04/67 Ph	A Shop Yard: D6354 (accident damage)
19/04/67	D6322/4/5/32/54
30/04/67	D6325 (incomplete list)
07/05/67	AE Shop: D6302/22/32 (being repainted)/54
16/05/67 PD	D6354
xx/06/67 Ph	AE Shop: D6302/22/33, Weigh Shop Yard: D6332
26/07/67 PD	D6322
27/07/67 PD	D6339
30/07/67	D6302/22/8/34/9/43
23/08/67	D6334
03/09/67	AE Shop: D6328/36/43
05/09/67 PD	D6328
13/09/67	D6328/36/7/43
11/10/67	AE Shop: D6337/40/3, Awaiting Despatch: D6336
12/10/67 PD	D6337
21/10/67	D6337/40/3
25/10/67	AE Shop: D6337/40/2
03/12/67	AE Shop: D6312/42 (repainted BFY)
26/01/68	Nil
04/02/68	Nil
10/03/68	Nil
06/04/68	Nil
04+31/08/68	Nil
08+22/09/68	Nil
24/11/68	Nil
01+16/12/68	Nil
26/01/69	Nil
16/03/69	Nil
27/04/69	Nil
18/05/69	Nil
01+08/06/69	Nil

Date	Works Sightings (excluding commissioning)
30/07/69	Nil
14/09/69	Nil
07+10/12/69	AE Shop: D6356
31/12/69	D6356
22/02/70	D6342
15/04/70 Ph	AE Shop: D6308
18/05/70 Ph	AE Shop Yard: D6336 (accident damage)
21/05/70 PD	D6308
29/07/70	AE Shop: D6348

Date	Works Sightings (excluding commissioning)
13/09/70 Ph	AE Shop: D6338 (stripped, awaiting repainting)
17/10/70	D6338
31/10/70	Nil
11/11/70	D6330
09/12/70 PD	D6330
13/12/70	D6330
19/04/71	D6319
22/04/71 PD	D6319
19/05/71 Ph	AE Shop: D6319

Notes:

1. Abbreviations:
   82C: Swindon,
   Ph: Photographic evidence, PD: Paint Date information (both therefore representing incomplete lists).
2. Swindon shed handled most locomotives bound for the Works and also immediately following release; as a consequence, observations at 82C Swindon are included. It should be noted that the D63xxs rarely, if ever, worked off 82C after initial commissioning.
3. Locomotives were often removed from the AE Shop during repairs when awaiting refurbished components. On the basis of sighting information, the Stock Shed (north-west of 82C Swindon depot) was a regular location used for short-term storage up to June 1962, with the Timber Yard (west of the Works complex) used during August to November 1962. This action was necessary to release space at the Works.
4. The sightings of the D63xx locomotives starkly illustrate how works visits came to an abrupt halt at the end of 1967 or very early 1968.

Following National Traction Plan guidance (see Volume 2), overhauls were suspended at this time; D6301 was withdrawn on 30 December 1967 and further withdrawals were planned during 1968 in the expectation that replacement diesel-electric locomotives from other Regions would be forthcoming.

5. Half of the D63xx fleet had been withdrawn by April 1969, but a general upturn in traffic levels stalled the continuation of diesel-electric transfers to the WR thereby preventing further withdrawals until mid-1971. Such was the demand for traction during that period eight D63xxs were put through Swindon Works for Classified repairs and one severely damaged locomotive was rebuilt.
6. Traffic levels, always cyclic in nature, deteriorated once again during 1971 and, as a consequence, further Works repairs were discontinued and withdrawals re-commenced.

D601 and D6308, Swindon Works (AE Shop), 17 April 1966. D63xx bogie in foreground, NBL/MAN engine left of D601.

(David Bromley)

Chapter 8

LOCOMOTIVE HISTORIES

8.1 Explanation of Information Provided

8.1.1 Sightings: Primary and Secondary Sources.

Locomotive histories have been built up for each of the D63xx locomotives, developed from primary sources (personal sightings and photographs) and secondary sources (magazine reports, archive depot/works visit sightings and other listings providing fully dated information).

Bill Hamilton has provided a list of locomotives seen at NBL Queen's Park Works, the only report that I have seen for this location; although undated, he states that the visit 'must have been September'. Most locomotives were identifiable by the order number painted on the buffer heads, as follows: D6305 (returned for attention), D6308 (complete) and L97/4 -L97/26 (D6309-30) in various stages of construction. D6306 and D6307 had been despatched ex-NBL on 24 and 29 September 1959 respectively with D6308 following on 5 October; this suggests that the date of the visit was between 29 September and 5 October 1959. Sightings are, therefore, given in the locomotive histories as 'we051059'.

Whilst Primary information is undoubtedly the best source of sighting details and associated anecdotal information, it is not without shortcomings; for example Swindon Works visits always covered the AE Shop and nearby yards, but visits to the Timber and Con Yards during 1971/72 were a bit 'hit and miss', dependent on the whim of the guide.

8.1.2 Works Information.

Works information from *Diesel Locomotive Record Cards* has been virtually impossible to track down and, for the one card I have seen, there was no Works information entered on the reverse side.

The Swindon Works 'Blue' Files are by far the best source of information although the files for the D63xx locomotives have been very difficult to come by in any number; partial records do exist for some locomotives but unfortunately no records at all have been found for others.

Given the component exchange philosophy adopted by the WR for its hydraulic fleet, great care is required with the 'Blue Files' with respect to pinning down actual *locomotive* visits to Swindon Works, as opposed to the major components from such locomotives sent to Swindon for repair (engines, transmissions, boilers, bogies, etc).

Other sources of Works information include:

- Sighting Reports. To achieve something close to a reasonably comprehensive history of Works visits by the D63xx locomotives required heavy reliance on sighting information (see Section 7). There are a number of known omissions as evidenced by external modifications and livery changes (specifically GNY to GSY) (see Volume 2), and there will undoubtedly be other omissions of which I am unaware. However, sightings do contribute substantially to the story.
- Stratford DRS Records. Two separate and complementary sources of information cover locomotive throughput at Stratford DRS during the period November 1963 to March 1971 and highlight London-allocated D63xx locomotive visits for tyre-turning.

8.1.3 Information from BR Fires on Diesel Train Locomotives Reports (1961-71).

All reported incidents are included (see also Volume 2).

8.2 Data Presentation

NBL Order Nos. and Progressive (Works) Nos. are provided for each locomotive.

Sighting Dates: The date format in the history logs is 'mmyy' or 'ddmmyy', as opposed to 'mm/yy' or 'dd/mm/yy', for clarity. The more conventional 'dd/mm/yy' format is, however, used in the locomotive 'Notes'.

Text colour coding is used as follows:

Blue	Key dates (e.g. New, Works information, Withdrawal and Disposal). N.B. Disposal information is sourced from either *Diesel & Electric Locomotives for Scrap* (A. Butlin) or BR.
Black	Locomotive sightings.
Purple	Dates when locomotives were <u>NOT</u> seen at a particular depot or works.

Red   Sighting conflicts with works information.
'Nil'   No sightings at the specified location.
'N/listed' Not listed (on specified date).

Various abbreviations are used as follows:

Depot Abbreviations:
81A: Old Oak Common, **81C**: Southall, **81D**: Reading,
81F: Oxford.
82A: Bristol Bath Road, **82C**: Swindon (SS: Stock Shed,
SSYd: Stock Shed Yard).
83A: Newton Abbot, **83B**: Taunton.
83D: Plymouth Laira, **83E**: St. Blazey, **83F**: Truro, **83G**:
Penzance (all up to 08/09/63).
83D: Exmouth Junction (from 09/09/63).
84A: Plymouth Laira, **84B**: St. Blazey, **84C**: Truro, **84D**:
Penzance (all from 09/09/63).
85A: Worcester, **85B** Gloucester Horton Road.

Other Location Abbreviations:
Bristol TM: Bristol Temple Meads station, **Exeter StD/
EStD**: Exeter St. Davids station, **Plymouth NR**: Plymouth
North Road station, **NA**: Newton Abbot station.
Newport ADJ: Newport Alexandra Dock Junction yard.
BMJ: Bristol Marsh Junction (**SPMCS**: St. Philip's Marsh
Coal Sidings, **CPS**: Cattle Pen Sidings, **VS**: Victoria Sidings).
S&D: Somerset & Dorset Joint Railway.

Works Information Abbreviations:
Information Sources:
BR Rcds: BR Records (including Swindon Works
'Blue' Files).
Derived Rcds: Derived Works Records.
SFR: Stratford DRS Records.

References to Works visits in the following logs (e.g. BR Rcds:
030362-110462 HC) specify 'Information Source', 'Date in
Works' to 'Date out of Works' and 'Class of Repair' (if known)
and/or 'Work done'.

Overhaul categories, or, Class of Repair:
Pre-1964:
HC: Heavy Casual, **LC**: Light Casual,
U: Unclassified/unscheduled.
From 1964 (locomotive repair level, not
individual components):

G: General, **I**: Intermediate, **C**: Classified (repair level not
specified), **Rect**: Rectification (i.e. re-call to Works to correct
faults), **U**: Unclassified/unscheduled.

Intra-Works locations:
Swindon Wks: Works (**ES**: Erecting Shop, **WksYd**: Works
Yard, **TYd**: Timber Yard, **ConYd**: Concentration Yard).
NBL QP Wks: NBL Queen's Park Works.

Paint Dates: Dates were recorded inside the locomotive
cab (usually above the A-end secondman's cab door);
painting details were usually presented in the form Works
Code/Date painted/Paint manufacturer and type of paint
(where applicable) although variations occurred in practice.
Abbreviations used:

Works Code: **SN, SWD, SWN, SDN**:
                       Swindon Works
Paint Manufacturer: **K**: R. Kearsley, **W**: T. & R. Williamson,
                       BS: Blundell Spence , **GW**:
                       Goodlass Wall.
Paint Type: **SYN**: Synthetic resin, **HPS**: Airless
                       spraying, **UROALKYD**: Urethane
                       modified by organic and alcohol acids.

Fires: Information from BR *Fires on Diesel Train Locomotives
Reports* are suffixed **FDTL**.

Other Abbreviations:
Jct: Junction, **CSdgs**: Carriage Sidings, **Sdgs**: Sidings.
Pass: Passenger service, **LE**: Light Engine.
STN: Special Traffic Notice.

And finally: Abbreviations of the sources used in the
'Disposal' and 'Notes' entries are explained in the 'Sources &
References' section in Volume 2.

8.3 Locomotive Histories
Locomotive histories are provided on the following pages.
Inevitably many of the non-Works sightings are Depot, rather
than in-traffic, observations; this obviously gives a somewhat
distorted view of the life and times of the D63xxs, but they
help significantly with respect to identifying locomotives
not on Works but awaiting attention, and, their locations
when stored.

D6300

NBL Order: L77/1, Progressive No.: 27665.

D6300, 83D Plymouth Laira, Undated. Pre-April 1963. (Lens of Sutton [The Transport Library])

D6300, 84A Plymouth Laira, Undated. Post-February 1967. BSY livery.
(Author's Collection)

Cannock, Wolverhampton: 131258
82C: 131258/141258
NBL Date Invoiced: 151258

Swindon Wks: 151258 (for fitting ATC apparatus, etc)/ 010159.
BR Rcds: 151258-120159 U.
82C: 110159

Date New: 120159

Swindon: 120159 (07.35 Swindon-Bristol running-in turn, continued on local trips to Bristol for circa 3 weeks)
Dauntsey: 190159 (17.00 Swindon-Bristol, failed at Dauntsey)
Bristol: 200159 (07.35 Swindon-Bristol)
Truro: 220259 (trials; load 11 (290t))
St. Ives branch: 030359 (gauging tests)
Looe branch: 040359 (gauging tests)
Newton Abbot: 100359 (trials in multiple with D6301 between Plymouth and NA on 50% fitted freight)
Penzance: xx0359 (regularly on 13.20 Penzance-Paddington (to Plymouth) and 11.10 Swansea-Penzance (from Plymouth) pass, with D6301)
Laira: 040459 (LE, with D6301)
Penzance: 120559 (up 'Royal Duchy', with D6302)
Chacewater: 160559 (11.40 Swansea-Penzance pass, with D6302)
83D: 170559 (with D6302)

Swindon Wks: Nil. N/listed 070659. BR Rcds:260559-060659 Repair category unknown.

Plymouth NR: 250659 (13.20 Penzance-Paddington (to Plymouth), 17.05 Plymouth-Penzance, both with D6303)
Newton Abbot: 040759 (08.15 Perranporth-Paddington pass, piloting D603 ex-Plymouth) / 11.00 down pass, piloting D601)
XX: 060759 (20.45 Oxley Sdgs-Tavistock freight, with D6301)
Dainton: 080859 (down pass, piloting 'King' 6003)
Dainton: 220859 (pass, piloting 'Castle' 5028)
83D: 250859
Marazion: 110959 (13.20 Penzance-Paddington, with D6303)
St Erth: 150959 (Penzance-Manchester pass, with D6304)
Saltash: 290959 (down 'Cornishman', with D6303)
Gwinear Road: 230460 (down pass, with D6305)
Truro: 200560 (07.55 Penzance-Swansea, with D6300)
83G: 210560

Swindon Wks: 110960 ('A' Shop)/ 091060 (WksYd)/ 161060 (WksYd)/ 191060. N/listed 131160. BR Rcds: 310860-281060 LC (5500hr examination). Returned to 83D: 041160.

Newton Abbot: 18 or 190661 (collision with D6313)

Swindon Works: Nil. Arrived 260661 ('B'-end mainframe bent, drooped cab; transmission transferred to D601[B]).
NBL, Glasgow: Nil. Arrived by 140761; collision damage repairs, mainframe straightened, 'B' cab rebuilt. Departed 301261.
82C: 301261 (Stock Shed)
Swindon Wks: Nil. BR Rcds: 020162-030162 U (after LC repair at NBL Glasgow).
83D: 050162 (arrived ex-Swindon Works)

84A: 150462
Plymouth NR: 250862 (pass, piloting 'Castle' 7037)

Swindon Wks: 230463/ 280463. N/listed 210463 & 120563. BR Rcds: 080463-010563 HC.

Tavistock Jct: 080763 (banking)/ 090763 (ditto)
84A: 110863/ 251263/ 090564/ 031064
Plymouth NR: 170465 (freight)/ 020565 (station pilot)/ 100765 (piloting D834)
84A: 030865/ 190965
Exeter StD: 070566 (freight)
Plymouth Laira: 180666 (up freight)
XX: 250766 (fire damage) (FDTL)
84B: 250766/ 210866
84A: 180966

Swindon Wks: 221066/ 131166/ 041266 ('A' Shop)/ 281266 ('A' Shop, BSY livery). N/listed 021066 & 120367. BR Rcds: 191066-060267 C

84B: 110667/ 180667/ 290767
Par: 290767

Stored: 1we110568 (xxxxxx)

84A: 180568

Withdrawn: 1we010668 (260568)

84A: 230668/300668 (steam shed sdgs)/ 310768 (steam shed sdgs)/ 100868/ 080968 (steam shed sdgs)/ 290968/ 171068/ 021168

STN Booked Transfer: 8Z79 12.00 131168 (Wednesday) Laira Jct-Newport ADJ (with D6302/3). N.B. D6302 failed to move, re-scheduled.

Ebbw Jct: 231168/011268 (sdgs near depot, with D6303/16)/ 131268

Received J. Cashmore, Newport: 201268 (with D6303/16)
J. Cashmore, Newport: Nil.
Disposal: 12/68 (D&ELfS).

General Note re. 'Pilot Scheme' Locomotives: There were numerous instances in the early years where 'Pilot Scheme' locomotives were taken out of service (effectively "Stored Unserviceable") for extended periods following collision damage or equipment failure and so awaiting repairs and/ or replacement equipment (most notably transmissions). There were also examples of 'healthy' locomotives deliberately being taken out of traffic to donate parts for use in the D600 "Warship" fleet, particularly transmissions which were in short supply during the 1960-62 period. Subsequent returns to traffic were frequently further delayed by repaired equipment being preferentially allocated to the D600s.

D6301

NBL Order: L77/2, Progressive No.: 27666.

D6301 and D803, Exeter St. Davids, circa 1959. D6301 was only available for traffic for three months over the two year period between 05/11/59 and 06/11/61. These long periods out of use will have delayed subsequent Classified Repairs and will no doubt have ultimately been a factor in D6301 never carrying headcode boxes and other front-end modifications, and its early demise. (Rail-Online)

D6301, 84A Plymouth Laira, 24 April 1968. Withdrawn: discs and two-piece gangway doors retained to the bitter end. (Jim Binnie)

NBL Date Invoiced: 301258
NBL, Glasgow: 311258 (departed with D6302)

82C: 110159
Tuffley Jct, Gloucester: 150159 (test train, with D6302)
Bristol: 050259 (10.05 Swindon-Bristol, with D6302)
Bathampton: 070259 (11.33 Bath-Swindon running-in turn, with D6302)
82C: 080259

Date New: 190259

Swindon: 210259 (07.50 Taunton-Paddington pass (from Sdn?), and, Paddington-?? parcels (to Sdn), with D6302)
82C: 080359
Swindon: 080359 (16.15 Paddington-Plymouth (from Sdn), with D6302)
Newton Abbot: 100359 (trials in multiple with D6300 between Plymouth and NA on 50% fitted freight)
Penzance: xx0359 (regularly on 13.20 Penzance-Paddington (to Plymouth) and 11.10 Swansea-Penzance (from Plymouth) pass, with D6300)
Plymouth Laira: 040459 (LE, with D6300)

Swindon Wks: 030559 ('A' Shop)/ 070659 ('A' Shop). BR Rcds: 270459-090659 U.

Plymouth: 250659(14.35 Plymouth-Exeter [via SR route])
Exeter StD: 270659 (14.35 Plymouth-Exeter Central via Okehampton)
Newton Abbot: 040759 (08.35 Falmouth-Paddington pass, piloting D802); (down 'Cornishman', piloting 'Hall' 6960)
XX: 060759 (20.45 Oxley Sdgs-Tavistock freight, with D6300)
Dainton: 220859 (pass, piloting 'Hall' 4931)
83D: 250859
Gwinear Road: 190959 (down relief pass, with D6302)
Truro: 210959 (07.45 Newton Abbot-Penzance pass, with D6302)
Penzance: 230959 (10.05 Penzance-Manchester pass, with D6302)
Par: 300959 (Manchester-Penzance pass, with D6304)

83D: 051159 (piston seizure)

Swindon Wks: 061159 (arrival)
82C: 081159/ 281159/ 131259 (SS)/ 311259 (SS)/ 070260 (SS)/ 010560 (SS)/ 190660 (SS). N.B. Deliberately kept out of service with engine No.141 kept as a spare following repairs.
Swindon Wks: 091060 ('A' Shop)/ 161060 ('A' Shop)/ 191060 (waiting engine and transmission)/ 061160 ('A' Shop)/ 131160 ('A' Shop)/ 051260 (Works Yard). N/listed 070960. BR Rcds: 161160-121260 LC. Returned to 83D 191260.

Swindon Wks: 090161 (arrival)/ 290161 ('A' Shop)/ 190261 ('A' Shop). Defective transmission; laid-up awaiting replacement. N/listed 260361/ 160461 and 280561 (at 82C?). BR Rcds: 090161-090561 LC. Returned to 83D 140561.

Tavistock Jct: 080761 (down pass, piloting 'Castle' 4037)

Swindon Wks: 270761 (arrival)/ 300761 ('A' Shop). Defective transmission; laid-up awaiting replacement. Not listed 200861/ 170961 (at 82C?).
82C: 291061
Swindon Wks: 051161 ('A' Shop). BR Rcds: 270761-061161 LC. Returned to 83D xx1161.

Newton Abbot: 280762 (down pass, with D6353)
Totnes: 080962 (pass, piloting 'Hall' 5904)
Kingsbridge: 150962 (pass)
Tavistock Jct: 080763 (banking)
84A: 251263/090564/ 120765/ 030865/ 040865/ 190965
XX: 230366 (fire damage) (FDTL)
84B: 250766
Par: 130866 (china clay, with D6303)
84B: 210866/180966
84A: 261266
84B: 290167
84A: 110667 (apparently stored, driver's windscreen wiper missing)/ 110767/ 290767/ 3010-011167 (open storage)

Stored: 1we111167 (091167)
Withdrawn: 1we301267 (301267)

84A: 030268/100468/ 240468/ 180568

Transfer 84A-G. Cohen, Morriston: xx0668

82A: xxxx68 (Breakdown Crane Road)

G. Cohen, Morriston: 220868/ 230868 (intact)
Disposal: 08/68 (D&ELfS).

Note:
1. 'I recall D6301 on Exeter shed for a time waiting passage to South Wales…..but I have no written record of this.' (S. Greenslade)

D6302

NBL Order: L77/3, Progressive No.: 27667.

D6302 and D6301, Bathampton, 7 February 1959. (Hugh Ballantyne [Rail-Photoprints])

D6302 and D6312, plus D6303, 84B. St.Blazey, Undated. Sometime between 05/66 (when D6312 was ex-Works with SI-HCB and GSY) and 12/66 (when D6303 went to Works for SI-HCB fitment and BSY repaint). Probably Summer 1966 given the foliage and condition of D6312. (Author's Collection)

NBL Date Invoiced: 301258
NBL, Glasgow: 311258 (departed with D6301)

82C: 110159
Tuffley Jct, Gloucester: 150159 (test train, with D6301)
Bristol: 050259 (07.35 Swindon-Bristol, and, 10.05 Bristol-Swindon, with D6301)
Bathampton: 070259 (11.33 Bath-Swindon running-in turn, with D6301)
82C: 080259

Date New: 190259

Swindon: 210259 (07.50 Taunton-Paddington pass (from Sdn?), and, Paddington-?? parcels (to Sdn), with D6301)
82C: 080359
Swindon: 080359 (16.15 Paddington-Plymouth (from Sdn), with D6301)
83D: 090359 (defects found, parts robbed for D602)/ 100359 (forwarded to Swindon Wks by steam loco)

Swindon Wks: 130359 (arrival)/ 150359 ('A' Shop)/ 260359 (out on trial). N/listed 030559. Dynastarter coupling failure.

Penzance: 120559 (up 'Royal Duchy', with D6300)
Chacewater: 160559 (11.40 Swansea-Penzance pass, with D6300)
83D: 170559 (with D6300)

Swindon Wks: 120659 (arrived, dynastarter coupling failure))/ 260659 (replacement dynastarter coupling and new type cylinder heads fitted)

Crediton: 180759 (14.45 Plymouth-Exeter Central pass, with D6303)
83D: 250859/010959
Gwinear Road: 190959 (down relief pass, with D6301)
Truro: 210959 (07.45 Newton Abbot-Penzance pass, with D6301)
Penzance: 230959 (10.05 Penzance-Manchester pass, with D6301)
Penzance: 060460 (17.50 Penzance-Acton milk, with D6304)
83D: 110460 (to Swindon Wks with D600, transmission governor issue)

Swindon Wks: Nil. Not listed 010560.

Swindon Wks: 150560 ('A'Shop)/ 190660 ('A' Shop)/ 240760 ('A' Shop)/ 240860 (WksYd)/ 110960 ('A' Shop). BR Rcds: 110560-190960 U (defective transmission; replacement transmission installed 080860)

83D: 300960/031060 (engine failure)

Swindon Wks: 091060 ('A' Shop)/ 061160 (WksYd). N/listed 131160. BR Rcds: 280960-091160 U (engine exchange). Returned to 83D: 131160.

83D: 310161 (collision with D6313, 'B'-end mainframe bent, drooped cab)

Swindon Wks: 050261 (arrival)/ 140261. BR Rcds: 190261-061261 C+Major Collision Damage Repairs; transmission transferred to D604[B]. N/listed: 190261/ 260361/ 160461/ 280561/ 250661/ 190761/ 200861/ 170961/ 121161. Work undertaken by NBL, Glasgow.
Gloucester: 190261 (en route NBL Glasgow, with D6324, hauled by Standard 5MT 73012)
NBL, Glasgow: Nil. Released xx1261 (collision damage reps, mainframe straightened, 'B' cab rebuilt).
Swindon Wks: Nil. BR Rcds: Released to traffic 061261.

83D: 150462/ 240562 (engine defects found)

Swindon Wks: 050662 (arrival). Transmission transferred to D602; laid up awaiting replacement.
82C: 170662 (SS)/ 240662 (SS)
Swindon Wks: 010762 ('A' Shop). N/listed 190862. BR Rcds: 240562-090862 HC. Returned to 83D xx0862.

Totnes: 080962 (pass, piloting 'Hall' 5904)
83D: 290563/190863 (LC repairs)
84A: 140963/251263
Callington: 031064
84A: 120765/030865/ 190965
84B: 250766   84A: 250966

Swindon Wks: 011266 (transmission change). N/listed 131166 and 041266.

Swindon Wks: 040567 (damaged)/ 070567 ('A' Shop)/ xx0667 ('A' Shop)/ 300767/ xx0867 ('A' Shop Yd, ex-Wks condition). N/listed 190467 & 030967. Derived Rcds: xx0567-xx0867.

Stored: 1we110568 (xxxxxx)

84A: 180568

Withdrawn: 1we010668 (260568)

84A: 230668/300668 (steam shed sdgs)/ 310768 (steam shed sdgs)/ 100868/ 080968 (steam shed sdgs)/ 290968/ 171068/ 021168

STN Booked Transfer: 8Z79 12.00 131168 (Wednesday) Laira Jct-Newport ADJ (with D6300/3). N.B. D6302 failed to move: re-scheduled.
STN Booked Transfer: 8Z79 12.00 201168 (Wednesday) Laira Jct-Newport ADJ (with D6304/5/13).

Received J. Cashmore, Newport: 21 or 231168 (with D6304/5/13)
J. Cashmore, Newport: 231168/ xx1268
Disposal: 12/68 (D&ELfS).

D6303

NBL Order: L77/4, Progressive No.: 27668.

D6303 piloting 'Hall' 4914, Dainton, 30 July 1960. 12.20p.m. Cardiff-Newquay. (Hugh Ballantyne [Rail-Photoprints])

D6303, Exeter St. Davids, August 1967. BSY livery. (Colour-Rail)

NBL Date Invoiced: 110559

Swindon Wks: Nil. BR Rcds: 270459-090659. Acceptance.

Date New: 220559

Swindon Wks: 010659. BR Rcds: 270459-090659 U (defective dynastarter).
82C: 070659

Kennington Jct: 100659 (freight)
Plymouth NR: 250659 (13.20 Penzance-Paddington (to Plymouth), 17.05 Plymouth-Penzance, with D6300)
Crediton: 180759 (14.45 Plymouth-Exeter Central pass, with D6302)
Meldon Jct: 010859 (Plymouth portion of 15.00 ex-Waterloo from Exeter, with D6304)
83D: 010959
Marazion: 110959 (13.20 Penzance-Paddington pass, with D6300)
Gwinear Road: 190959 (10.05 Penzance-Manchester pass, with D6304)
Saltash: 290959 (down 'Cornishman', with D6300)
83D: 111059
Hemerdon: 240260 (banking)

Swindon Wks: 280260 (WksYd)/ xx0360. Engine change. N/listed 010560. In Works 28 days during period 12 we260360 (B. Penney).

Newton Abbot: 160760 (waiting next duty)
Par: 210760 (pass, with D63xx)
Dainton: 300760 (12.20 Cardiff-Newquay pass, piloting 'Hall' 4914)
Stoneycombe: 030960 (08.05 Newquay-Newcastle, piloting 'Hall' 4932)

Swindon Wks: 071160 (arrival)/ 131160 ('A' Shop)/ 051260 ('A' Shop). N/listed 091060. BR Rcds: 161160-121260 LC (defective transmission, awaiting replacement).

Swindon Wks: 290161 ('A' Shop)/ 050261 ('A' Shop)/ 190261 ('A' Shop)/ 260361 ('A' Shop)/ 160461/ 060561 ('A' Shop Yd). N/listed 280561. BR Rcds: 090161-090561 LC (defective transmission, awaiting replacement). Returned to 83D: 140561.

82C: 190761 (SSYd)

Tigley (Totnes): 220761 ('Royal Duchy', piloting 'Hall' 5979)

Swindon Wks: 240761 (arrival)/ 300761 ('A' Shop)/ 200861 ('A' Shop). BR Rcds: 270761-061161 LC (defective transmission; laid up awaiting replacement).
82C: 170961 (SS)/ 240961 (SSYd). At Stock Shed between 260861 and 311061 awaiting transmission from NBL.

Swindon Wks: 051161 ('A' Shop)/ 101161 (Badminton trial)/ 121161 (WksYd)/ 131161 (Stoke Gifford trial)/ 141161 (ditto). N/listed 070162. BR Rcds: xxxxxx-141161.

83D: 150462
Exeter StD: 260762 (with D10xx)
Plymouth NR: 250862 (pass, piloting D811)

Swindon Wks: 090663 ('A' Shop)/ 210663. N/listed 120563.

Tavistock Jct: 080763 (banking)
Newton Abbot: 240863 (Plymouth-NA pass, piloting 'County' 1011)
84A: 251263

Swindon Wks: 060464. N/listed 010464 & 120464.

84A: 090564/031064/ 120765/ 040865/ 190965/ 240766
Par: 130866 (china clay, with D6301)
84B: 210866/180966

Swindon Wks: 120367. N/listed 041266. BR Rcds: 211266-010467 C.

84B: 040467 (ex-Wks)
St Budeaux East: xx0667 (trip-freight from Bull Point MoD)
84A: 170667/060767
Treffry (Luxulyan): 120867 (11.45 Newquay-York pass, piloting D854)
84A: 240967

Stored: 1we110568 (xxxxx)

84A: 180568

Withdrawn: 1we010668 (260568)

84A: 230668/300668 (steam shed sdgs)/ 310768 (steam shed sdgs)/ 100868/ 080968 (steam shed sdgs)/ 290968/ 171068/ 021168

STN Booked Transfer: 8Z79 12.00 131168 (Wednesday) Laira Jct-Newport ADJ (with D6300/2). N.B. D6302 failed to move, re-scheduled.

Ebbw Jct: 231168/011268 (sdgs near depot, with D6300/16)/ 131268

Received J. Cashmore, Newport: 201268 (with D6300/16)
J. Cashmore, Newport: Nil.
Disposal: 12/68 (D&ELfS).

D6304

NBL Order: L77/5, Progressive No.: 27669.

D6304, Market Drayton,
18 June 1959. On delivery
from NBL Glasgow
to Swindon Works.

(Brian Penney)

D6304, 84A Plymouth
Laira, 14 April 1967.

(Transport Treasury)

Market Drayton: 180659
NBL Date Invoiced: 230659

Date New: 230659

Meldon Jct: 010859 (Plymouth portion of 15.00 ex-Waterloo from Exeter, with D6303)
Trerule: 150959 (down 'Cornishman', with D63xx)
St Erth: 150959 (Penzance-Manchester pass, with D6300)
Gwinear Road: 190959 (10.05 Penzance-Manchester pass, with D6303)
Par: 300959 (Manchester-Penzance pass, with D6301)
Penzance: 060460 (17.50 Penzance-Acton milk, with D6302)
Truro: 200560 (07.55 Penzance-Swansea, with D6300)
83G: 210560

Swindon Wks: 110960 (WksYd)/ 180960 (WksYd). N/listed 190660 & 091060. BR Rcds: 020860-200960 LC (defective transmission, awaiting replacement). Returned to 83D: 280960.

83D: 060861

Swindon Wks: 240961. N/listed 170961 & 121161. BR Rcds: 250961-231061 HC (serviceable transmission transferred to D604; laid up awaiting transmission). Returned to 83D: 011161.

Swindon Wks: 130462 (arrival). N/listed 040362 & 060562. BR Rcds: 120462-300462 HC (partially seized engine replaced).

Plymouth NR: 250862 (vans)
Tavistock Jct: 080763/ 090763 (both banking)
84A: 251263
XX: 210164 (fire damage) (FDTL)

Swindon Wks: 230264 ('A' Shop)/ 010364/ 220364 ('A' Shop)/ 010464/ 120464 ('A' Shop). N/listed 280164 & 260464. BR Rcds: 030264-170464 U.

84A: 090564/120765
Plymouth NR: 040865

Swindon Wks: 190965 ('A' Shop)/ 260965 ('A' Shop)/ 031065 ('A' Shop)/ 101065 ('A' Shop)/ 051265 ('A' Shop)/ 121265 ('A' Shop). N/listed 080865 & 230166. BR Rcds: xxxxxx-110166.

Truro Yard: 210866
84A: 180966
84B: 110667/290767
XX: 190867 (fire damage) (FDTL)
84A: 100468

Stored: 1we110568 (xxxxxx)

84A: 180568

Withdrawn: 1we010668 (260568)

84A: 230668/300668 (steam shed sdgs)/ 310768 (steam shed sdgs)/ 100868/ 080968 (steam shed sdgs)/ 290968/ 171068/ 021168

STN Booked Transfer: 8Z79 12.00 201168 (Wednesday) Laira Jct-Newport ADJ (with D6302/5/13)

Received J. Cashmore, Newport: 21 or 231168 (with D6302/5/13)
J. Cashmore, Newport: 231168/ xx1268
Disposal: 12/68 (D&ELfS).

D6304, Swindon Works ('A' Shop Yard), 18 September 1960.
(Brian Stephenson [Rail-Online])

D6305

NBL Order: L77/6, Progressive No.: 27670 1959.

D6305 and D6310, 83D Plymouth Laira, 25 September 1960. (R.C. Riley [The Transport Library])

D6305, 83D Plymouth Laira, Undated. Between January 1962 and August 1966. (Transport Topics)

NBL Date Invoiced: 070859

Birmingham Snow Hill: 070859

Swindon Wks: 080859 (arrival)/ 110859 (trials)/ 120859 (trials, failed with forward/reverse fault). Returned to NBL, Glasgow.

Preston: 180859 (hauled dead Swindon-Preston; spent night at Preston)/ 190859 (departed for NBL, Glasgow)

NBL, Glasgow: 040959/ we051059. Forward/reverse fault; additional faults found requiring replacement of transmission bottom casting, causing several weeks delay; additional modifications undertaken (e.g. temperature controls).

Swindon Wks: 051259 (arrival)/ 131259 ('A' Shop)/ 311259 ('A' Shop). Minor faults rectified; commenced working 110160.

Date New: 110160

82C: 070260
Swindon Wks: Nil. N/listed 280260.
In Works 56 days during period 12we260360 (B. Penney); included trial runs with new radiator fan thermal control switches between Swindon and Gloucester on 020360.

83D: 290360 (to Swindon Wks for dynastarter change)

Swindon Wks: Nil. BR Rcds: 300360-080460 U (defective dynastarter).

Gwinear Road: 230460 (down pass, with D6300)
Dainton: 300760 (13.30 Paddington-Penzance pass, piloting 'Hall' 5969)

Swindon Wks: 090161 (arrival)/ 290161 ('A' Shop)/ 050261 ('A' Shop)/ 190261 ('A' Shop)/ 280561 ('A' Shop). N/listed 051260 & 260361/ 160461 (82C?). BR Rcds: 090161-020661 LC (defective transmission; laid up awaiting replacement).
82C: 250661 (SSYd). Returned to 83D: 010761.

83D: 090761/ 060861/ 250861
Laira Jct: 300861 (up freight)
83D: 221061

Swindon Wks: 171261 (arrival). N/listed 031261, 070162 & 040262. BR Rcds: 181261-120162 LC (defective transmission).

Badminton: 100162 (trial)
Stoke Gifford: 110162 (trial)

83D: 040662

Swindon Wks: 060663 ('A' Shop Yd). N/listed 120563 & 090663.

83D: 070763
Tavistock Jct: 080763 (banking)

Swindon Wks: 280763 ('A' Shop)/ 180863 ('A' Shop)/ 210863 ('A' Shop). BR Rcds: 230763-300863 HC.

84A: 140963/ 251263/ 090564/ 120765/ 040865
Plympton: 060965 (down freight)
84A: 190965   **84B:** 250766

Swindon Wks: 310866/ 040966 ('A' Shop)/ 140966/ 190966 ('A' Shop)/ 021066/ 221066/ 131166/ 041266 ('A' Shop). N/listed 120367. BR Rcds: 100866-221266 C(I).

84A: 030767/ 290767/ 190867
84B: 3010-011167
84A: 100468

Stored: 1we110568 (xxxxxx)

84A: 180568

Withdrawn: 1we010668 (260568)

84A: 230668/ 300668 (steam shed sdgs)/ 310768 (steam shed sdgs)/ 100868/ 080968 (steam shed sdgs)/ 290968/ 171068/ 021168

STN Booked Transfer: 8Z79 12.00 201168 (Wednesday) Laira Jct-Newport ADJ (with D6302/4/13)

Received J. Cashmore, Newport: 21 or 231168 (with D6302/4/13)
J. Cashmore, Newport: 231168/ 011268 (rems)
Disposal: 12/68 (D&ELfS).

D6306

NBL Order: L97/1, Progressive No.: 27879.

D6306, 83D Plymouth Laira, 4 June 1960. (Peter Groom)

D6306, Truro, 23 August 1965. Bolt-on headcode boxes. (Richard Lewis [Rail-Photoprints])

NBL Date Invoiced: 240959

Swindon Wks: 230959 (arrival)
82C: 270959
Swindon: 071059 (07.05 Cheltenham-Paddington pass (from Sdn?)/
Kensington-Whitland milk empties (to Sdn), with D6307)/ 091059
(ditto)

Date New: 121059

Swindon: 121059 (as 071059)/ 131059 (07.50 Taunton-Paddington
pass (from Sdn?), and, 14.20 Paddington-?? parcels (to Sdn), with
D6307)/ 141059 (07.05 Cheltenham-Paddington pass (from Sdn?), and,
Kensington-Whitland milk empties (to Sdn), with D6307)/ 161059
(ditto)

Swindon Wks: 041259 (arrival). In Works 16 days during period
12we260360 (B. Penney).

83G: 210560
83D: 220560/040660
Redruth: 040760 (13.55 Penzance-Paddington, with D6308)/ 160760 (13.20
Penzance-Paddington pass, with D6309; one NBL failed on Hayle
bank, assisted by Pannier Tank to Redruth, then by 'Manor' 7813 to
Plymouth)
83D: 310760

Swindon Wks: Nil. N/listed 110960. BR Rcds: 030860-170860 LC.

Cowley Bridge Jct: 040761 (Exeter-Plymouth pass, via Okehampton)

Swindon Wks: 190761 ('A' Shop)/ 230761 ('A' Shop)/ 300761 ('A' Shop)/
170961 ('A' Shop)/ 240961 (WksYd). N/listed 200861. BR Rcds: 180761-
250961 LC.

83D: 221061

Swindon Wks: 031261 ('A' Shop). N/listed 121161 & 070162. BR Rcds:
241161-151261 LC.

83F: 150462
Royal Albert Bridge, Saltash: 130862 (up freight, with D6319)
Kingswear: 040563 (10.30 ex-Paddington, Kingswear portion)
83D: 050763/080763
Bideford: 060964 (Exeter-Torrington pass)

Swindon Wks: 310165/ 140365 ('A' Shop). N/listed 240165 & 280365.

84A: 120765
Redruth: 030865 (e.c.s.)
Truro: 230865 (parcels)
83A: 190965

Swindon Wks: 070566. N/listed 240466 & 050666.

84B: 180966
Bodmin General: 190966 (08.16 Padstow-Bodmin)
84B: 290167/110667/ 180667/ 290767
XX: 140867 (fire damage) (FDTL)
XX: 111067 (fire damage) (FDTL)
84B: 3010-011167
Truro: 230568 (07.45 Truro-Penzance pass, with D6315)
84A: 300668   **84B:** 080868
Par: 100868 (assisting failed 09.05 Manchester-Penzance pass (Par-Truro))
84B: 080968

Withdrawn: 1we211268 (211268)

84A: 281268/220269/ 050369/ 120469/ 130469/ end-0469/ 100569/
140569

STN Booked Transfer: 8Z31 03.05 270569 (Tuesday) Laira Jct-Newport
ADJ (with D6311/7)

Newport: 270569 (hauled by D6981, with D6311/7)

Received J. Cashmore, Newport: 280569 (with D6311/7)
J. Cashmore, Newport: 310569 (cabs)
Disposal: 05/69 (D&ELfS).

D6307

NBL Order: L97/2, Progressive No.: 27880.

D6307 piloting D813,
Aller Junction, Undated.
(Gordon Turner [David
Dunn Collection])

NBL Date Invoiced: 290959

Swindon Wks: 290959 (arrival)
Swindon: 071059 (07.05 Cheltenham-Paddington pass (from Swindon?)/
Kensington-Whitland milk empties (to Swindon), with D6306)/ 091059
(ditto)

Date New: 121059

Swindon: 121059 (as 071059)/ 131059 (07.50 Taunton-Paddington pass
(from Swindon?), and, 14.20 Paddington-?? parcels (to Swindon), with
D6306)/ 141059 (07.05 Cheltenham-Paddington pass (from Swindon?),
and, Kensington-Whitland milk empties (to Swindon), with D6306)/
161059 (ditto)

Swindon Wks: 041259 (arrival)
82C: 131259 (SS)
Plymouth NR: 110560 (03.10 Plymouth-Penzance parcels, with D6316)

Newton Abbot: 020760 (down 'Cornish Riviera Express', piloting D815 to
Plymouth)
Bodmin Road: 260860 (BR-Liskeard pass, with D6316)
83D: 300461
Chacewater: 220561 (07.20 Newquay-Chacewater pass)
Tavistock Jct: 080761 (up milk, piloting D811)
Hemerdon: 220761 (08.20 Penzance-Paddington pass, piloting D867)
83D: 060861   **83E:** 150462
St Dennis Jct: 080763 (freight, with D6339)
Par Bridge: 040963 (LE, with D6312)
84B: 200864/031064

Swindon Wks: 041164/ 081164 ('A' Shop)/ 221164 ('A' Shop)/ 291164 ('A'
Shop)/ 131264/ 170165/ 240165 ('A' Shop)/ 310165. N/listed 251064 &
140265.

Par: 040865

D6307 and D6309, Swindon Works (Timber Yard), 30 June 1971. Withdrawn. Bolt-on headcode boxes. Spoked wheels readily apparent.

(Adrian Booth)

Gunnislake: 010166 (pass)
84A: 240766   **84B:** 210866
XX: 050966 (fire damage) (FDTL)
84B: 180966
XX: 031066 (fire damage) (FDTL)
Par: 290767
84A: 190867
84B: 3010-011167
Truro: 240568 (07.45 Truro-Penzance DMU replacement, with D6339)
84A: 230668/300668/ 270768
Penzance: 130868
84A: 080968/220269
84B: 030569
84A: 100569   **83A:** 140569
Exeter s.p.: 170569
Saltash: 290869 (W'bound clay, with D6318)
Newquay branch: 220969 (china clay, with D6312)
84B: 071069   **84D:** 101169
84A: 270370/280670/ 130870/ 140870/ 160870/ 260970
84B: 221170

Withdrawn: 1we270371 (270371)

84A: 030471/070471/ 010571

Transfer 84A-Exeter South Devon Sdgs: 120571 (with D6309/12/5)

Exeter StD Carriage Shed: 120571/ 150571/ 260571

Transfer Exeter-BMJ: 270571 (with D6309/12/5)

BMJ: 010671 (Albert Rd Yd)/ 150671 (VS)/ 160671 (SPMCS)

Transfer BMJ-Swindon Wks: 220671 (with D6309/12/52)
Chippenham: xxxx71 (with D6309/12 [D6352 not listed], hauled by D853)

Swindon Wks: 250671/ 300671/ 020871 (TYd, whole)/ 110871 (TYd)/ 140871 (TYd, whole)/ 180871 (TYd)/ 111071 ('A' Shop Yd, whole)/ 181071/ 311071/ 041271/ 121271 (Dump, gutted bodyshell, on bogies)/ 291271. N/listed 050172.
Disposal: By 301271 (BR).

D6308

NBL Order: L97/3, Progressive No.: 27881.

D6308, 84A Plymouth Laira, 17 June 1969. Stored out-of-use. NBL Works plates removed, never to be replaced despite subsequent Works attention and re-instatement to traffic. (Peter Foster)

D6308, 85B Gloucester Horton Road, 11 November 1970. Cab-end letters visible below the steps immediately below the kick-plates ('A'-end nearest), a feature of BFY(v2) liveried locomotives. (Norman Preedy [Jim Binnie Collection])

NBL QP Wks: we051059 (numbered D6308)
NBL Date Invoiced: 051059

Swindon Wks: 081059 (arrival)/ 011159 (WksYd)
82C: 081159

Date New: 070160

Swindon: 070160 (07.50 Taunton-Paddington pass (from Sdn?), and, Paddington-?? parcels (to Sdn), with D6311)/ 080160 (ditto)/ 090160 (ditto)/ 180160 (07.50 Taunton-Paddington pass (from Sdn?), with D6312)
83D: 220560
Redruth: 040760 (13.55 Penzance-Paddington, with D6306)
83D: 250960

Swindon Wks: 101060 (arrival)/ 161060 ('A' Shop)/ 191060/ 061160 ('A'Shop)/ 131160 ('A' Shop). N/listed 091060 & 051260. BR Rcds: 101060-161160 U (transmission failure).

Swindon Wks: 190761 ('A' Shop)/ 200861 ('A' Shop)/ 170961 ('A' Shop)/ 240961 (TYd). N/listed 250661 & 121161. BR Rcds: 080861-041061 LC.

83D: 150462
Gwinear Road: 031162 (16.11 GR-Helston pass, last day pass traffic)
Carn Brea: 080763 (shunting)
84A: 251263/090564
Exeter StD: 080864 (16.00 Plymouth- Waterloo (EStD-Exeter Central), with West Country Pacific 34108)
84A: 031064/ 030865

Swindon Wks: 130366/ 130466/ 170466 ('A' Shop)/ 240466/ 050666 ('A' Shop)/ 260666. N/listed 230166 & 070566. BR Rcds: xxxxxx-250766.

84A: 240766
Plymouth NR: 250766 (ex-Wks)
84B: 210866/180966/ 180667
Menheniot: 150767 (rescuing failed D1063 on 06.55 Plymouth-Penzance pass (Menheniot-Liskeard))
84A: 190867   84D: 230668
84A: 310768   84B: 080968
Exeter s.p.: 261068
84B: 120469/ 030569/ 100569
Paignton: 140569 (17.46 Paignton-Kingswear pass)

Stored: 1we140669 (xx0669)

84A: 170669/250669
83A: 190869/200969/ xx1069/ 070270 (by traverser, cannibalised)/ 220270/ 280270 (Factory Yd). Departed xx0370 (to Swindon, with D862). N/listed 070370.

Reinst. (Wks): 1we140370 (090370)

Swindon Wks: 150470. BR Rcds: xxxxxx-050670 C. Paint Date: GOODLASS WALL S.W.N. 21/5/70 UROAL KYD.

Reinst. (Traffic): 1we060670 (050670)

82A: 100670/ 020970/ 171070
85B: 111170/221170/ 131270
82A: 200271
Bath: 160371 (13.35 Bristol-Portsmouth (Bath-Westbury) after failure of D7012)
82A: 280371/190471
Exeter: 020571 (with D6328/43/8)
84A: 020571 (ex-82A with D6328/43/8)
Exeter s.p.: 220571/240571
84A: 300571   Exeter s.p.: 110771
Newton Abbot: 150771 (freight from Heathfield)
Exeter Riverside: 190771 (ER-Hemyock milk)
Par: 020871 (china clay)
84B: 090871

Stored: 1we140871 (110871)

84A: 250871

Withdrawn: 1we110971 (110971)

84A: 220971/250971/ end-0971

Transfer 84A-83A: ?
Hackney Yd, NA: (101071). See Note.
Transfer 83A-BMJ: ?

BMJ: 211071/ 221071 (CPS)/ 271071/ 301071 (CPS)/ 031171 (CPS)/ 141171 (VS)/ 301171/ 041271 (VS)/ 121271/ 181271/ 291271/ 010172/ 040172/ 090172/ 150172 (VS)/ 260172 (VS)/ 130272/ 190272/ 220272/ 260272/ 040372/ 120372

Transfer BMJ-Swindon Wks: 130372 (with D6334/7/48)

Swindon Wks: 150372 ('A' Shop, being stripped)/ 180372 ('A'Shop Yd)/ 220372 ('A' Shop Yd, gutted bodyshell, on bogies)/ 260372 (ditto)/ 050472 (ConYd)/ 100472/ 150472 (ConYd)/ 270472 (ConYd Cutting Area, being cut-up). N/listed 170572.
Disposal: By 050572 (BR).

Note:
1. Photo: D6319/28, Hackney Yard (NA), 10/10/71 (MLI197). '.....there were seven Class 22s spread around the vicinity', i.e. D6318/22/3 already in the NA area, D6319/28 recently ex-84A, plus D6308/48?

D6309

NBL Order: L97/4, Progressive No.: 27882.

D6309, Fowey, Undated.
(Brian Morgan [Kidderminster Railway Museum])

D6309, 84B St.Blazey,
25 September 1969.
(John Chalcraft [Rail-Photoprints])

NBL QP Wks: we051059 (L97/4)
NBL Date Invoiced: 131059

Preston: 131059 (LE)

82C: 011159
Swindon Wks: 311259 ('A' Shop). N/listed 191259.

Date New: 120160

Swindon: 130160 (07.50 Taunton-Paddington pass (from Sdn?), and, Paddington-?? parcels (to Sdn), with D6313)
83D: 220560
Redruth: 160760 (13.20 Penzance-Paddington pass, with D6306; one NBL failed on Hayle bank, assisted by 0-6-0PT to Redruth, then by 'Manor' 7813 to Plymouth)
83D: 030860

Swindon Wks: 121060 (arrival)/ 161060 (WksYd)/ 191060. N/listed 091060. BR Rcds: 151060-311060 U.
82C: 061160 (ex-Wks)

Swindon Wks: 290161 ('A' Shop)/ 050261 ('A' Shop). N/listed 051260 & 190261. BR Rcds: 301260-080261 LC.
Swindon-Gloucester: Early-0261 (ex-Wks, test train, with D6310)

Swindon Wks: 280561 ('A' Shop)/ 250661 (WksYd). N/listed 160461 & 190761. BR Rcds: 160561-040761 LC.

83E: 060861   83G: 150462
Helston: 230462/ 180862
83D: 160962
Truro/Penzance: 080763/ 090763
Dunmere: 140863 (tests on Wenford branch, subsequently aborted)
84A: 030865
Wadebridge: xx0865 (pass)

Swindon Wks: 230166 ('A' Shop)/ 130366 ('A' Shop). N/listed 121265 & 130466.

84A: 240766   84B: 210866
84A: 180966
Bodmin General: 280167 (Bodmin General-Wadebridge/Padstow, last pass service in lieu of DMU)

Par: 290167   84B: 110667
Truro: 030767 (engine+van)
84B: 290767
84A: 190867/021267
84B: 230668
Truro Yard: 290668 (shunting)
84A: 310768
Plymouth NR: 100868 (Penzance-Liverpool pass, with D6315)
Truro: 130868 (e.c.s., with D6315)
84B: 080968   84A: 220269
Plymouth NR: 110469
84A: 120469/130469
84B: 100569/220769
84A: 290769/200969
84B: 250969   Par: 091169
84A: 270370   Par: 020870
84A: 160870/210870
82A: 021170   84B: 221170
XX: 050171 (fire damage) (FDTL)
84B: 030471   84A: 010571

Stored: 1we080571 (020571)

Transfer 84A-Exeter South Devon Sdgs: 120571 (with D6307/12/5)

Exeter StD Carriage Shed: 120571/ 150571

Withdrawn: 1we220571 (220571)

Exeter StD Carriage Shed: 260571

Transfer Exeter-BMJ: 270571 (with D6307/12/5)

BMJ: 010671 (Diesel Depot [SPMCS?])/ 180671 (DMU Sdgs). N/listed 160671 (SPMCS).

Transfer BMJ-Swindon Wks: 220671 (with D6307/12/52)
Chippenham: xxxx71 (with D6307/12 [D6352 not listed], hauled by D853)

Swindon Wks: 230671 ('A' Shop)/ 250671/ 300671 / 020871 (TYd, whole)/ 110871 (TYd)/ 140871 (TYd, whole)/ 180871 (TYd)/ 181071/ 311071/ 041271/ 121271 (Dump, gutted bodyshell, on bogies)/ 231271 (ConYd Cutting Area, being cut-up)/ 291271. N/listed 050172.
Disposal: By 301271 (BR).

D6310

NBL Order: L97/5, Progressive No.: 27883.

D6310 and D6331, 83G Penzance, 26 October 1960. Earlier in the year the *Railway Observer* (June 1960) noted: "Only one locomotive is employed on Hemerdon banking duties, D6310 being the most frequent as it is running without its Clayton steam generator which has been put to stationary use for instructional purposes". (Rail-Online)

D6310 and D6331, Bristol Marsh Junction, Undated.
(Amyus Crump Collection)

NBL QP Wks: we051059 (L97/5)
NBL Date Invoiced: 201059

82C: 011159/081159
Swindon Wks: 311259 ('A' Shop). N/listed 191259.

Date New: 050160

83D: 090160 (arrived Laira)
Hemerdon: xx0160 (banking)
Newton Abbot: 120260 (up 'Mayflower' (to NA), with D6315)
83D: 220560
Saltash: 020760 (pass, with D6319)
Newton Abbot: 160760 (waiting next duty)

Swindon Wks: 161060 ('A' Shop). N/listed 091060. BR Rcds: 101060-201060 U.

83G: 261060

Swindon Wks: 290161 ('A' Shop)/ 050261 ('A' Shop). N/listed 190261. BR Rcds: 160161-100261 LC.
Swindon-Gloucester: Early-0261 (ex-Wks, test train, with D6309)

83D: 090761
Hemerdon: 220761 (pass, piloting D600)
83A: 060861
Laira Jct: 240861 (china clay, with D6311)
XX: 160162 (fire damage) (FDTL)
83F: 150462
Hayle Wharf: 080763 (shunting)
Truro/Penzance: 090763
Cambourne: 240863 (local pass)
Kingsbridge: 161063 (removing remaining wagons after line closure)
84A: 251263
Yelverton: 010664 (demolition)
84A: 031064
XX: 120465 (severe fire damage) (FDTL)

Swindon Wks: 090565 ('A' Shop)/ 300565 ('A' Shop)/ 060665/ 200665 ('A' Shop)/ 270665/ 150765 ('A' Shop)/ 080865 ('A' Shop)/ 110865/ 190965 ('A' Shop)/ 260965 ('A' Shop)/ 031065 ('A' Shop)/ 101065 ('A' Shop)/ 051265 ('A' Shop). N/listed 121265. Derived Rcds: xx0465-xx1265 C+ Fire damage reps.

Plymouth NR: 280566 (freight)
84D: 250766   **84B:** 180667
Plymouth NR: 160867 (St.Blazey-Tavistock Jct Yard engineers)
82A: 281067   **83A:** 180568
Exeter s.p.: 110668
83A: 290668
Exeter StD/Exeter s.p.: 060768
83A: 310768
Exeter StD: 170868 (shunting)/ 240868 (16.45 Ilfracombe-Exeter pass, with D6333)
Exeter s.p.: 080968
Exeter StD: 091068 (16.30 Paddington-Paignton (from Exeter))/ 311268 (12.30 Paddington-Paignton (from Exeter))
Teignbridge/ Heathfield: 010469 (Newton Abbot-Bovey Tracey freight)
83A: 110469
Exeter StD: 130469/ 100569
Exeter s.p.: 140569
82A: 240769/020869/ 010969/ 140969/ 121069/ 181069/ 201069
85B: 161269 /250170
Newland: 140270 (p.way, with D6320)
85B: 150270/250570/ 140670
82A: 090870/020970/ 190970
85B: 151070/131270
82A: 200271/220271

Withdrawn: 1we270371 (270371)

82A: 040471/ 190471/ 150571

BMJ: 010671 (Albert Rd Yd)/ 020771/ 030871 (DMU Shed)/ 130871/ 140871 (DMU shed) / 250971 (DMU shed)/ 231071/ 031171 (DMU Shed)/ 041271 (DMU Shed)/ 051271 (DMU Shed) . N/listed 180671 (Albert Rd Yd).

Transfer BMJ-Swindon Wks: 101271 (with D865, D6320)

Swindon Wks: 121271 ('A' Shop Yd, complete)/ 291271/ 050172 (Dump/ Yds)/ 090172/ 130172/ 210172/ 120272 (TYd)/ 270272 (Yard)/ 120372 (TYd, gutted shell, on bogies)/ 150372/ 180372/ 220372/ 040472/ 050472/ 100472/ 120472/ 270472 (ConYd Cutting Area, being cut-up). N/listed 170572.
Disposal: By 120572 (BR).

D6311

NBL Order: L97/6, Progressive No.: 27884.

D6311, Swindon Works ('A' Shop Yard, outside south-west doors), 30 July 1961. (RCTS)

NBL QP Wks: we051059 (L97/6)
NBL Date Invoiced: 181259

Swindon Wks: 191259 (WksYd)/ 311259 ('A' Shop)

Date New: 070160

Swindon: 070160 (07.50 Taunton-Paddington pass (from Sdn?), and, Paddington-?? parcels (to Sdn), with D6308)/ 080160 (ditto)/ 090160 (ditto)
81A: 070560
Par: 120560 (06.45 Par-Newquay pass)
83G: 210560
XX: 180660 (07.50 Newquay-Manchester pass, with D6324 and 'Warship')
Newton Abbot: 090760 (10.35 down pass, piloting D600)/ 060860 (down 'Cornish Riviera', piloting 'Grange' 6800, both from NA)
83E St.Blazey: 050261

Swindon Wks: 230761 ('A' Shop)/ 300761 (WksYd)/ 010861 (Badminton trial)/ 020861 (Gloucester trial). N/listed 250661 & 200861. BR Rcds: 140661-020861 LC.

Laira Jct: 240861 (china clay, with D6310)
Newquay: 230462

Helston: 240762 (Helston-Gwinear Road pass)
St.Blazey/Tregoss: 120263 (severe fire damage) (FDTL); virtual write-off
83D: 180263 (left 83D hauled by 'Prairie' 5569 for Swindon Works)

Swindon Wks: xx0363 (engine compartment gutted by fire)/ 170363 ('A' Shop)/ 240363 ('A' Shop)/ 210463/ 280463/ 120563 ('A' Shop)/ 060663 ('A' Shop Yd). BR Rcds: 190263-020763 HC (fire damage reps).

83D: 060763/080763/ 110863
Exeter Central: 270863 (pass)
St Austell: 050964 (up freight)
84B: 031064
Heathfield: 180665 (freight)
84A: 120765
Bodmin Road: 030865 (pass)
84C: 040865   **84A:** 190965
Par: 230965 (assisting D601 up 'Cornish Riviera Express' (Par-Plymouth), with D6315)

Swindon Wks: 070566/ 050666 ('A' Shop)/ 260666. N/listed 240466. BR Rcds: 130566-020866 C(I)+ Mods.

84D: 210866/290167
Bere Ferrers: 290567 (freight)

D6311, Bere Ferrers, 29 May 1967. (Colour-Rail)

83A: 290767
Bristol TM: 071067
82A: 151067
Laira Sdgs: 100468 (cement)
84B: 180568
84A: 230668 / 300668
84B: 070868
Par: 100868 (Newquay-Newcastle pass, piloting D1061, detached Par)

Stored: 1we140968 (xx0968)

84A: 080968

Withdrawn: 1we280968 (230968)

84A: 290968 / 171068 / 021168 / mid-1168 / 281268 / 220269 (part of nose-end / buffer-beam valance removed) / 050369 / 070369 / 120469 / 130469 / end-0469 / 100569 / 140569

STN Booked Transfer: 8Z31 03.05 270569 (Tuesday) Laira Jct-Newport ADJ (with D6306 / 17)

Newport: 270569 (hauled by D6981, with D6306 / 17)

Received J. Cashmore, Newport: 280569 (with D6306 / 17)
J. Cashmore, Newport: 310569 / 010669 (by Wall) / 070669 / 090669
Disposal: 05 / 69 (D&ELfS).

D6312

NBL Order: L97/7, Progressive No.: 27885.

D6312, Penzance, Undated. Between August 1963 and March 1966. (Rail-Online)

D6312 and D6338, 84B St.Blazey, October 1966. (Colour-Rail)

NBL QP Wks: we051059 (L97/7)
NBL Date Invoiced: 291259

Swindon Wks: 311259 (WksYd)

Date New: 140160

Swindon: 180160 (07.50 Taunton-Paddington pass (from Sdn?), with D6308)
Truro: 220760 (pass, with D6316, piloted by 'Prairie' 4549)
Bodmin Road: 190860 (down 'Cornishman', with D6322)
Truro: 020960 (up pass, with D6322)

Swindon Wks: 051260 (WksYd). N/listed 131160 & 290161. BR Rcds: 031260-221260 LC.

Dainton: 190861 (up pass, piloting D868)
XX: 230162 (fire damage) (FDTL)
83D: 150462
Royal Albert Bridge, Saltash: 290462 (engineer's train)
Boscarne: 080662 (trip-freight)
Helston/Praze: 031162 (20.45 Helston-Gwinear Rd pass, last day pass traffic)
83D: 030763/080763
Exeter Central: 270763

Swindon Wks (?): Nil. N/listed 210863. BR Rcds: After 140863-260863 HC.

Par Bridge: 040963 (LE, with D6307)
84A: 251263   **84B** 031064
84A: 190965

Swindon Wks: 130366 ('A' Shop)/ 130466/ 240466. N/listed 230166 and 070566.
82C: 220566
Swindon Wks: 050666 ('A' Shop). N/listed 250666.

84A: 240766
84B: 180966/290167
Dainton: 170667 (07.50 Penzance-Paddington (Plymouth-Newton Abbot), piloting D1070)
83A: 170667   **82A:** 281067
Evercreech Jct: 061167 (demolition)

Swindon Wks: 031267 ('A' Shop). N/listed 260168. BR Rcds: xxxxxx-141267 Minor collision reps ('B' end).

84B: 180568/230668/ 070868
Truro: 130868 (freight)
84D: 080968
84A: 290968/281268
Redruth: 120469
84D: 120469/130469
Laira Jct: 250469 (freight)
84A: 270469/100569
Truro: 250669 (stabled)
84B: 220769   **84A:** 020869
Newquay branch: 220969 (china clay, with D6307)
Lostwithiel: 071069
84B: 091169
Grampound Road: 240270
84B: 020570
Lostwithiel: 030670 (stabled)
84A: 280670   **84B:** 020870
Plymouth NR: 270870
Exeter s.p.: 270271
84B: 030471/010571

Stored: 1we080571 (020571)

Exeter s.p.: 030571
84A: Nil

Transfer 84A-Exeter South Devon Sdgs: 120571 (with D6307/9/15)

Exeter StD Carriage Shed: 120571/ 150571

Withdrawn: 1we220571 (220571)

Exeter StD Carriage Shed: 260571

Transfer Exeter-BMJ: 270571 (with D6307/9/15)

BMJ: 010671 (Albert Rd Yd)/ 150671 (VS)/ 160671 (SPM Coal Sdgs)

Transfer BMJ-Swindon Wks: 220671 (with D6307/9/52)
Chippenham: xxxx71 (with D6307/9 [D6352 not listed], hauled by D853)

Swindon Wks: 230671 ('A' Shop)/ 250671/ 300671/ 020871 (TYd, whole)/ 110871 (TYd)/ 140871 (TYd, whole)/ 180871 (TYd)/ 181071/ 311071/ 021171/ 041271/ 121271 (Dump, gutted bodyshell, on bogies)/ 291271/ 050172 (ConYd Cutting Area)/ 090172 (ConYd Cutting Area, being cut-up). N/listed 210172.
Disposal: By 150172 (BR).

D6313

NBL Order: L97/8, Progressive No.: 27886.

D6313, 72A Exmouth Junction, June 1963. Depot re-coded 83D three months later under Western Region jurisdiction.
(Rex Conway [Rail-Online])

NBL QP Wks: we051059 (L97/8)
NBL Date Invoiced: 191259

Swindon Wks: Nil. N/listed 191259 & 311259. BR Rcds: 311259-080160 Acceptance.

Date New: 120160

Swindon: 130160 (07.50 Taunton-Paddington pass (from Swindon?), and, Paddington-?? parcels (to Swindon), with D6309)
St Budeaux: 150360 (Plymouth-Exeter (via Okehampton) pass (failed))

Swindon Wks: 010560 (Weigh Shop). BR Rcds: 050460-020560 LC.

83G: 210560
Penzance: 130660 (up 'Cornishman', with D6323)
Saltash: 020760 (pass, with D6318)
Newton Abbot: 090760 (10.30 down pass, piloting D807)

Swindon Wks: 280860 ('A' Shop Yard)

83D: 310161 (collision with D6302)

Swindon Wks: 180361 (trial to Gloucester). N/listed 190261. BR Rcds: 200261-200361 LC (collision damage reps; mainframe straightened).
82C: 260361 (ex-Wks)

Newton Abbot: 18 or 190661 (collision with D6300). (N.B. No subsequent BR official info found re visit to Swindon Wks for examination/repairs.)

83D: 060861
Laira Jct: 240861 (trip-freight)
Wadebridge: 161261
83D: 150462/060763/080763
Tavistock: 310864 (pass)
84C: 031064   **84A:** 120765

D6313, Bristol Temple Meads, 24 April 1968.

(Jim Binnie)

Swindon Wks: 070566/ 050666 ('A' Shop)/ 260666. N/listed 240466 & 310866. BR Rcds: 020566-080866 C(I).

Exeter s.p.: 180867
84A: 290867
Exeter StD: 020967 (pass, with D6315)
83A: 040967
82A: 071067/151067/281067
Bedminster: 130168 (mixed freight)
82A: 210168/150368/060468
Bristol TM: 240468 (up freight)
82A: 260468 (derailed)
Exeter StD: 110568 (with D6315, transfer 82A-84A)

Stored: 1we150668 (xx0668)

84A: 230668/300668 (steam shed sdgs)/ 310768 (steam shed sdgs)

Withdrawn: 1we030868 (030868)

84A: 100868/080968 (steam depot sdgs)/ 290968/ 171068/ 021168

STN Booked Transfer: 8Z79 12.00 201168 (Wednesday) Laira Jct-Newport ADJ (with D6302/4/5)

Received J. Cashmore, Newport: 21 or 231168 (with D6302/4/5)
J. Cashmore, Newport: 231168/ xx1268
Disposal: 12/68 (D&ELfS).

D6314

NBL Order: L97/9, Progressive No.: 27887.

D6314, Plymouth North Road, Undated. Rake of six-wheeled milk tanks.
(Author's Collection)

D6314, 84D Penzance, 18 October 1968. BSY livery.
(K.C.H. Fairey [Colour-Rail])

NBL QP Works: we051059 (L97/9)
NBL Date Invoiced: 311259

Swindon Wks: 140160 (arrival)

Date New: 250160

Kemble: 250160 (Gloucester-Swindon running-in turn, with D6315)
Swindon: 260160 (07.50 Taunton-Paddington pass (from Sdn?), and, Paddington-?? parcels (to Sdn), with D6315)
83D: 230260 (engine fire investigation)/ 240260 (ditto)
83G: 210560
Devonport: 260860 (Devonport-Plymouth pass, with D6319)
83A: 060861
Laira Jct: 240861 (e.c.s.)
Tavistock Jct: 290861 (engine & van)
83E: 150462
Nanstallon Halt: 250462 (09.03 Padstow-Bodmin General pass)
Plymouth: 080763 (Plymouth-Waterloo pass (to Exeter))
84C: 031064/030865
Redruth: 040865
84A: 240766
Plymouth NR: 280566 (LE)
84B: 210866

Swindon Wks: 131166/ 041266 ('A' Shop). N/listed 221066. BR Rcds: xxxxxx-xx1266 I.

Moorswater: 290167 (ex-Wks)
84A: 040367
Dainton: 170667 (09.15 Bristol-Penzance (SO) pass, piloting D836)
84A: 290767/270867
Dawlish: 310867 (down pass, piloting D1033)
84A: 240967
84B: 3010-011167/ 180568/ 230668
84A: 310768
Penzance: 130868
84A: 180968 (transmission change)/ 290968
84D: 181068
84A: 281268/220269/ 120469/ 130469

Stored: 1we190469 (180469)
Withdrawn: 1we260469 (260469)

84A: End-0469/100569/ 140569/ 250669

STN Booked Transfer: No information found. N.B. Pencil annotation on **Sale of Surplus Locomotives** document dated 080769 indicates 'Sunday 13/7 ex-Westbury' (with D800/63).

Gloucester: 180769 (with D800/63, hauled by D1680)

Received J. Cashmore, Newport: 220769 (with D800/63, D6353)
J. Cashmore, Newport: 220769/ 240769/ 270769. N/listed 290769.
Disposal: 07/69 (D&ELfS).

D6314, Tavistock Junction, 29 August 1961. (R.C. Riley [The Transport Library])

D6315

NBL Order: L97/10, Progressive No.: 27888.

D6315, High Street (north-west of Burngullow Junction), circa 1962. (M. Roberts [Kidderminster Railway Museum])

D6315. 84B St.Blazey, 27 March 1970. (Peter Foster)

NBL QP Wks: we051059 (L97/10)
NBL Date Invoiced: 130160

Swindon Wks: 140160 (arrival)

Date New: 250160

Kemble: 250160 (Gloucester-Swindon running-in turn, with D6314)
Swindon: 260160 (07.50 Taunton-Paddington pass (from Sdn?), and, Paddington-?? parcels (to Sdn), with D6314)
Newton Abbot: 120260 (up 'Mayflower' (to NA), with D6310)
83D: 260260 (engine overspeed trips)
83G: 210560   **83D:** 220560

Swindon Wks: 110960 (WksYd, arrived during visit)

Perranporth: 040661 (16.35 Chacewater-Newquay pass)
Newton Abbot: 020961 (11.30 Liverpool Lime St-Penzance (NA-Plymouth), with D852)

Swindon Wks: 070162 ('A' Shop)/ 040262 ('A' Shop)/ 040362 ('A' Shop). N/listed 121161. BR Rcds: 050162-080362 LC.

83D: 150462
Royal Albert Bridge, Saltash: 130862 (down pass, piloting D826)
XX: 140862 (fire damage) (FDTL)
Quintrell Downs: 280962 (15.50 Par-Newquay pass)
Plymouth NR: 070763 (Paddington-Penzance pass (Newton Abbot to Plymouth), piloting D1039)
Bodmin Road: 140863
84A: 090564
Plymouth NR: 100765 (with D6340)
Hayle: 040865 (freight)
Par: 230965 (assisting D601 up 'Cornish Riviera Express' (Par-Plymouth), with D6311)

Swindon Wks: 051265 ('A' Shop)/ 121265 ('A' Shop)/ 230166/ xx0266 ('A' Shop). N/listed 101065 & 130366. Paint date: 19/1/66.

84B: 250766/210866/ 180966
Heathfield: 240667 (oil tanks, with D6321)
Exeter s.p.: 010767
Exeter StD: 050767 (LE)
Par: 290767
Exeter StD: 260867 (e.c.s. EStD-Exeter Central, with D6316)/ 020967 (pass, with D6313)
83A: 040967
Exeter StD: 140967 (21.00 EStD-Paignton pass, with D6317)

82A: 071067/151067
Midford (S&D): 291167 (demolition)
82A: 210168/040268/ 060468
Exeter StD: 110568 (with D6313, transfer 82A-84A)
84A: 180568
Truro: 230568 (07.45 Truro-Penzance pass, with D6306)
84B: 230668
Plymouth: 100868 (Penzance-Liverpool pass, with D6309)
Truro: 130868 (e.c.s., with D6309)
84B: 080968/180968
Plymouth NR: 301168 (LE)/ 250169 (milk)
84B: 120469/100569
Par: 140569
Drinnick Mill: 160569 (china clay)
84A: 220769/290869
84B: 071069/270370/ 020870
84A: 130870/160870
Stoke Canon: 270371 (16.06 Hemyock-Exeter milk)
Exeter: 050471 (D6333 hauling failed D6315/8 on 16.40 Torrington-Exeter freight)

Stored: 1we080571 (020571)

84A: Nil

Transfer 84A-Exeter South Devon Sdgs: 120571 (with D6307/9/12)

Exeter StD Carriage Shed: 120571/ 150571

Withdrawn: 1we220571 (220571)

Exeter StD Carriage Shed: 260571

Transfer Exeter-BMJ: 270571 (with D6307/9/12)

BMJ: 010671 (Diesel Depot [SPMCS?])/ 160671 (SPMCS)/ 270671 (SPMCS)/ 020771/ 310771 (SPMCS)/ 110871/ 130871/ 300871 (SPMCS)/ 250971 (SPMCS)/ 260971 (SPMCS)/ 091071/ 221071/ 271071/ 301071 (SPMCS)/ 031171 (SPMCS)/ 141171 (SPMCS). N/listed 301171.

Transfer BMJ-Swindon Wks: 021271 (with D6327/31/54)

Swindon Wks: 121271 ('A' Shop, complete)/ 050172 ('A' Shop)/ 090172 ('A' Shop, being stripped)/ 210172 (ConYd Cutting Area, being cut-up). N/listed 120272.
Disposal: By 280172 (BR).

D6316

NBL Order: L97/11, Progressive No.: 27889.

D6316, Swindon Works (Timber Yard), Undated. Circa-July/August 1962. Waiting transmission. (Colour-Rail)

NBL QP Wks: we051059 (L97/11)
NBL Date Invoiced: 170260

Date New: 010360

Plymouth NR: 110560 (03.10 Plymouth-Penzance parcels, with D6307)
Newton Abbot: 020760 (08.05 Newquay-Newcastle, piloting Std 5MT 73041)
83A: 030760
Newton Abbot: 160760 (waiting next turn of duty)
Truro: 220760 (pass, with D6312, piloted by 'Prairie' 4549)
Bodmin Road: 260860 (Bodmin Road-Liskeard pass, with D6307)
Tolcarn East Jct: 230561 (16.40 Par-Newquay pass)
83A: 060861
Goonhavern Halt: 290961 (16.40 Newquay-Chacewater pass)

83D: 221061   **83E:** 150462
Bodmin: 230462

Swindon Wks: 120862 (TYd)/ 190862 (TYd)/ 260862 (TYd)/ 090962 ('A' Shop)/ 160962 (WksYd). N/listed 010762 & 300962. BR Rcds: 270662-101062 HC (transmission reps/ replacement).

Bodmin General: 080763 (shunting)
XX: 280564 (fire damage) (FDTL)
Barnstaple: 260764
Barnstaple Jct: 180864 (pass to Ilfracombe)
Exeter s.p.: 190864
84C: 031064   **84A:** 190965

D6316, Swindon Works (Weigh Shop Yard), 16 September 1962. (A. Linaker [Kidderminster Railway Museum])

Swindon Wks: 130466/ 240466/ 070566/ 050666 ('A' Shop). N/listed 130366 & 260666. Derived Rcds: xxxxxx-xx0666.

83D Exmouth Jct: 230766
Exeter s.p.: 270766
St. Ives: 070966 (up 'Limited' (last through service from St.Ives), with D6321)
84B: 180966   **84A:** 190867
Exeter StD: 260867 (e.c.s. EStD-Exeter Central, with D6315)
82A: 071067/ 211067/ 281067
85B: 040268/240268

Stored: 1we230368 (xx0368)
Withdrawn: 1we060468 (310368)

85A: 120468/160468/ 230568/ 080668/ 090668/ 220668/ 290668/ 180768/ 210768/ 240768/ 260768/ 250868/ 070968/ 291068. Not listed 180868 & 241168.

STN <u>**Booked Transfer:**</u> 7V55 04.12 221168 (Friday) Bescot-STJ (from Worcester, reduced to Class 8); 8A94 19.00 221168 (Friday) STJ-Newport Ebbw Jct

Ebbw Jct: 231168/ 011268 (sdgs near depot, with D6300/3)/ 131268

Received J. Cashmore, Newport: 201268 (with D6300/3)
J. Cashmore, Newport: Nil.
Disposal: 12/68 (D&ELfS).

D6317

NBL Order: L97/12, Progressive No.: 27890.

D6317 and D851, 83G
Penzance, 26 August
1963. (Colour-Rail)

NBL QP Wks: we051059 (L97/12)
NBL Date Invoiced: 170260

Date New: 010360

83D: 220560

Swindon Wks: 190660 ('A' Shop). N/listed 110960.

83E: 050261
XX: 080261 (fire damage) (FDTL)
XX: 030661 (fire damage) (FDTL)
Bodmin Road: 130761 (pass)
Bodmin General: 140761 (pass)
Tolcarne Jct: 150761 (11.15 Newquay-Wolverhampton pass, piloting 'Castle' 5058)
83D: 060861   **83G:** 230861

Swindon Wks: Nil. N/listed 170961 & 121161.
    BR Rcds: 091061-241061 LC.

83E: 150462
Helston: 240762 (freight)
83G: 260863   **84A:** 251263
St. Blazey/Fowey Docks: 031064

Swindon Wks: 280365/ 030465/ 100465/ 090565 ('A' Shop)/ 300565 ('A' Shop)/ 060665/ 200665 ('A' Shop). N/listed 140365 & 150765. BR Rcds: 150365-150765 C.

84A: 190965
Lydford: 311265 (freight from Launceston)
84A: 240766   **84B:** 250766
83D Exmouth Jct: 210866/ 180966/ 050367

84B: 110667
Dainton Bank: 170667 (09.15 Bristol-Penzance (Newton Abbot-Plymouth), piloting D836)
84B: 180667
Exeter StD: 250867 (banking 16.30 Tavistock Jct-Exeter Central cement (from EStD to EC), with D6319)/ 140967 (21.00 EStD-Paignton pass, with D6315)
82A: 151067/ 211067/ 281067
85B: 040268/240268
82A: 150368/060468
Exeter StD: 110568 (with D6318, transfer 82A-84A)
84A: 230668/300668/ 310768
84B: 070868

Store: 1we070968 (xx0968)

XX (china clay drier, Cornwall): 040968 (recently sustained derailment/ collision damage)
84A: 080968 (steam depot sdgs)

Withdrawn: 1we280968 (230968)

84A: 290968/171068/ 021168/ 281268 (old steam shed)/ 220269/ 050369/ 070369/ 120469/ 130469/ end-0469/ 100569/ 140569

STN Booked Transfer: 8Z31 03.05 270569 (Tuesday) Laira Jct-Newport ADJ (with D6306/11)

Newport: 270569 (hauled by D6981, with D6306/11)

Received J. Cashmore, Newport: 280569 (with D6306/11)
J. Cashmore, Newport: 310569/ 010669 (by Wall)/ 070669/ 090669
Disposal: 05/69 (D&ELfS).

D6317, Swindon Works ('AE' Shop), Undated. Circa-June/ July 1965 during Classified body overhaul. Bolt-on headcode boxes. (Rail-Online)

D6318

NBL Order: L97/13, Progressive No.: 27891.

D6318, 83A Newton
Abbot, 18 September
1966. (M.J. Burnett [RCTS])

D6318, 84A Plymouth
Laira, 10 May
1970. (Rail-Online)

NBL QP Wks: we051059 (L97/13)
NBL Date Invoiced: 220260

Swindon Wks: 280260 ('A' Shop)

Date New: 140360

Swindon Wks: 270360 ('A' Shop)

83D: 120460 (arrived with D6319)
Newquay: 120560 (Newquay-St. Dennis Jct pick-up freight and return)
83G: 210560   **83D:** 220560
Saltash: 020760 (pass, with D6313)

Swindon Wks: 091060 (TYd)/ 161060 (WksYd). N/listed 110960.
82C: 061160 (ex-Wks)

83E: 050261
Totnes: 220761 (11.40 Paddington-Penzance pass, piloting 'Hall' 6963)
Laira Jct: 270861 (down pass, piloting D808)
83D: 221061

Swindon Wks: Nil. N/listed 040362. BR Rcds: 220362-140462 LC.

83E: 150462
Helston: 180862
Drinnick Mill: 080763 (shunting)
Bampton: 280963 (SO pass)
84A: 251263
Totnes: 080864 (11.17 Cardiff-Penzance, piloting D7046)
Penzance: 031064
XX: 050665 (fire damage) (FDTL)
84A: 120765   **Par:** 040865
84B: 250766
83D Exmouth Jct: 210866
83A: 180966

Swindon Wks: 120367/ 020467 ('A' Shop). N/listed 061266. BR Rcds: xxxxxx-140467 C. Paint Date: SWD 31.3.67 (K) SYN.

Exeter s.p.: 220467
Barnstaple: 080667 (stabled)

Exeter s.p.: 010767
82A: 071067/ 151067/ 281067/ 150368/ 240468
Ashchurch: 040568 (breakdown train)
Exeter StD: 110568 (with D6317, transfer 82A-84A)
84A: 180568   **84B:** 230668
83B: 050868
84B: 070868/080968
84A: 130469
84B: 100569/220769
84A: 020869/060869
Saltash: 290869 (W'bound clay, with D6307)
84B: 071069/091169
84A: 270370/100570/ 170570/ 020870/ 130870
84A: 260970
XX: 281070 (fire damage) (FDTL)
Exeter StD: 050471 (D6333 hauling failed D6315/8 on 16.40 Torrington-Exeter freight)
84B: 010571

Stored: 1we080571 (020571)
Withdrawn: 1we220571 (220571)

83A: 310571
Hackney Yard, NA: 010671/ 230671
83A: 280771
Newton Abbot CS: 080871

Transfer 83A-BMJ: 211071 (with D6322/3, D815)

BMJ: 211071/ 221071 (CPS)/ 271071/ 301071 (CPS)/ 031171 (CPS/ 141171/ 301171/ 041271 (VS)/ 121271/ 181271/ 241271/ 291271/ 010172/ 040172 (VS)/ 090172 (VS)/ 150172 (VS)/ 260172 (VS)

Transfer BMJ-Swindon Wks: 030272 (with D6322/3, D7002)

Swindon Works: 100272/ 120272 ('A' Shop Yd, by SW door)/ 270272 (Yd)/ 120372 (ConYd Cutting Area, gutted internally, off bogies)/ 150372 (ConYd Cutting Area, gutted internally, bodyshell part cut, off bogies)/ 220372 (baseframe remains). N/listed 050472.
Disposal: By 240372 (BR).

D6319

NBL Order: L97/14, Progressive No.: 27892.

D6319, Swindon Works ('A' Shop Yard), 26 July 1961. (Author's Collection)

D6319, Bristol Marsh Junction (Victoria Sidings), 1972. D6319 was the last of the Class to be overhauled at Swindon Works (outshopped 11/06/71 after Intermediate repair). DTG Website comment: "During its overhaul … the decision was made to withdraw it from service. Because of the level of work already carried out … this instruction was over-ruled and the overhaul continued". D6319 was subsequently withdrawn three months later on 11 September 1971 with transmission defects. (Author's Collection)

NBL QP Wks: we051059 (L97/14)
NBL Date Invoiced: 280360

Preston: 280360 (with D6322)

Date New: 110460

83D: 120460 (arrived with D6318)
Saltash: 020760 (pass, with D6310)
Devonport: 260860 (Devonport-Plymouth pass, with D6314)

Swindon Wks: 110960 (WksYd, arrived during visit). N/listed 091060.
  BR Rcds: 100960-260960 U.

Swindon Wks: 051260 ('A' Shop). N/listed 131160 & 290161. BR Rcds:
  211160-161260 LC.

83E: 050261

82C: 280561 (SSYd)/ 250661 (SSYd)
Swindon Wks: 190761 ('A' Shop)/ 230761 ('A' Shop)/ 260761 ('A' Shop
  Yd)/ 300761 ('A' Shop). BR Rcds: 290661-030861 LC.

Plymouth NR: 020961 (up pass, piloting 'Castle' 5090)
83G: 221061

Swindon Wks: xx1161 ('A' Shop Yd). N/listed 121161/ 070162.

83F: 150462
Saltash: 130862 (up freight, with D6306)/ 010663 (up pass, with D6334,
  piloting D603)
Tiverton: 060863 (shunting)
84A: 251263   **84B:** 031064

Swindon Wks: 150765 ('A' Shop)/ 080865 ('A' Shop)/ 110865/ 190965 ('A'
  Shop)/ 260965 ('A' Shop)/ 031065/ 101065 ('A' Shop)/ 051265
  ('A' Shop). N/listed 200665, 121265 & 230166. BR Rcds: 230765-181265
  C+ damage reps.

83D Exmouth Jct: 210866/ 180966
Exeter StD: 290167
83A: 290767
Exeter StD: 250867 (banking 16.30 Tavistock Jct-Exeter Central cement
  (EStD-EC), with D6317)
82A: 210168/150368/ 060468
85B: 020668/080668
Marsh Sdgs, Parkend: 100668
85B: 290668/130768/ 040868

Stored: 1we100868 (xxxxxx)
Reinstated: 1we170868 (xx0868)

Wellington: 170868 (fire damage)
84D: 080968
St.Austell: 081068 (up china clay, with D6336)
84B: 020569   **84A:** 260970

Swindon Wks: Nil. Not listed 131270.
Stored: 1we270371 (270371)
Swindon Wks: 190471
Reinstated: 1we080571 (020571)
Swindon Wks: 190571 ('A' Shop, re-painted). BR Rcds: 180271-110671 I.
  Paint Date: G&W UROL 22.4.71 SDN.

82A: 150671 (ex-Wks)
Portishead: 160671 (Portishead-Marsh Pound woodpulp)
Bristol-Plymouth Laira: 170671
Par: 190671 (09.45 Cardiff-Penzance (from Plymouth), with D6330)
Truro: 080771 (LE)
Lostwithiel: 170771 (shunting)
84B: 220771
Aller Jct: 050871 (vans, piloting D819)
Exeter StD: 080871 (milk)
83A: 140871
St.Blazey: 180871 (china clay)
84A: 280871 (transmission fault)/ 010971 (ditto)

Stored: 1we040971 (020971)
Withdrawn: 1we110971 (110971)

84A: 110971 (dump sdgs)/ 220971/ 250971/ end-0971

Transfer 84A-83A: ?
Hackney Yd, NA: 101071
Transfer 83A-BMJ: ?

BMJ: 211071/ 221071 (CPS)/ 301071 (CPS)/ 031171 (CPS/ 041271 (VS)/
  241271 (VS)/ 040172 (VS)/ 150172 (VS)/ 260172 (VS)/ 130272 (VS)/
  260272 (VS)/ 160372 (VS)/ 020472 (VS)/ 120472 (VS)/ 220672 (VS)/
  260772 (VS)/ 090972

Transfer BMJ-Swindon Wks: 051072 (with D807/25, D7099: D807/
  25 ex-84A, D6319 & D7099 ex-82A)

Swindon Wks: 071072 (Triangle)/ 111072 (Triangle)/ 211072 (WksYd,
  partially stripped)/ 251072 (ConYd, on bogies)/ 271072/ 211172
  (ConYd Cutting Area, part cut/off bogies)/ 241172 (ConYd Cutting
  Area, rems)
Disposal: By 101172 (BR).

D6320

NBL Order: L97/15, Progressive No.: 27893.

D6320 and D6327,
Aller Junction, Undated.
Probably July/August 1960
given condition of D6327.

(David Dunn Collection)

D6320, 85B Gloucester
Horton Road, 14
September 1968.

(Norman Preedy [Kidderminster
Railway Museum])

NBL QP Wks: we051059 (L97/15)
NBL Date Invoiced: 110360

Date New: 230360

83D: 220560

Swindon Wks: 190660 ('A' Shop)/ 240760 ('A' Shop). N/listed 110960.
 BR Rcds: 020660-230660 U.

83E: 060861
St.Budeaux: 280861 (down freight)
Tolcarn Jct: 031061 (Chacewater-Newquay pass)
St.Dennis Jct: 041061 (Newquay-Par pass)

82C: 291061
Swindon Wks: 051161 ('A' Shop)/ 121161 ('A' Shop). N/listed 070162.
 BR Rcds: 311061-301161 LC.

83F: 150462
Falmouth: 230462
83G: 150862
Moorswater: 050763 (china clay)
XX: 240964 (fire damage) (FDTL)
Exeter StD: 050665 (pass)
Newton Abbot: 280665 (12.30 Paddington-Kingswear (from NA))
84A: 030865
Scorrier: 110865 (freight)
84A: 190965
83A: 240766/180966

Swindon Wks: 021066/ 221066/ 131166. N/listed 041266.

Exeter StD: 290167
Torrington: 200367 (shunting)/ 230367 (china clay ex-Meeth)
Newton Abbot: 130667 (Exeter Riverside-Hackney Yard freight)
82A: 160767/300767/ 190867
Sharpness Docks: 080967 (freight)
85B: 040268/240268
82A: 090668/300668/ 060768

Gloucester: 250768/ 310768
85B: 040868
Gloucester: 040968 (inspection saloon)
85B: 140968/191068/ 260169/ 020269
Ashchurch: 080369 (breakdown train)
85B: 160369/200469/ 270469/ 040569/ 110569
82A: 240769/020869/ 010969
85B: 091069/171169/ 291169/ 161269/ 250170
Newland: 140270 (track train, with D6310)
85B: 150270

86A Cardiff Canton: 100570 (tyre-turning?)

82A: 170570
85B: 250570/140670
82A: 280670/131270
Bristol area: 281270
XX: 291270 (fire damage) (FDTL)
82A: 200271/220271/ 140371/ 280371/ 170471

Stored: 1we080571 (020571)

82A: 150571

Withdrawn: 1we220571 (220571)

82A: end-0571/end-0671
BMJ: 020771/ 030871 (DMU Shed)/ 130871/ 140871 (DMU Shed)/ 250971
 (DMU Shed)/ 231071/ 031171 (DMU Shed)/ 041271 (DMU Shed)/
 051271 (DMU Shed)

Transfer BMJ-Swindon Wks: 101271 (with D865, D6310)

Swindon Wks: 121271 ('A' Shop Yd, complete)/ 291271/ 050172 (Dump/
 Yds)/ 090172/ 210172/ 260172/ 120272 (TYd)/ 270272 (Yard)/ 120372
 (TYd)/ 150372 (TYd, gutted internally, on bogies)/ 220372 (TYd, gutted
 internally, on bogies)/ 050472 (TYd)/ 100472/ 170572 (TYd)/ 200572/
 230572 (TYd)/ 260572 (ConYd Cutting Area, being cut-up)/ 310572.
 N/listed 200672.
Disposal: By 160672 (BR).

D6321

NBL Order: L97/16, Progressive No.: 27894.

D6321 and GW 2-8-0 4705, Dainton, 5 August 1961. (Hugh Ballantyne [Rail-Photoprints])

D6321, Exeter Central, Undated. Between January 1963 and August 1966. (Rail-Online)

NBL QP Wks: we051059 (L97/16)
NBL Date Invoiced: 210360

Date New: 070460

Swindon Wks: 051260 (WksYd). N/listed 131160 & 290161. BR Rcds: 111160-051260 LC.
82C: xx1260

Swindon Wks: 260361 ('A' Shop Yd). N/listed 190261 & 160461. BR Rcds: 070361-300361 LC.

82C: 280561 (SSYd)
Swindon Works: 250661 (Works Yd)/ 190761 ('A' Shop). BR Rcds: 030661-280661 LC.

Totnes: 220761 (pass, piloting 'Hall' 5999; pass, piloting 'Grange' 6848; pass, piloting D842)
Dainton: 050861 (07.43 Nottingham-Plymouth pass, piloting 2-8-0 4705)
Chippenham: 120961 (LE, with D845)

Swindon Wks: 170961 ('A' Shop)/ 240961 ('A' Shop). N/listed 121161. BR Rcds: 120961-301061 LC.

83E: 150462
Bodmin: 170662
Wadebridge: 250662 (pass)

Swindon Wks: 091262 ('A' Shop). N/listed 181162 & 270163. BR Rcds: 041262-220163 HC.
82C: 270163
Swindon Wks: 100263 ('A' Shop). N/listed 170363. BR Rcds: 060263-130263 HC.

Newquay: 080763 (shunting)
Torrington: 310864 (pass, 13.15 from Barnstaple Jct)
84A: 120765   **84C:** 030865

Swindon Wks: 310866/ 040966 ('A' Shop)/ 140966. N/listed 260666 & 021066.

St. Ives: 070966 (up 'Limited' (last through service from St. Ives), with D6316)
Dawlish: 220467 (down freight, with D6323)
Cowley Bridge: 070567 (Torrington-Exeter Riverside milk)
Heathfield: 240667 (oil tanks, with D6315)
83B: 290767
82A: 190867/030967/ 071067/ 131067/ 151067/ 211067/ 281067
Wellow (S&D): 021167 (demolition)
Westbury: 220268 (Tiverton Jct-Westbury-Tiverton Jct, ballast cleaner)
85B: 020668/ 080668/ 090668

Stored: 1we150668 (xx0668)

85A: 220668/ 290668/ 180768/ 210768/ 240768/ 260768

Withdrawn: 1we030868 (030868)

85A: 250868/070968/ 291068/ 241168/ 260169/ 020269/ 120469/ 200469/ 270469/ 040569/ 250569

STN Booked Transfer: 8Z39 03.00 290569 (Thursday) 85A-Newport ADJ (with D6324/5/9)

Received J. Cashmore, Newport: 040669 (with D6350/1/5)
J. Cashmore, Newport: 070669/ 090669
Disposal: 06/69 (D&ELfS)

D6321, Wadebridge, 25 June 1962. (Rail-Online)

D6322

NBL Order: L97/17, Progressive No.: 27895.

D6322, Paignton, July 1966. (Rail-Online)

D6322, Barnstaple Junction, 24 June 1971.
(John Medley [Rail-Photoprints])

NBL QP Wks: we051059 (L97/17)
NBL Date Invoiced: 280360

Preston: 280360 (with D6319, on delivery)

Date New: 070460

Plymouth NR: 190560 (09.10 Plymouth-Penzance pass)
Par-Newquay: 210560
Bodmin Road: 190860 (down 'Cornishman', with D6312)
Truro: 020960 (up pass, with D6312)
Newton Abbot: 030960 (pass, piloting 'Grange' 6831)

82C: 110960/ 091060/ 161060 (SS)
Swindon Works: 191060/ 131160 ('A' Shop). N/listed 051260.
    BR Rcds: 021160-251160 LC.

Luxulyan: 120861 (pass, with D6323)
Laira Jct: 270861 (up pass, piloting 'Castle' 5022)
Dainton Tunnel: 020961 (piloting 'Castle' 5043)
XX: 080162 (fire damage) (FDTL)
83D: 150462/080763
Doublebois: 090763 (Tavistock Jct-Doublebois freight, failed, hauled back
    to 84A by D862 LE)
Barnstaple Jct: 040764 (pass)
St. Blazey/Fowey Docks: 031064
Newquay: 310765 (10.05 Newquay-Paddington, with D6349, piloted by
    D6325 to Par)
84C: 030865
83D Exmouth Jct: 161065
83A: 250466
83D Exmouth Jct: 210866
Exmouth: 150966 (freight)
83D Exmouth Jct: 180966
83A: xxxxxx (accident damaged, see Volume 2)

Swindon Wks: 130267 ('A'Shop, severe accident damage)/ 120367/
    020467 ('A' Shop)/ 190467/ 070567 ('A' Shop)/ xx0667 ('A' Shop)/
    300767. N/listed 041266. Derived Rcds: xxxxxx-xx0867 C + accident
    damage repairs. Paint Date: SN 26.7.67 K (SYN).

Newton Abbot: 170867 (pass)
84B: 301067-011167

84A: 100468/180568/ 230668/ 300668
84B: 070868   84A: 080968
Exeter s.p.: 211268
84A: 281268
Burngullow: 120469 (6C57 off Newquay branch)
84B: 120469 (ex-Burngullow)/ 030569
Truro s.p.: 100569
84A: 140569/220769
84B: 180969   84A: 200969
84B: 091169
St. Blazey: 160770 (13.15 Bugle-Par Harbour freight)
84A: 020870
Penryn (Falmouth branch): 020970 (shunting vans)
84B: 221170
Exeter s.p.: 070271
84A: 030471   84B: 130671
Barnstaple Jct: 240671 (04.30 Exeter Riverside-Barnstaple freight)
Tiverton Jct: 090771 (LE)
Exeter StD: 170771 (milk)
84B: 250771
Exeter s.p.: 290871
Exeter StD: 040971 (W'bound milk)
84A: 220971
Hemyock: 240971 (milk)
Exeter: 250971

Withdrawn: 1we091071 (031071)

83A: 171071 (active)

Transfer 83A-BMJ: 211071 (with D6318/23, D815)

BMJ: 211071/ 221071 (CPS)/ 271071/ 301071 (CPS)/ 031171 (CPS)/
    141171/ 301171/ 041271 (VS)/ 121271/ 181271/ 291271/ 010172/
    040172 (VS)/ 090172 (VS)/ 150172 (VS)/ 260172 (VS)

Transfer BMJ-Swindon Wks: 030272 (with D6318/23, D7002)

Swindon Wks: 100272/ 120272 (Reception Shed Yd(W)?) / 270272 (Yd)/
    120372 (TYd)/ 150372 (TYd, gutted internally, on bogies)/ 220372
    (TYd)/ 050472 (TYd)/ 100472/ 170572 (TYd)/ 260572 (ConYd Cutting
    Area, being cut-up). N/listed 310572.
Disposal: By 020672 (BR).

D6323

NBL Order: L97/18, Progressive No.: 27896.

D6323, Gloucester Central, April 1961.
(Norman Preedy [Kidderminster Railway Museum])

D6323, Swindon Works ('A' Shop Yard), October 1966. Ex-Works condition with 'A'-end nearest. Locomotive seen at 82A Bristol Bath Road on 7 September 1966 and at 83D Exmouth Junction on 18 September, so the photograph was probably taken slightly earlier than quoted by Colour-Rail. D6323 has obviously received a significant amount of 'panel-bashing' to the 'A-B' side following 'side-swipe' accident damage; a photograph of D6323 taken by Robin Lush on 7 September shows the 'B-A' side to be in pristine condition. The 'A' end cab is a replacement D6333-57 style cab, with the HCBs at a very slightly lower position. See Volume 2 for further explanation. (Colour-Rail)

NBL QP Wks: we051059 (L97/18)
NBL Date Invoiced: 050460

Date New: 250460

82C: 010560

83G: 210560
Penzance: 130660 (up 'Cornishman', with D6313)

Swindon Wks: 110960 (WksYd, arrived during visit)

83D: 250960   **83A:** 060861
Luxulyan: 120861 (pass, with D6322)

Swindon Wks: Nil. N/listed 170961 & 121161. BR Rcds: 250961-111061
      LC.

Swindon Wks: 070162 ('A' Shop)/ 040262 ('A' Shop)/ 040362 ('A' Shop).
      BR Rcds: 020162-280362 LC.

83E: 150462
Carn Brea Yd: 080763
84A: 251263
Callington: 070964 (17.24 Bere-Alston-Callington pass)
84A: 031064
Exeter StD: 081164 (pass)
84A: 120765
Exeter StD: 020865 (freight)
St Austell: 030865
Seaton Jct: 270366 (milk)

Swindon Wks: 310866/ 040966 (WksYd). N/listed 260666 & 110966.
      Paint date: SN 8.66 K SYN.

82A Bristol Bath Road: 070966 (ex-Works, presumably en route from
      Swindon Works to 83A Newton Abbot)
83D Exmouth Jct: 180966
Dawlish: 220467 (down freight, with D6321)
82A: 040667/100667/ 160767/ 300767/ 190867
Bristol TM: 240867
Bristol Marsh Jct: 030967
Radstock North: 070967 (demolition, with D6331)
82A: 071067/151067/ 211067/ 281067
85B: 040268/240268
82A: 090668/300668/ 060768/ 210768

Bristol TM: 300768
82A: 010868
84A: 120469/130469/ 100569
Truro: 140569
Moorswater: 180969 (china clay)
Plymouth NR: 200969
84B: 071069
Par: 091169
84B: 020570
84A: 170570/280670
Laira Jct: 130870
84A: 140870
Liskeard: 260970
XX: 281070 (fire damage) (FDTL)
Liskeard: 131170 (freight)
Exeter Riverside: 130271 (Barnstaple-Exeter vans)
84A: 030471/010571

Stored: 1we080571 (020571)

84A: 020571

Withdrawn: 1we220571 (220571)

83A: 310571
Hackney Yard, NA: 010671/ 230671
83A: 050771
Newton Abbot CS: 080871

Transfer 83A-BMJ: 211071 (with D6318/22, D815)

BMJ: 211071/ 221071 (CPS)/ 271071/ 301071 (CPS)/ 031171 (CPS)/
      141171/ 301171/ 041271 (VS)/ 121271/ 181271/ 291271/ 010172/
      040172 (VS)/ 090172 (VS)/ 150172 (VS)/ 260172 (VS)

Transfer BMJ-Swindon Wks: 030272 (with D6318/22, D7002)

Swindon Wks: 100272/ 120272 (Reception Shed Yd (W)?)/ 270272 (Yd)/
      120372 (TYd, gutted internally, on bogies)/ 150372 (TYd)/ 220372 (TYd,
      gutted internally, on bogies)/ 050472 (TYd)/ 100472/ 080572 (TYd)/
      170572 (TYd)/ 200572 (TYd)/ 260572/ 310572/ 030672 (TYd, gutted
      bodyshell, on bogies)/ 200672 (TYd, gutted bodyshell, on bogies)/
      210672 (TYd)/ 020772/ 240772 (ConYd Cutting Area, off-bogies, part-
      cut). N/listed 170872.
Disposal: By 040872 (BR).

D6324

NBL Order: L97/19, Progressive No.: 27897.

D6324, 83F Truro, 15 April 1962. Bolt-on headcode boxes. (Colour-Rail)

NBL QP Wks: we051059 (L97/19)
Newton: 060560 (09.45 Newton-Kingsknowe test train)
NBL Date Invoiced: 190560

Wigan: xx0560

Date New: 010660

XX: 180660 (07.50 Newquay-Manchester pass, with D6311 and 'Warship')

Swindon Wks: 280860 ('A' Shop). N/listed 110960.
BR Rcds: 160860-310860 U.

Wiveliscombe: 300161 (2C74 05.10 St.Austell-Plymouth pass, derailed in landslip)

Swindon Wks: Nil (arrived xx0261). N/listed: 190261/ 260361/ 160461/ 280561/ 250661/ 190761/ 200861/ 170961 (Work undertaken at NBL, Glasgow.)
Gloucester: 190261 (en route NBL Glasgow, with D6302, hauled by Standard 5MT 73012)
NBL Glasgow: Nil. Released xx1061 (derailment damage repairs).
Wigan: 12 or 131061 (LE ex-NBL, with D855)
Swindon Wks: Nil. Arrived 131061, released to traffic 231061. Derived Rcds (Swindon+NBL): xx0261-231061.

83F: 150462
St.Agnes: 150862 (freight)
Exeter s.p.: 210963
XX: 250464 (fire damage) (FDTL)
84A: 090564   **84D:** 031064

D6324 and D6325,
82A Bristol Bath Road,
August 1968.

(D. Cobbe [Rail-Photoprints])

Falmouth Docks: 120665 (pass)
84B: 190665   **84A:** 120765
Sidmouth Jct: 240765 (pass)
Exeter StD: 210865 (pass)
83A: 190965
83D Exmouth Jct: 161065/ 230766
Yeovil Town: 280766
83D Exmouth Jct: 210866

Swindon Wks: 021066/ 221066. N/listed 140966 & 131166.

82A: 290167

Swindon Wks: 020467 ('A' Shop)/ 190467. N/listed 120367 & 070567.

XX: 220567 (fire damage) (FDTL)
82A: 100667
Chilcompton: 290667 (demolition)
82A: 160767/300767
Taunton: 260867 (LE)

82A: 211067/281067/ 210168/ 060468
85B: 080668
82A: 300668/060768/ 210768/ 010868

Stored: 1we100868 (xx0868)

82A: 040868/080968

Withdrawn: 1we140968 (140968)

85A: 291068/241168/ 260169/ 020269/ 120469/ 200469/ 270469/ 040569/ 250569

STN Booked Transfer: 8Z39 03.00 290569 (Thursday) 85A-Newport ADJ (with D6321/5/9)

Received J. Cashmore, Newport: 290569 (with D6325/9/42)
J. Cashmore, Newport: 310569/ 010669 (by Wall)/ 070669/ 090669
Disposal: 05/69 (D&ELfS).

D6325

NBL Order: L97/20, Progressive No.: 27898.

D6325 and 'Castle' 7026, Tavistock Junction, 8 July 1961. (R.C. Riley [Transport Treasury])

NBL QP Wks: we051059 (L97/20)
NBL Date Invoiced: 280560

Date New: 140660

Saltash: 020760 (pass, with D63xx)

Swindon Wks: 240860 (WksYd). N/listed 110960.
   BR Rcds: 270760-220860 U.

Tavistock Jct: 080761 (down pass, piloting 'Castle' 7026)
Laira Jct: 290861 (freight)

Swindon Wks: 051161 (WksYd). N/listed 170961 & 121161.
   BR Rcds: 191061-081161 LC.

83F: 150462
Clinnick: 260462 (09.20 Falmouth-Plymouth pass)
Bodmin Road: 230762 (shunting)
St. Blazey: 050763 (mixed freight)
83E: 080763
Exeter StD: 280964
Newton Abbot: 031064
Newquay: 310765 (10.05 Newquay-Paddington, pilot engine to D6322/49, to Par)
83A: 240766
83D Exmouth Jct: 210866
Taunton: 060167 (11.00 PW special Taunton-Theale (with D6334), returned to Taunton LE)
82A: 290167

D6325, 82A Bristol Bath Road, April 1967.
(M. Jefferies [Rail-Photoprints])

Swindon Wks: 020467 ('A' Shop) / 190467 / 300467 (WksYd, repainted BFY). N/listed 120367 & 070567. BR Rcds: xxxxxx-xx0567 C.

82A: 040667

82C: 300767

82A: 190867
Evercreech Jct: 250867 (demolition)
82A: 071067 / 151067 / 211067 / 281067
Bath/Midford (S&D): 221167 (demolition)
82A: 210168 / 060468 / 090668
Keynsham: 180668 (shunting)
85B: 290668 / 010768
82A: 210768

Bristol TM: 300768
82A: 010868 / 040868 / 080968

Stored: 1we280968 (xx0968)
Withdrawn: 1we051068 (051068)

85A: 291068 / 241168 / 260169 / 020269 / 120469 / 200469 / 270469 / 040569 / 250569

STN <u>Booked</u> **Transfer:** 8Z39 03.00 290569 (Thursday) 85A-Newport ADJ (with D6321/4/9)

Received J. Cashmore, Newport: 290569 (with D6324/9/42)
J. Cashmore, Newport: 310569 / 010669 (by Wall) / 070669 / 090669
Disposal: 05/69 (D&ELfS).

D6326

NBL Order: L97/21, Progressive No.: 27899.

D6326, 81A Old Oak Common, Undated. Old Oak's longest resident (7½ years, between September 1963 and March 1971). (R.M. Himsworth)

D6326, 84B St.Blazey, 16 June 1971. (K.C.H. Fairey [Colour-Rail])

NBL QP Wks: we051059 (L97/21)
NBL Date Invoiced: 040560

82C: 150560

Date New: 160560

Swindon Wks: 240760 ('A' Shop). N/listed 190660. BR Rcds: 250660-090860 U.

Plymouth NR: 150860 (09.30 Bristol-Plymouth pass, with D6326/32 piloting 'Castle' 4098 [D6326/32 en route from Swindon Wks to 83D])
Dainton: 200860 (down pass, piloting 'Castle' 5085)
83A: 060861
Plymouth NR: 020961 (Newquay-Paddington pass, piloting 'Castle' 5060)
83D: 301061   **83F:** 150462
Helston: 210662 (pass)
Boscarne Jct: 250662 (pass)/ 200762 (pass)
Exeter Central: 020763 (pass)
Bodmin General: 060963 (pass/milk)
81A: 061063
Scrubs Lane: 091163 (e.c.s.)
Paddington: 071263
81A: 050164/160264 / 080364
Paddington: 310364
81A: 020564/190764/ 160864
Paddington: wc021164

Transfer 81A-Swindon Wks: 171164 (for boiler mods)
Swindon Wks: 221164 (WksYd)/ 291164 ('A' Shop)/ 170165/ 240165 ('A' Shop)/ 140265 (WksYd). N/listed 310165.

81A: 270265/130365 (ex-Wks)
Old Oak Common: 030465 (e.c.s.)
Paddington: 140465
81A: 271165

Swindon Wks: xxxxxx ('A' Shop Yd, accident damage [droop nose])/ 051265 (Weigh House)/ 121265 ('A' Shop)/ 230166 ('A' Shop). N/listed 130366. Collision damage reps.

Paddington: 130466
81F: 170466
81A: 240466/030666/ 030766/ 100766/ 280866/ 020966
Leamington Spa: 271066 (oil tanks ex-Warwick)
81A: 111266/251266
Leamington Spa: 050167/ 260467
81A: 240767/141067/ 070168
Southall: 080368
81A: 080368/270368/ 060468/ 120568
81F: 250568

81A: 060868/170868/ 080968/ 290968/ 051068/ 221068/ 190169
81D: 260169   **81A:** 290669
81F: 050769/060769
81A: 100869

Stratford DRS: Nil. SFR: 131069-161069 Tyre turning.

81D: 221169
81A: 261269/030170
Witney Goods Yd: 130270 (shunting)

Swindon Wks: Nil. N/listed 220270. Derived Rcds: xxxxxx-xx0470 C.

Moreton Cutting: 190470 (ballast)
81A: 250470 (ex-Wks)
81F: 160570
Cholsey & Moulsford Yd: 230670
81C: 270670   **81D:** 090870
81A: 220870/241070/ 251070
Reading: 311070
Hayes: 111170
81A: 250271
84B: 010571
Exeter StD: 150571 (14.55 Exeter-Chard Jct milk)
84B: 130671/160671
Exeter StD: 190671 (LE)/ 260671 (milk)
XX: 030771 (hauled 82A-84A by D828 for fire damage inspection)
Exeter StD: 070771 (08.00 Paignton-Liverpool pass, piloting D1601 to Exeter)
Tiverton Jct: 070771 (Hemyock milk)/100771 (Hemyock milk)
Exeter s.p.: 110771
84A: 170771/280771
Exeter s.p.: 180971
Tiverton Jct: 260971 (Hemyock milk)
84A: 290971 (engine overheated)

Stored: 1we021071 (300971)
Withdrawn: 1we091071 (031071)

84A: 041071

Transfer 84A-Swindon Wks: 061071 (with D804, D6343/56, hauled by D841, noted at Dawlish in transit)

Swindon Wks: 111071 ('A' Shop Yd, whole)/ 181071/ 201071 ('A' Shop Yd)/ 311071/ 021171/ 121271 (Dump, gutted bodyshell, on bogies)/ 040172 (ConYd)/ 050172 (Dump/ Yards)/ 090172/ 210172/ 120272 (ConYd)/ 260272 (ConYd)/ 270272 (Yard)/ 120372 (ConYd Cutting Area, rems). N/listed 150372.
Disposal: By 100372 (BR).

D6327

NBL Order: L97/22, Progressive No.: 27900.

D6327 and D6309, Plymouth North Road, circa 1961. (Rail-Online)

D6327 and D5579, Stratford DRS, 1 November 1969. BSY livery. (John Grey Turner)

NBL QP Wks: we051059 (L97/22)
NBL Date Invoiced: 150660

Carlisle: 150660 (LE)

Swindon Works: 190660 ('A' Shop)

Date New: 300660

Swindon Wks: 141060 (arrival)/ 191060 (transmission)

Swindon Wks: Nil. N/listed 260361 & 160461. BR Rcds: 060461-080561 LC.
82C: 280561

83A: 240661/060861/ 150462
Churston: 020762
Penzance: 150862 (up pass, with D6349)
Plymouth NR: 010663 (down pass, piloting 'Castle' 5057)
Totnes: 080763 (banking)/ 090763 (banking)
Paignton: 130863 (Newton Abbot-Kingswear pass, with D6329)/ 140863
(LE)/ 150863 (Newton Abbot-Kingswear pass, with D6330)
Newton Abbot: 140963 (down goods)
83B: 290963
Exeter StD: 121063 (13.35 Exeter-Kingswear pass)
83A: 151263
Churston: 070464 (Kingswear portion of down 'Cornish Riviera')
Ilfracombe: 220764 (shunting stock for 10.20 Ilfracombe-Exeter pass)
84A: 031064
Plymouth NR: 031064
Launceston: 090265 (fire dam) (FDTL)
84B: 120765
Redruth: 040865
81A: 090166/110166
Paddington: 220166
81A: 280366/110466
Paddington: 130466/150566
81A: 100766
Warwick: 010966
81A: 131166/171266/ 251266
Southall: 281266

Swindon Wks: Nil. Derived Rcds: xxxxxx-xx0367. Paint date: 26/2/67.

81A: 020367/110367/ 230467
Westbury: 280467 (weed-killing train)
81A: 040667/180667/ 120767
Warwick: 020967
81A: 141067/070168/ 080368/ 060468
81D: 090668   **81A:** 170868
81D: 250868

81A: 080968/290968/ 051068/ 081268
Paddington: 211268
81A: 050169   **81F:** 230269
Paddington: 070469
81A: 050769/120769/ 060969

Stratford DRS: Nil. SFR: 180969-190969 Tyre turning.

Oxford: 210969 (17.45 Oxford-Birmingham New Street pass and 19.55
Birmingham NS-Reading pass (hauling failed DMU))

Stratford DRS: 011169. SFR: 011169-031169 Tyre turning.

81A: 261269
Paddington: 010170
81A: 030170
Reading West: 270170 (freight)
Westbury: 130270 (ballast)
82A: 220270
Bristol TM: 280270/ 020370
82A: 310370/290470/ 170570/ 100670/ 280670/ 090870/ 020970/ 250970/
260970/ 171070/ 131270
XX: 291270 (fire damage) (FDTL)
85B: 100171/250371
Ashchurch: 240471
Barry: 280471 (ballast)

Stored: 1we080571 (020571)

85B: 130571. N/listed 050571.
82A: Nil. N/listed 150571.

Withdrawn: 1we220571 (220571)

BMJ: 010671 (Diesel Depot [SPMCS?])/ 160671 (SPMCS)/ 270671
(SPMCS)/ 020771/ 290771 (SPMCS)/ 310771 (SPMCS)/ 130871/
300871 (SPMCS)/ 250971 (SPMCS)/ 260971 (SPMCS)/ 221071/
271071/ 301071 (SPMCS)/ 031171 (SPMCS)/ 141171 (SPMCS).
N/listed 301171.

Transfer BMJ-Swindon Wks: 021271 (with D6315/31/54)

Swindon Wks: 121271 ('A' Shop Yd, complete)/ 291271/ 050172 ('A'
Shop)/ 090172 ('A' Shop, being stripped)/ 210172/ 120272 (TYd)/
270272 (Yard)/ 120372 (TYd, gutted shell, on bogies)/ 150372 (TYd)/
220372 (TYd)/ 260372 (TYd, gutted shell, on bogies)/ 050472 (TYd)/
100472/ 120472/ 170572 (TYd)/ 200572 (TYd)/ 260572/ 310572/
200672 (TYd)/ 210672 (TYd)/ 280672 (ConYd Cutting Area, gutted
internally, off bogies)/ 020772. N/listed 240772.
Disposal: By 070772 (BR).

D6328

NBL Order: L97/23, Progressive No.: 27901.

D6328, Newton Abbot, Undated. Flat-topped profile to yellow panel.
(Fred Caster)

D6328, Kensington Olympia, October 1969. (Rail-Online)

NBL QP Wks: we051059 (L97/23)
NBL Date Invoiced: 030660

Date New: 180660

Combe Fishacre: 300760 (08.05 Newquay-Newcastle pass, piloting 'Hall' 6982)
Plymouth NR: 010860

Swindon Wks: 300761 ('A' Shop). N/listed 250661 & 200861. BR Rcds: 240761-100861 LC.

Ivybridge: 080962 (pass, piloting 'Castle' 4037)
Teignmouth: 210663 (Exeter-Torquay pass)
83A: 080763

Swindon Wks: 280763 ('A' Shop). BR Rcds: 150763-060863 HC.

83A: xx0863

Swindon Wks: 011263 ('A' Shop)/ 151263 ('A' Shop)/ 221263/ 190164 ('A' Shop)/ 260164 ('A' Shop)/ 280164 ('A' Shop). N/listed 101163 & 230264. BR Rcds: 141163-310164 Casual.

Dawlish Warren: 170564 (19.00 [16th] Glasgow Central-Plymouth pass, with D6338)
Barnstaple Jct: 170664 (towed into BJ by 'N' 2-6-0 31853 after catching fire at Bideford)
Wadebridge: 130864 (15.55 Bodmin Road-Padstow pass)
84B: 120765   **83A:** 030865
83D Exmouth Jct: 190965
81C: 020166
81A: 090266/280366/ 110466
Paddington: 130466
81C: 240466

Swindon Wks: 050666 (WksYd). N/listed 070566 & 290666.

81A: 030766/ 100766/ 170766
Paddington: 290766 (ex-Wks)
81A: 020966/300966/ 111266
81C: 251266
Leamington Spa: 110167
81A: 230467
XX: 280467 (fire damage) (FDTL)

Swindon Wks: 300767/ 030967 ('A' Shop)/ 130967. N/listed 070567. Derived Rcds: xxxxxx-xx0967 C. Paint Date: SWD 5.9.67 K (SYN).

81A: 170967 (ex-Wks)
81D: 211067
81A: 270368/060468/ 050568
Paddington: 220668/220868
81A: 250868/290968/ 201068
81C: 151268
81D: 260169/230269
Paddington: 030469/190469
81F: 200469   **81A:** 030569
81F: 180569   **81A:** 080669
West Ruislip/Denham: 240969 (empty coal; failed, rescued by DMU, propelled to Gerrards Cross)
81A: 021169/231169/ 071269
Witney: 141269 (track recovery?)
81A: 070270
Chearsley Bridge: 080270 (engineer's train)
81A: 280270/250470
81C: 050470   **Didcot:** 090870
81A: 091070/241070/ 031170
Paddington: 251170
82A: 220271/280371/ 150471/ 170471
Exeter: 020571 (with D6308/43/8)
84A: 020571 (ex-82A with D6308/43/8)/ 150571
Bodmin General: 160571 (weed-killing train)
83A: 310571   **84A:** 190671

Stored: 1we100771 (080771)
Withdrawn: 1we170771 (170771)

84A: 280771 (sdgs between depot and main line)/ 290771/ 080871/ 250871/ 110971 (dump sdgs)/ 220971/ 250971/ end-0971

Transfer 84A-83A: ?
83A: end-xx0971
Hackney Yd, NA: 101071
Transfer 83A-BMJ: ?

BMJ: 211071/ 221071 (CPS)/ 271071/ 301071 (CPS)/ 031171 (CPS)/ 141171/ 301171/ 041271 (VS)/ 121271/ 181271/ 241271 (VS)/ 291271/ 010172/ 040172/ 090172/ 150172/ 260172 (VS)/ 130272/ 190272/ 220272/ 260272 (VS)/ 040372/ 120372

Transfer BMJ-Swindon Wks: 160372 (with D831/69, D6330)

Swindon Works: 220372 ('A' Shop Yd, gutted internally, on bogies)/ 260372 ditto/ 050472 (ConYard)/ 150472 (ConYd)/ 170572 (ConYd Cutting Area, gutted internally, off bogies). N/listed 100472 & 310572.
Disposal: By 260572 (BR).

D6329

NBL Order: L97/24, Progressive No.: 27902.

D6329, 83D Plymouth Laira, 27 June 1960.

(Norman Preedy [Kidderminster Railway Museum])

D6329, 83A Newton Abbot, 28 June 1966.

(Alec Swain [Transport Treasury])

NBL QP Wks: Nil. N/listed we051059.
NBL Date Invoiced: 100660

XX (in transit): 100660

Date New: 180660

83D: 270660

Totnes: 220761 (pass, piloting 'Castle' 5029)
Hemerdon: 220761 (07.40 St.Austell-Birmingham pass, piloting 'Hall' 7914)

Swindon Wks: 200861 ('A' Shop). Not listed 170961.
   BR Rcds: 020861-060961 LC.

83D: 150462
Newton Abbot: 070762 (with D838)
Lostwithiel: 080763 (shunting)
Brent: 200763 (pass, piloting D800)
Coombe Farm: 310763 (14.22 Kingsbridge-Hackney freight)
Paignton: 130863 (Newton Abbot-Kingswear pass, with D6327)
Taunton: 250764 (pass)
83D: 190864
XX: 041164 (fire damage) (FDTL)
83A: 030865   **82A:** 030865
Bristol TM: 070865 (N'bound 'Devonian' (to Bristol), with D6342)
XX: 070865 (fire damage) (FDTL)
82A: 080865   **83A:** 190965

Swindon Wks: 121265 ('A' Shop)/ xx0266 ('A' Shop)/ 130366 ('A' Shop)/ 130466/ 240466. N/listed 051265 & 070566.

83A: 280666 (ex-Wks)
83D Exmouth Jct: 230766
Dawlish: 260766 (up freight)
83D Exmouth Jct: 180966
82A: 290167 (BLS)
Whitecliff/Coleford Jct: 260467 (ballast from Whitecliff Quarry)
85B: 300667
Coleford: 060767 (LE, en route Whitecliff)
Cinderford: 110767 (shunting)
85B: 220767
Coaley Jct: 130967(freight)
Tiverton Jct: 160368 (milk)
Exeter StD: 280668 (LE to 83A, with D811/67, D7037)
83A: 290668
Exeter s.p.: 050868

Stored: 1we021168 (xx1168)

82A: 031168
85A: 241168

Withdrawn: 1we301168 (301168)

85A: 260169/020269/ 120469 (OD)/ 200469/ 270469/ 040569/ 250569

STN <u>Booked</u> **Transfer:** 8Z39 03.00 290569 (Thursday) 85A-Newport ADJ (with D6321/4/5)

Received J. Cashmore, Newport: 290569 (with D6324/5/42)
J. Cashmore, Newport: 310569/ 010669 (by Wall). N/listed 070669.
Disposal: 05/69 (D&ELfS).

D6329, D855 and D7050, Swindon Works ('AE' Shop), 17 April 1966.
(David Bromley)

D6330

NBL Order: L97/25, Progressive No.: 27903.

D6330, Swindon Works (A Shop Yard), 14 February 1965. Bolt-on headcode boxes.
(Transport Treasury)

D6330, 84A Plymouth Laira, 7 July 1971. (Dave Jolly)

NBL QP Wks: we051059 (L97/25)
NBL Date Invoiced: 170660

Date New: 230760 (260660 per B.Reed book)

Swindon Wks: 240760 (WksYd)

Newton Abbot: 120860 (up LE)

Swindon Wks: 240860 (WksYd)/ 280860/ 040960 ('A' Shop).
  BR Rcds: 190860-080960 U.

Gloucester Central: 070960 (14.40 GC-Swindon (GC-Kemble)
XX: 230361 (fire damage) (FDTL)
Totnes: 220761 (11.00 Paddington- Penzance pass, piloting D845)
Dainton: 190861 (down pass, piloting 'Hall' 6963)
83D: 150462
Kingsbridge: 230662 (pass)
XX: 070762 (fire damage) (FDTL)
Lostwithiel: 280762 (freight)
Newton Abbot: 221262 (freight)
Aller Jct.: 090763 (banking)
Starcross: 280763 (down pass, with D6337)
Paignton: 150863 (Newton Abbot-Kingswear pass, with D6327)
Starcross: 180863 (p.way)
83B: 290963   **83A:** 151263
Yeovil Town: 180564 (pass from Taunton)
83A: 031064
Goodrington: 071064 (13.30 Exeter-Kingswear pass)

Swindon Wks: 181064 (WksYd)/ 251064/ 041164/ 081164 ('A' Shop/
  221164 ('A' Shop)/ 291164 ('A' Shop)/ 131264/ 170165/ 240165 ('A'
  Shop)/ 300165/ 140265 (WksYd). N/listed 111064 & 140365.

Dawlish: 240465 (engineer's train)
XX: 070865 (fire damage) (FDTL)

Swindon Wks: 230166 ('A' Shop). N/listed 121265 & 130366.

83D Exmouth Jct: 250466
83A: 180966
Shillingstone (S&D): 170267 (demolition)
82A: 040667/160767/ 030967
Exeter StD: 091267 (snow clearance)
84A: 230668   **84B:** 080968

Stored: 1we140968 (xx0968)
Withdrawn: 1we280968 (230968)

84A: 290968/171068/ 021168/ 281268 (old steam shed)/ 220269/ 050369/
  120469/ 100569/ 250669/ 220769/ 020869/ 060869

Re-instated: 1we130969 (080969)

Truro: 140969 (milk)
Exeter StD: 111169 (boiler fire)
Newton Abbot: 230170 (replacement 16.03 Paignton-Exeter DMU service
  from NA; 17.42 NA-Ilfracombe & 19.55 Ilfracombe-Exeter)
Exeter StD: 230270 (21.42 EStD-NA pass)/ 040570 (20.10 EStD-NA pass)
Exeter s.p.: 230570
Exeter StD: 090770 (20.10 Exeter-NA pass, with D6339)
Hemyock: 150770 (shunting)
Yeoford: 031070 (up parcels)
Exeter s.p.: 161070

Swindon Wks: 111170/ 131270. N/listed 311070. Derived Rcds: xxxxxx-
  xx1270 C. Paint Date: SDN 9/12/70 UROAL KYD WILLIAMSONS.

Tiverton Jct: 050171 (12.20 Exeter-Hemyock, failed)
Newton Abbot: 060171 (assisted D825 from NA to Plymouth on 19.30
  Paddington-Plymouth)
Exeter s.p.: 270271
84B: 030471/010571
84A: 190671 (with D6319)
Par: 190671 (09.45 Cardiff-Penzance (from Plymouth), with D6319)
84B: 170771/220771/ 250771
St Austell: 130971 (Parkandillack-St Blazey freight, with D6356)

Withdrawn: 1we091071 (031071)

XX (in traffic): 041071/ 051071/ 071071/ 081071/131071
Truro Yard: 181071 (in traffic)

BMJ: 211071/ 221071 (CPS)/ 301071 (CPS)/ 031171 (CPS)/ 141171/
  301171/ 041271 (VS)/ 121271/ 291271/ 010172/ 090172 (VS)/ 260172
  (VS)/ 190272/ 260272/ 040372/ 120372

Transfer BMJ-Swindon Wks: 160372 (with D831/69, D6328)

Swindon Wks: 220372 ('A' Shop Yd, gutted bodyshell, on bogies)/ 260372
  (ditto)/ 050472 (ConYd)/ 100472/ 150472 (ConYd)/ 170572 (ConYd
  Cutting Area, gutted bodyshell, off bogies)/ 200572 (ConYd Cutting
  Area, gutted bodyshell, off bogies, part-cut)/ 230572 (ditto).
  N/listed 310572.
Disposal: By 020672 (BR).

D6331

NBL Order: L97/26, Progressive No.: 27904.

D6331, 85B Gloucester
Horton Road, Undated.
Between July 1969
and circa-March 1970.
(Norman Preedy [Kidderminster
Railway Museum])

D6331, 85B Gloucester
Horton Road, Undated.
Full yellow ends looking
to be recently applied;
circa April 1970.
(Norman Preedy [Kidderminster
Railway Museum])

NBL QP Wks: we051059 (L97/26)
NBL Date Invoiced: 240660

Swindon Wks: 240760 (WksYd)

Date New: 260760 (260660 per B. Reed book)

82C: 091060

83G: 261060

82C: 061160
Swindon Wks: 051260 ('A' Shop). N/listed 131160. BR Rcds: 211160-091260 U.
82C: xx1260

Swindon Wks: Nil. N/listed 290161, 050261 & 190261. BR Rcds: 060261-170261 LC.

Dawlish: 010761 (up pass, piloting D807; down pass, piloting 'Castle' 7037)
Newton Abbot: 200761 (freight)
Dainton: 050861 (07.43 Nottingham-Plymouth pass, piloting 'Castle' 4098)
83A: 060861
Laira Jct: 300861 (Penzance-Paddington pass, piloting D868)
Torquay: 070762 (pass)
Aller Jct.: 080763 (banking)
83F Barnstaple Jct: 170664 (derailed)
84B: 200864   **83A:** 031064
Churston: 131064 (engineer's train)
83A: 190965

Swindon Wks: 051265 ('A' Shop)/ 121265 ('A' Shop)/ 230166. N/listed 101065 & 130366.

83A: 180966
82A: 111266/300767/ 190867
Severn Tunnel Jct: 290867 (freight to Stoke Gifford)
82A: 030967
Radstock North: 070967 (demolition, with D6323)
83A: 3010-011167
Exeter StD: 141267 (Exeter Riverside-Newton Abbot freight, with D6336/7)
83A: 180568/120668
Newton Abbot: 150668
Exeter StD: 290668/ 310768/ 050968 (parcels)/ 080968/ 120968 (parcels)

85B: 260169/020269/ 070369/ 160369/ 110469 (ex-Parkend)/ 270469/ 110569
Gloucester Yd: 150769
85B: 290769/291169/ 161269/ 250170

Swindon Wks: ??? (see Note 1). N/listed 220270.

85B: 290470/230570/ 250570
Abbotswood: 200670 (p.way)
Chepstow: 180870
82A: 171070
Bristol TM: 170171/ 220271

Withdrawn: 1we270371 (270371)

82A: 150471/190471/ 220471
Sampford Peverell: 020571 (withdrawn D6331 apparently hauling D6336/56 ex-82A, D6331 caught fire at Sampford Peverell, removed from train at Exeter)

Exeter s.p.: 030571/ 050571/ 120571/ 150571/ 180571/ 220571/ 250571. N/listed 260571 (17.00).

STN <u>**Booked**</u> **Transfer:** LA loco & crew 06.00 LE Laira-Exeter SP 26/5/71, pick up D6331 & haul to 82A

Transfer Exeter s.p.-BMJ: xx0571 (hauled by D827)

BMJ: 010671 (Diesel Depot [SPMCS?])/ 160671 (SPMCS)/ 270671 (SPMCS)/ 020771/ 310771 (SPMCS)/ 110871/ 130871/ 300871 (SPMCS)/ 250971/ 260971 (SPMCS)/ 091071/ 221071/ 271071/ 301071/ 031171 (SPMCS)/ 141171 (SPMCS). N/listed 301171.

Transfer BMJ-Swindon Wks: 021271 (with D6315/27/54)

Swindon Wks: 121271 ('A' Shop, complete)/ 050172 (Dump/Yds)/ 090172/ 210172/ 120272 (ConYd)/ 260272 (ConYd)/ 270272 (ConYd). N/listed 120372.
Disposal: By 030372 (BR).

Notes:
1. D6331 GSY 29/07/69, GFY by 29/04/70 (recently applied). Possibility of visit to Swindon Works 02-04/70?
2. Questions: Did D6331 haul D6336/56 on 02/05/71? Or, was it destined to provide spares for other D63xxs at 84A? Or, was it due for re-instatement?

D6332

NBL Order: L97/27, Progressive No.: 27905.

D6332, 81A Old Oak
Common, September
1966. 'Warship'-style
yellow warning panels.
(Grahame Wareham)

D6332, 81A Old Oak
Common, 26 March 1970.
(Anthony Sayer)

NBL Date Invoiced: 010760

Swindon Wks: 240760 (Wks Yd)

Date New: 280760

Plymouth NR: 150860 (09.30 Bristol-Plymouth pass, with D6326/32 piloting 'Castle' 4098 [D6326/32 en route from Swindon Works to 83D])

Swindon Wks: 121060 (arrival)/ 161060 (WksYd)/ 191060. N/listed 091060 & 131160. BR Rcds: 151060-131160 U (transmission failure).
82C: 061160 (ex-Wks)

83F: 050261
Plymouth NR: 020961 (13.20 Penzance-Paddington (Plymouth-Newton Abbot), with D809)
83A: 150462
Newton Abbot: 180662 (freight)/ 250762 (10.40 Paddington-Penzance relief pass, piloting' King' 6021)
Brent: 080663 (LE)
Laira Jct: 050763 (down pass, piloting D827)
Aller Jct: 090763 (banking)
83A: 151263   83D: 190864
Totnes: 031064
Bovey: 010565 (demolition)
Milverton: 190665 (pass to Ilfracombe)
Wiveliscombe: 190665 (10.20 Ilfracombe-Cardiff pass)
83A: 030865   84A: 040865
83D Exmouth Jct: 190965
81A: 280366/290366
Didcot: 130466

Swindon Wks: 240466. N/listed 070566.

81A: 030766/170766/ 261166/ 111266/ 010167

Swindon Wks: 070567 ('A' Shop, being repainted blue)/ xx0667 (Weigh Shop Yd). N/listed 190467. Derived Rcds: xxxxxx-xx0667 C.

81A: 150767/070168/ 270368/ 060468/ 050568/ 030668/ 170868
Reading: 220868
81A: 270868/290968/ 051068/ 201068
Paddington: 081268
81A: 081268/211268/ 050169/ 020269/ 200269/ 260369/ 200469
Didcot: 270469
Reading: 290469 (parcels)
Kensington Olympia: 060669 (S'bound coal)
81A: 290669/050769/ 100869/ 190869/ 221169/ 261269/ 280270/ 150370/ 260370/ 310370/ 050470
Saunderton/Princes Risborough: 070470 (19.00 Thame-Acton freight, caught fire, attended by fire brigade)
XX: 100470 (fire damage) (FDTL)
81A: 110470/200470/ 250470
81D: 300570
Reading: 060870
81D: 090870
81A: 280970/031070/ 091070
81F: 241070
Witney Goods Yd: 301070/ 031170 (last day)
Didcot: 111170
81A: 011270/051270/ 150271/ 200271
Reading: 200371

Stored: 1we240471 (200471)
Withdrawn: 1we220571 (220571)

81A: Nil

Transfer 81A-Swindon Wks: By 250671

Swindon Wks: 250671/ 300671/ 280771/ 020871 (TYd)/ 110871 (TYd)/ 140871 (TYd, whole)/ 180871 (TYd)/ 181071/ 311071/ 041271. N/listed 121271.
Disposal: By 111271 (BR).

D6333

NBL Order: L97/28, Progressive No.: 27906.

D6333, Dawlish Warren, 22 July 1966. Return of the two ventilation slats above the driving cab windows after an absence since D6312! It is believed that D6333 never carried yellow panels and ultimately went straight to BFY. Inspection saloon. (Rail-Photoprints)

D6333, Hemyock, 12 September 1970. Survived until the bitter end. On 1 January 1972 D6333 worked the 04.30 Exeter Riverside-Barnstaple freight (with D6339), then trips to Meeth/ Torrington (alone) and 16.35 Torrington/ Lapford-Exeter (milk) before finally being switched off on arrival at Exeter. (Author's Collection)

NBL Date Invoiced: 150760

Swindon Wks: 240760 ('A' Shop) (wheel flats). BR Rcds: 200760-160860 (Commissioning, replacement bogies).

Date New: 030860

Swindon Wks: 280860/180960 ('A' Shop). N/listed 110960. BR Rcds: 220860-070960 U.

Swindon Wks: 181060 (arrival)/ 191060/ 061160 ('A' Shop). N/listed 091060 & 131160. BR Rcds: 181060-091160 LC.

Torquay: 020861 (Manchester-Kingswear pass (from Newton Abbot))
83A: 060861
XX: 130961 (fire damage) (FDTL)
83A: 050462
Dainton: 030762 (Goodrington-Saltash excursion)
Taunton: 200163
Exeter Riverside Yard: 250263
Gara Bridge: 090863 (14.22 Kingsbridge-Hackney freight)
Brent: 030963 (06.30 Hackney-Kingsbridge freight)
Exeter StD: 211263 (down pass, piloting 'Castle' 7035)
83D Exmouth Jct: 120765
Ilfracombe: 280865 (11.10 Ilfracombe-Wolverhampton [to Taunton])
83A: 190965
Dawlish Warren: 220766 (inspection saloon)
83D Exmouth Jct: 230766
Dawlish: 260766 (freight, with D63xx)
83D Exmouth Jct: 210866/ 180966
82A: 111266   83B: 290167

Swindon Wks: xx0667 ('A' Shop). N/listed 070567. BR Rcds: 140567-210767 C(I).

82A: 300767/070867 (ex-Wks)
Keynsham: 150867 (trip-freight)
Exeter StD: 240867 (pass, with D6337)
Radstock: 250867 (demolition)
Aller Jct: 291267 (engine+van)
83A: 180568
Exeter s.p.: 110668/ 290668
Newton Abbot: 090768 (freight)
84A: 310768
Exeter StD: 240868 (assist failed D6545 on 12.30 EStD-Waterloo pass (EStD to Exeter Central) [with D6337])/ 14.15 Exeter C-Ilfracombe pass [with D6337]/ 16.45 I'combe-Exeter pass [with D6310])
Exeter s.p.: 050968
83A: 080968   84A: 220269
Tiverton Jct: 080469 (Hemyock milk)
83A: 130469
Hemyock: 190469 (shunting tanks)
Cowley Bridge: 020569 (ex-Hemyock)
Exeter StD: 290769 (evening pass to NA, with D6338)
Exeter s.p.: 070869

Dawlish Warren: 220869 (21.42 Exeter StD-NA pass, with D6339; caught fire at DW, detached)
Exeter s.p.: 200969
Exeter StD: 090370 (21.42 EStD-NA pass)/ 280470 (ditto)
83A: 170570   Exeter s.p.: 280670
Teignmouth: 110770 (LE NA-Exeter, failed T'mouth, propelled to Exeter West by D1740 (on Motorail), to Exeter s.p.)
Exeter s.p.: 200770 (with D6339, towed D802/30 Exeter s.p.-Exeter StD c.s.)
Torrington: 220770 (milk to Exeter)
83A: 130870
Exeter StD: 280870 (20.10 EStD-NA pass, with D6339)
Hemyock: 120970 (shunting milk)
Umberleigh: 190970 (milk)
Exeter s.p.: 260970
Barnstaple Jct: 031070
Exeter: 071070 (06.55 Exeter-Honiton DMU replacement)
XX: 121170 (fire damage) (FDTL)
Exeter StD: 151270 (18.57 EStD-Paignton DMU replacement)
84A: 030471
Exeter: 050471 (16.40 Torrington-Exeter freight, hauling failed D6315/8)
84B: 010571   84A: 190671
Exeter s.p.: 010771
Dawlish Warren: 060771 (vans)/ 140771 (14.50 Ponsandane-Exeter Riverside freight, piloting D810)
Exeter StD: 160771 (milk from Chard)
St.Budeaux Jct.: 130971 (trip-freight)
Newton Abbot: 240971 (up freight piloting D832)
84B: 021071   Exeter: 131171
Exeter s.p.: 041271

Stored: 1we181271 (181271)

Exeter s.p.: 191271 (booked Chard milk)
Exeter: 301271 (in traffic, 15.41 Exeter-Lapford & rtn/ 20.10 Exeter-NA pass)/010172 (in traffic, local trips)

Withdrawn: 1we010172 (010172)

Exeter s.p.: Nil

Transfer 84B/Exeter-BMJ: 030172 (D6336/8 ex-84B (04.05) picking up D6333/9 ex-Exeter, hauled by D5180)

BMJ: 040172 (CPS)/ 090172. N/listed 150172./ 260172.

Transfer BMJ-Swindon Wks: 270172 (with D6336/8/9)

Swindon Wks: 100272/ 270272 (Yd)/ 120372 (TYd, gutted internally, on bogies)/ 150372 (TYd)/ 050472 (TYd)/ 080572 (TYd)/ 170572 (TYd)/ 260572/ 030672 (TYd, gutted internally, on bogies)/ 200672 (ditto)/ 210672 (TYd)/ 020772/ 240772 (ConYd Cutting Area, off-bogies, part-cut). N/listed 170872.
Disposal: By 040872 (BR).

D6334

NBL Order: L97/29, Progressive No.: 27907.

D6334, Newton Abbot, Undated. (Colour-Rail)

D6334, Exeter St. Davids, 15 September 1971.

(John Medley [Rail-Photoprints])

NBL Date Invoiced: 111160

Date New: 011260

Laira Jct: 230761 (up pass, piloting 'Castle' 7030)
83A: 060861
Laira Jct: 300861 (05.30 Paddington-Penzance pass, piloting 'Castle' 5090)

Swindon Wks: 031261 ('A' Shop)/ 171261/ 070162 (Weigh House)/ 040262 ('A' Shop, Rect?). N/listed 121161 & 040362. BR Rcds: 161161-080162 LC.

Saltash: 010663 (up pass, with D6319, piloting D603)
Yeovil Jct: 180564 (pass)
Taunton: 250664 (pass)
84B: 031064
Exeter s.p.: 020165 (propelling railcar W79975 onto depot)
83D Exmouth Jct: 020865
Newton Abbot: 030865 (freight)
Barnstaple: 020965 (Ilfracombe-Exeter pass)
83A: 190965

Swindon Wks: 031065 ('A' Shop). N/listed 260965 & 101065.

83D Exmouth Jct: 230766
83A: 180966   **82A:** 221066
Taunton: 060167 (11.00 PW special Taunton-Theale, with D6325)
82A: 040667

Swindon Wks: 300767/230867 ('A' Shop Yard). BR Rcds: xxxxxx-300867 C. Paint Date: SN 8.67 D (SYN).

82A: 030967
Exeter StD: 270168 (LE, with D6337)
83A: 180568
Exeter StD/Exeter s.p.: 290668
Newton Abbot: 070868 (Paddington-Torbay pass, from Exeter StD)
Exeter: 260868 (removed failed D6545 from Exeter Goods Yard to the SR via Taunton/Westbury)
Exeter StD: 050968 (milk)
Exeter s.p.: 080968
Torrington: 091168 (shunting tanks)
Exeter StD: 110469
Newton Abbot: 110469
Exeter Riverside: 130469
Exeter s.p.: 100569/ 240669
Plymouth NR: 290769
Newton Abbot: 300769 (stabled between duties)
Paignton: 020869 (stock)
Exeter s.p.: 070869

Tiverton Jct: 060969 (rescued failed D820 on down 'Devonian' (TJ-Exeter StD); taken off Hemyock milk)
Petrockstow: 141069 (china-clay)
Hemyock: 291269 (shunting)
Exeter s.p.: 280370
Newton Abbot: 270470 (vans)
XX: 090670 (fire damage) (FDTL)
Aller Jct: 250770 (LE)
83A: 130870/150870
Exeter StD: 120970 (milk)
83A: 260970
Newton Abbot: 161070 (freight)
Exeter StD: 281070 (20.10 EStD-NA pass with D6339, both failed at City Basin Jct, propelled to NA by D847)/ 160171 (assisting D1960 on 00.40 Exeter-Plymouth Friary, failed Totnes/Rattery; assisted by D829)
Torrington: 130271 (16.40 Torrington-Exeter milk, failed at Eggesford, rescued by D864)
84A: 010571
Goonbarrow Jct: 160671 (shunting china-clay wagons)
83A: 300671/110771
Exeter StD: 080871 (milk)
Plymouth: 090871/ 130871 (Ponsandane-Exeter Riverside freight, assisting D855 Plymouth-Exeter)
Exeter s.p.: 220871
Exeter: 250871 (14.50 Ponsandane-Exeter Riverside freight, piloting D814)
Torrington: 270871 (08.50 Barnstaple-Torrington/Meeth china clay & 12.00 rtn)
Exeter s.p.: 290871
Exeter StD: 150971 (15.20 Exmouth Jct-Exeter Riverside freight)
84A: 250971   **84B:** 021071

Withdrawn: 1we091071 (031071)

Devonport Jct: 071071 (in traffic, LE to 84A)/ 081071 (in traffic, LE to 84A)
Exeter s.p.: 091071/ 101071 (shunting stock)
Truro Yard: 141071 (in traffic)

84A: Nil

Transfer 84A-BMJ: 181071 (with D831/69, D6337)

BMJ: 211071/ 221071 (CPS)/ 301071 (CPS)/ 031171 (CPS)/ 041271 (VS)/ 121271/ 291271/ 040172/ 090172/ 150172/ 260172 (VS)/ 130272/ 190272/ 260272/ 040372/ 120372

Transfer BMJ-Swindon Wks: 130372 (with D6308/37/48)

Swindon Wks: 150372/ 180372/ 220372/ 040472/ 050472/ 100472. N/listed 270472.
Disposal: By 210472 (BR).

D6335

NBL Order: L97/30, Progressive No.: 27908.

D6335, 83A Newton
Abbot, 7 April 1963.
(Peter Groom)

D6335, 83A Newton Abbot, 7 April 1963. (Peter Groom)

NBL Date Invoiced: 251160

Swindon Wks: 051260 (WksYd). N/listed 290161.
NBL, Glasgow: Nil. Rectification?
Dumfries: xx0261 (trials)
XX: xxxxxx (on delivery with D844)
Swindon Works: Nil

Date New: 220261

Luxulyan: 030461 (pass)
Newton Abbot: 130761 (pass, piloting 'Warship')
83F: 060861
Chacewater: 060861 (Truro-Perranporth pass)
XX: 160762 (fire damage) (FDTL)
Kingswear: 080862 (pass)

Swindon Wks: 090962 (WksYd). N/listed 190862 & 300962.

83A: 070463
Dawlish: 190963 (pass)
83A: 241163
Bishops Nympton: 060364 (pass)
83A: 190564
Paddington: 310864

Swindon Wks: 060964/ 130964 (WksYd)/ 200964 ('A' Shop)/ 270964
('A' Shop)/ 111064 ('A' Shop)/ 181064 ('A' Shop). N/listed 251064.

Paddington: wc021164 (ex-Wks)/ 231264/ 270265/ 010565/ 310865
81A: 180965

Swindon Wks: 031065 ('A' Shop)/ 101065 ('A' Shop)/ 051265 ('A' Shop).
N/listed 260965 & 121265.

81A: 160166/110466
Paddington: 030766/170766
81A: 251266
Leamington Spa: 220267/ 010367
81A: 020367/110367
Leamington Spa: 070667
81A: 180667/150767/ 141067

Stratford DRS: Nil. SFR: 061167-241167 Collision damage.

81A: 070168/020368/270368/ 050568
Paddington: 060568 (Paddington-Newton Abbot weed killing)
Westbury: 170568 (weed killing)
81A: 020668/030668

Stored: 1we100868 (xx0868)

81A: 060868/170868/ 080968

Withdrawn: 1we140968 (140968)

81A: 290968/221068/ 071268/ 151268/ 040169/ 190169/ 280169 (CSdgs)/ 020269/ 020369/ 140369 (CSdgs)/ 260369 (CSdgs)/ 300369/ 060469/ 200469/ 030569/ 250569

STN **Booked** **Transfer:** 0Z33 11.45 290569 (Thursday) 81A-Newport ADJ (with D6341/4)

Reading/Burnham: 290569 (hauled by D7073, with D6341/4)

Received J. Cashmore, Newport: 300569 (with D6341/4)
J. Cashmore, Newport: 310569
Disposal: 05/69 (D&ELfS).

Note:
1. Photo: D6335, Dumfries, xx02/61 (MLI197). Caption: 'The less than pristine condition of the locomotive suggests that it was being trialled following return to the maker's works for rectification'.

D6335 and D6345, 81A Old Oak Common (Carriage Sidings), Undated. Probably late-1968 given D6345's lack of side-swipe damage.

(Author's Collection)

D6336

NBL Order: L97/31, Progressive No.: 27909.

D6336 and 'Castle' 5070, Plymouth Mutley, 8 July 1961. (R.C. Riley [The Transport Library])

D6336, 81A Old Oak Common, 17 February 1969. (C. Campbell [David Dunn Collection])

Preston: xxxx61

Date New: 030761

Plymouth NR: 080761 (07.00 Swindon-Penzance pass, piloting 'Castle' 5070)
Aller Jct: 290961 (05.30 Paddington-Penzance pass, piloting 'Castle' 7037)

Swindon Wks: 120862 (WksYd)/ 190862 (WksYd)/260862 ('A' Shop Yard). N/listed 010762 & 090962. BR Rcds: 100762-190962 HC.

Aller Jct.: 080763 (banking)
Totnes: 090763 (banking)
83A: 151263/190564
Exeter s.p.: 260664/ 020864
Bishops Lydeard: 220864 (08.10 Taunton-Minehead pass, piloting 'Prairie' 6148)/ 09.25 Minehead-Manchester pass [to Taunton])
Exeter StD: 280964
Churston: 131064 (pass)
Maiden Newton: 310765 (pass, piloting Std 5MT 73018)
Seaton: 020865 (freight)
83A: 030865
Bristol TM: 070865 (Plymouth-Newcastle pass [to Bristol]; 06.55 Wolverhampton-Paignton pass [from Bristol], both with D6346)
83A: 250466
Exeter StD: 280666 (freight)
83D Exmouth Jct: 230766
82A: 221066/ 111266

Stored: 5we280567 (080567)

82A: 040667/100667

Reinstated: 4we220767 (260667)

82A: 160767/300767

Swindon Wks: 030967 ('A' Shop)/ 130967/ 111067 (ex-Wks). N/listed 211067. BR Rcds: 170867-131067 I.

Exeter StD: 141267 (Exeter Riverside-Newton Abbot freight, with D6331/7)
84A: 230668/300668
Exeter s.p.: 050868
84D: 080968
St.Austell: 081068 (clay, with D6319)
81A: 071268/ 190169/ 220269
81F: 070469
81A: 200469/250569/ 290669
Bledlow: 050969 (mineral wagons)
Oxford: 031269 (assisting failed D1664 on 13.15 Paddington-Hereford pass [Oxford-Worcester])
81A: 030170/080270
81F: 080370/xx0370 (collision with D7029, to Swindon Wks 180370)

Swindon Wks: 180570 ('A' Shop Yd, acc dam). N/listed 290770. BR Rcds: 170370-290570 U (Col Damage).

81D: 300570
Didcot: 060870
81A: 220870/280970/ 031070/ 241070/ 281270/ 060271/ 150271
Southcote Jct: 190271 (rock salt)
81A: 170471
84A: Arrived 020571 (with D6356; D6331 apparently hauling D6336/56) removed from consist at Exeter after catching fire at Sampford Peverell)
Exeter s.p.: 070571
XX: 080571 (16.55 Chard-South Morden milk, failed, assisted by D805 to Exeter)
Exeter s.p.: 150571/ 240571/ 310571
84B: 170771/220771/ 250771
Truro: 280771 (freight/shunting)
St. Blazey Yard: 030871
Exeter StD: 080871 (mineral wagons)
Exeter s.p.: 290871/ 040971
Exeter Central: 110971 (Chard milk)
Tiverton Jct: 150971 (Hemyock milk)
Hemyock: 200971/220971 (milk)
Barnstaple: 280971
Exeter s.p.: 031071

Withdrawn: 1we091071 (031071)

Devonport Jct: 061071 (in traffic, LE to 84A)/ 081071 (in traffic, freight)
Plymouth: 171071 (with D6338)

Reinstated: 1we231071 (211071)

Exeter s.p.: 271071
Exeter StD: 191171 (20.10 EStD-NA pass)
Exeter s.p.: 011271 (sent to 84B)

Stored: 1we181271 (181271)

Lostwithiel: 191271 (in traffic, milk)
St. Blazey: 311271 (in traffic, trip-freights)

Withdrawn: 1we010172 (010172)

84B: Nil

Transfer 84B/Exeter-BMJ: 030172 (D6336/8 ex-84B (04.05) picking up D6333/9 ex-Exeter, hauled by D5180)

BMJ: 040172 (CPS)/ 090172. N/listed 150172/ 260172.

Transfer BMJ-Swindon Wks: 270172 (with D6333/8/9)

Swindon Wks: 100272/ 120272 (TYd)/ 270272 (TYd)/ 120372 (TYd)/ 150372 (TYd, gutted internally, on bogies)/ 220372 (TYd)/ 050472 (TYard)/ 100472/ 120472/ 170572 (TYd, gutted internally, on bogies)/ 200572 (TYd)/ 230572 (TYd)/ 260572 (ConYd Cutting Area, being cut-up)/ 310572. N/listed 200672.
Disposal: By 090672 (BR).

D6337

NBL Order: L97/32, Progressive No.: 27910.

D6337, 84A Plymouth Laira, 29 April 1962.
(Dave Cobbe [Rail-Photoprints])

D6337 (with D6339), Exeter s.p., 8 February 1969. (RCTS)

Crewe South: xxxx62 (LE, on delivery with D862)

Swindon Wks: 040362 ('A' Shop). N/listed 040262.

Date New: 130362

83A: 130362   **83D:** 290462
Newton Abbot: 210762 (pass, piloting steam loco)
Brent: 280762 (12.40 Newquay-Cardiff, piloting D802)
Kingswear: 080862 (pass)
83B: 070763
Exeter StD: 280763 (banking freight to Exeter Central, with Ivatt 2MT 41296)
Starcross: 280763 (down pass, with D6330)
Paignton: 130863 (Kingswear-Newton Abbot pass)
83A: 151263
Venn Cross: 230665 (engine & van)
84A: 120765
83D Exmouth Jct: 040865
82A: 140866/ 221066/ 111266
Templecombe: 040667 (demolition, en route to Sturminster Newton)
Templecombe Lower Yd/ Stalbridge/ Sturminster Newton: 240667 (demolition)
82A: 300767
Exeter StD: 240867 (up pass, with D6333)
82A: 030967

Swindon Wks: 130967/ 111067 ('A' Shop)/ 211067/ 251067. N/listed 031267. Derived Rcds: xxxxxx-xx1167 C. Paint Date: (SDN) 12.10.67 K (SYN).

Exeter StD: 141267 (Exeter Riverside-Newton Abbot freight, with D6331/6)/ 270168 (LE, with D6334)
Exeter s.p.: 110668
Exeter StD/Exeter s.p.: 290668
Exeter StD: 240868 (assist failed D6545 on 12.30 EStD-Waterloo pass from EStD to Exeter Central, with D6337); 14.15 Exeter Central-Ilfracombe pass, with D6337)
83A: 080968
Exeter s.p.: 080269
84A: 120469/130469
Teignmouth: 010569 (Paddington-Paignton pass [from Exeter])

Exeter s.p.: 100569
Newton Abbot: 130669 (NA-Paignton relief pass)
Exeter StD: 290769/ 020869 (LE)
83A: 200969
Starcross: 230969 (21.42 Exeter StD-Newton Abbot pass with D6339, failed at Starcross)
Newton Abbot: 071069
84B: 020570/130870
84A: 260970
Lostwithiel: 131170 (china clay)
84B: 221170/030471
Exeter StD: 240471 (LE)
84A: 150571
Newton Abbot: 210571 (parcels)
84A: 300571
Newton Abbot: 020771 (engine+van)
83A: 050771   **84A:** 250771
83A: 080871/090871
Honiton: 110871 (17.03 Exeter StD-Axminster [DMU substitute])
Exeter: 130871
83A: 220871
Exeter StD: 200971
Newton Abbot: 250971

Withdrawn: 1we231071 (211071)

84A: Nil

Transfer 84A-BMJ: 181071 (with D831/69, D6334)

BMJ: 211071/221071 (CPS)/ 271071/ 301071 (CPS)/ 031171(CPS)/ 141171/ 301171/ 041271 (VS)/ 121271/ 181271/ 291271/ 010172/ 090172 (VS)/ 150172/ 260172 (VS)/ 130272/ 190272/ 220272/ 260272/ 040372/ 120372

Transfer BMJ-Swindon Wks: 130372 (with D6308/34/48)

Swindon Wks: 150372 ('A' Shop, being stripped)/ 180372 ('A' Shop Yd)/ 220372 ('A' Shop Yd, gutted internally, on bogies)/ 260372 (ditto)/ 050472 (ConYd)/ 100472/ 150472 (ConYd)/ 110572 (ConYd Cutting Area, being cut-up)/ 170572. N/listed 260572.
Disposal: By 260572 (BR).

D6338

NBL Order: L97/33, Progressive No.: 27911.

D6338, Exeter s.p., 27 March 1970. (Peter Foster)

D6338, 85B Gloucester Horton Road, 19 November 1970. Air-intake apertures in the aluminium castings still just about visible through the front-end circular grilles, despite Classified body repair work undertaken in 1970. Plating-over would have been expected. (Rail-Online)

Date New: 290362

83G: 150462
St. Ives: 230462
Plymouth NR: 230662 (pass, piloting D810)
Dainton: 120463 (13.30 Bristol-Plymouth pass, piloting 'Hall')
Paignton: 140863 (Kingswear-Newton Abbot pass)
Newton Abbot: 140963
83A: 151263
Dawlish Warren: 170564 (19.00 [16th] Glasgow Central-Plymouth pass, with D6328)

Swindon Wks: 170165/ 240165 ('A' Shop). N/listed 291164 & 310165.

Callington: 280565 (pass)
Evershot: 260665 (Wolverhampton-Weymouth (SO) pass, piloting Std 5MT 73020)
83A: 030865   **84A:** 040865
83D Exmouth Jct: 190965
83A: 250466
82A: 140866/150866

Stored: 4we270567 (080567)

82A: 040667/100667

Reinstated: 4we220767 (260667)

82A: 160767/300767/090867/190867/030967/071067/151067/211067/
281067/210168/040268/150368/060468/090668
Exeter StD/Exeter s.p.: 060768/ 310768
Exeter s.p.: 210968/ 220269
Newton Abbot: 030469 (Paignton-NA pass)
Stoke Canon: 110469 (6C03 freight)
Exeter Riverside: 130469
84A: 100569
Exeter s.p.: 230769
Exeter StD: 290769 (evening EStD-NA pass, with D6333)
Exeter s.p.: 200969
Newton Abbot: 260370 (piloting defective D1018 on 08.30 Paddington-Penzance pass (NA-Plymouth): LE to NA)
Exeter s.p.: 270370
Hemyock: 290370 (milk tain)
Barnstaple Jct: 300370

83A: 170570
Exeter s.p.: 280670
Exeter StD: 070770 (20.20 EStD-Newton Abbot pass, with D6339)/ 070970 (20.20 EStD-Newton Abbot pass, with D6339)

Swindon Wks: 130970 (stripped, awaiting repaint)/ 171070. Derived Rcds: xx0970-xx1070 C.

Marsh Sdgs, Parkend: 291070 (shunting)
Gloucester: 301070 (Gloucester-Cheltenham pass, in lieu of failed 16.00 Swindon-Cheltenham DMU)
85B: 191170 (ex-Wks)
84B: 030471
Penryn: 190471 (Falmouth Docks-Truro freight)
84B: 010571
Exeter s.p.: 120571/ 220571/ 290571
Liskeard Goods Yd: 130771 (freight)
83A: 030871/080871
Exeter s.p.: 220871
Menheniot: 220971 (LE)
Plymouth: 171071 (with D6336)
Par Bridge: 061171 (LE)

Stored: 1we181271 (181271)

84B: 191271
St. Blazey/St Austell: 291271 (in traffic, St. Blazey trips, 16.11 Drinnick Mill-St. Blazey freight, piloting D806, caught fire at St Austell, fire brigade in attendance)

Withdrawn: 1we010172 (010172)

84B: Nil

Transfer 84B/Exeter-BMJ: 030172 (D6336/8 ex-84B (04.05) picking up D6333/9 ex-Exeter, hauled by D5180)

BMJ: 040172 (CPS)/ 090172. N/listed 150172/ 260172.

Transfer BMJ-Swindon Wks: 270172 (with D6333/6/9)

Swindon Wks: 100272/ 120272 ('A' Shop Yd)/ xx0272 ('A' Shop'). N/listed 270272.
Disposal: By 250272 (BR).

D6339

NBL Order: L97/34, Progressive No.: 27912.

Date New: 020462

82C: 010462 (SSYd)

83E: 150462   **Newquay:** 230462
Grogley Halt: 240462 (13.25 Wadebridge-Bodmin General pass)
Torquay: 310762 (11.50 Paignton-Paddington pass (to Newton Abbot))
Totnes: 080962 (down pass, piloting 'King' 6026)
St.Dennis Jct: 080763 (freight, with D6307)
84A: 251263/090564
84C: 031064
Yeovil Pen Mill: 260665 (Wolverhampton-Weymouth pass, piloting 'Grange' 6803)
XX: 140765 (fire damage) (FDTL)
83D Exmouth Jct: 020865
Bristol TM: 080865 (pass, with D6342)
Totnes: 140566 (weed-killing)
83A: 240766/180966
Tavistock North: 300467 (inspection saloon)

Swindon Wks: 300767. N/listed 070567 & 030967. Derived Rcds: xxxxxx-xx0867 C. Paint Date: SN 27/7/67 K (SYN).

83A: 040967 (ex-Wks)
Newton Abbot: 181067 (14.30 Paddington-Penzance pass, piloting ailing D1059 from NA to Plymouth)
Heathfield: 291267 (trip-freight)
84A: 180568
Truro: 240568 (07.45 Truro-Penzance DMU replacement, with D6307)
Exeter s.p.: 110668/060768/ 050868
Exeter Central: 050968 (freight)
Exeter s.p.: 080968/ 080269/ 220269
Coldharbour: 080369 (Hemyock milk)
Lapford: 130469 (shunting tanks)
83A: 100569/140569
Exeter StD: 170569 (milk)/ 290769
Dawlish Warren: 220869 (21.42 Exeter StD-NA pass, with D6333; D6333 caught fire at DW and detached)
Exeter StD: 300869 (LE)
Exeter s.p.: 200969
Starcross: 230969 (21.42 Exeter StD-NA pass with D6337, failed at Starcross)
84B: 250969
Newton Abbot: 081069
Exeter StD: 240270 (12.38 Barnstaple-Exeter pass)
Exeter s.p.: 280670
Exeter StD: 070770 (20.10 EStD-NA pass, with D6338)/ 090770 (20.10 EStD-NA pass, with D6330)
Exeter s.p.: 200770 (with D6333, towed D802/30 from Exeter s.p. to Exeter StD Carriage Sdgs).
Torrington/Meeth: 220770 (china clay)

Exeter s.p.: 310770/020870
83A: 150870
Exeter StD: 280870 (20.10 EStD-NA pass, with D6333)
83A: 260970   **Exeter s.p.:** 081070
Exeter StD: 281070 (20.10 EStD-NA pass with D6334, both failed at City Basin Jct, propelled to NA by D847)
XX: 260571 (fire damage) (FDTL)
Exeter s.p.: 290671/ 010871/ 020871
84B: 090871   **Exeter s.p.:** 220871
Lostwithiel: 290871 (milk)
Truro: 011071 (shunting)

Withdrawn: 1we091071 (031071)

Wadebridge: 171071 (in traffic,ballast empties)

Bristol Marsh Jct: 211071/ 221071 (CPS)/ 231071. N/listed 271071.

Reinstated: 1we301071 (251071)

Devonport Jct: 081171 (freight)
Exeter StD: 171171 (17.03 EStD-Axminster DMU replacement)
Barnstaple: 231171 (assisting failed D811 on 17.55 Barnstaple-Exeter pass)

Stored: 1we181271 (181271)

Exeter StD: 291271 (in traffic, 20.10 Exeter-NA pass)/ 311271 (in traffic, 13.15 Plymouth-Exeter, 20.10 Exeter-NA pass, 23.30 NA-Exeter e.c.s.)
Exeter StD: 010172 (in traffic, 04.30 Exeter Riverside-Barnstaple freight (with D6333), 09.20 Barnstaple-Exeter (alone), 14.30 Exeter-Tiverton Jct-Hemyock & 16.45 return (milk), switched off on arrival at Exeter)

Withdrawn: 1we010172 (010172)

Exeter s.p.: Nil

Transfer 84B/Exeter-BMJ: 030172 (D6336/8 ex-84B (04.05) picking up D6333/9 ex-Exeter, hauled by D5180)

BMJ: 040172 (CPS)/ 090172. N/listed 150172/ 260172.

Transfer BMJ-Swindon Wks: 270172 (with D6333/6/8)

Swindon Works: 100272/ 120272 ('A' Shop Yd)/ 270272 (Yd)/ 120372 (TYd, gutted internally, on bogies)/ 150372 (TYd)/ 220372 (TYd)/ 050472 (TYd)/ 100472/ 120472/ 170572 (TYd)/ 200572 (TYd)/ 260572/ 310572/ 030672 (TYd, gutted bodyshell, on bogies)/ 200672 (ConYd Cutting Area, gutted bodyshell, off bogies)/ 210672 (ConYd Cutting Area, being cut-up)/ 230672 (ditto). N/listed 020772.
Disposal: By 300672 (BR).

D6340

NBL Order: L97/35, Progressive No.: 27913.

D6340, Swindon Works (Timber Yard), 4 November 1962. Awaiting replacement transmission. (L.W. Perkins [Kidderminster Railway Museum])

D6340, Bristol Marsh Junction (SPM Coal Sidings), 3 November 1971. Withdrawn. 81A metal shed plates still fitted on cabside valance.
(Norman Preedy [Kidderminster Railway Museum])

Swindon Wks: 010462 (newly delivered ex-NBL)

Date New: 030462

83F: 150462

Swindon Wks: 120862 (TYd)/ 190862 (TYd)/ 020962 (TYd)/ 090962 (TYd)/ 160962 (TYd)/ 230962 (TYd)/ 300962 (TYd)/ 211062 (TYd)/ 041162 (TYd). N/listed 010762 & 181162. BR Rcds: 270762-291162 HC (transmission reps/replacement).

Exeter StD: 150663 (pass)
Newton Abbot: 070763 (Paddington-Penzance pass (NA to Plymouth), piloting D811)
Aller Jct.: 080763 (banking)
Plymouth NR: 080763 (Paddington-Penzance pass (NA to Plymouth), piloting D812); Penzance-Manchester pass (Plymouth to NA), piloting D831
Newton Abbot: 090763 (Paddington-Penzance pass (NA to Plymouth), piloting D1008)
Ilfracombe: 160863 (General Manager's saloon; 12.15 Ilfracombe-Exeter pass, piloting SR Pacific 34110)
84A: 251263
XX: 110365 (fire damage) (FDTL)

Swindon Wks: 030465. N/listed 280365 & 100465.

Plymouth NR: 100765 (with D6315)
XX: 220765 (fire damage) (FDTL)
84C: 040865
Padstow: 270865 (pass)
83D Exmouth Jct: 190965
81C: 240466
Kensington Olympia: 100566 (inter-regional freight)
81A: 030766/170766/ 131166/ 261166/ 111266/ 010167
Leamington Spa: 260167
82A: 040667/100667/ 160767/ 300767

Swindon Wks: 111067 ('A' Shop)/ 211067/ 251067. N/listed 130967 & 031267. Derived Rcds: xxxxxx-xx1267 C.

81A: 070168/270368/ 050568/ 120568/ 030668
Paddington: 220668
81A: 060868/170868/ 080968/ 290968/ 051068/ 221068/ 071268
Paddington: 081268
81A: 081268
Paddington: 150169
81A: 220269
Cricklewood Yd: 010469
Paddington: 250469
81A: 250569/290669/ 060769/ 300869
Paddington: 270969 (engineer's train)/ 111069
81A: 221169/261269
Paddington: 010170
81A: 030170/ 250170/ 080270/ 310370/ 050470
Paddington: 290670 (e.c.s.)
81A: 220870   **81F:** 270970
81A: 251070
Hayes: 021170
Paddington: 141270
81A: 250271/140371
Paddington: 300471 (14.38 Paddington-Bristol parcels)

Stored: 1we080571 (040571)
Withdrawn: 1we220571 (220571)

BMJ: 010671 (Diesel Depot [SPMCS?])/ 160671 (SPMCS)/ 270671 (SPMCS)/ 020771/ 310771 (SPMCS)/ 130871/ 300871 (SPMCS)/ 250971 (SPMCS)/ 260971 (SPMCS)/ 091071/ 221071/ 271071/ 301071 (SPMCS)/ 031171 (SPMCS)/ 141171 (SPMCS)

Transfer BMJ-Swindon Wks: 301171 (with D834/45/58)

Swindon Wks: 121271 (Dump, complete)/ 090172/ 210172/ 120272 (TYd)/ 270272 (Yard)/ 120372 (TYd, gutted shell, on bogies)/ 150372 (ConYd, gutted internally, on bogies, under gantry awaiting removal from bogies)/ 180372 (ConYd Cutting Area, gutted shell, off bogies)/ 220372 (ditto)/050472 (ConYd Cutting Area, rems). N/listed 100472.
Disposal: By 140472 (BR).

D6341

NBL Order: L97/36, Progressive No.: 27914.

Swindon Wks: 060562 ('A' Shop Yard). N/listed 040362 & 270562.

Date New: 120562

Swindon Wks: 120862 (TYd)/ 190862 (TYd)/ 090962 (TYd)/ 160962 (TYd)/ 230962 (TYd)/ 300962 (TYd)/ 211062 (TYd)/ 041162 ('A' Shop). N/listed 010762 & 181162. BR Rcds: 090762-131162 HC (transmission reps/ replacement).

Falmouth: 080763 (Falmouth-Paddington pass (to Plymouth))
84C: 031064
Exeter Central: 020865 (freight)
Exeter StD: 110865 (assisting failed DMU on 09.45 Yeovil Jct-EStD; failed, further assisted by Std 4MT 80039)

Swindon Wks: ???
82C: 220566
Swindon Wks: ???

Paddington: 030766
81A: 100766/111266/ 251266/ 010167
Leamington Spa: 010267
81A: 110367

Stored: 4we200567 (080567)

81A: 030667/ 180667

Reinstated: 4we220767 (260667)

82A: 160767
81A: 280767/141067/ 070168
Southall: 080368
81A: 270368   **81C:** 050568
81A: 120568   **81D:** 090668

Stored: 1we100868 (xxxxxx)

81A: 170868. N/listed 080868.

Reinstated: 1we170868 (xxxxxx)

81A: 080968/290968/ 051068

Stored: 1we021168 (291068)
Withdrawn: 1we301168 (301168)

81A: 071268/151268/ 040169/ 190169/ 280169 (CSdgs) / 020269/ 020369/ 140369 (CSdgs)/ 260369 (CSdgs)/ 060469/ 030569/ 250569

STN <u>Booked</u> Transfer: 0Z33 11.45 290569 (Thursday) 81A-Newport ADJ (with D6335/44).

Reading/Burnham: 290569 (hauled by D7073, with D6335/44)

Received J. Cashmore, Newport: 300569 (with D6335/44)
J. Cashmore, Newport: 310569/ 010669 (by Wall)
Disposal: 05/69 (D&ELfS).

D6341, Swindon Works (Timber Yard), 9 September 1962. Awaiting replacement transmission. (RCTS)

D6342

NBL Order: L97/37, Progressive No.: 27915.

D6342, Unknown location/date. Relatively recently ex-Works condition. (Geoff Sharpe)

D6342, 85B Gloucester Horton Road, 9 April 1968. (Norman Preedy [Kidderminster Railway Museum])

Swindon Works: 060562 (Diesel Test Bay). N/listed 040362 & 270562.

Date New: 110562

Dawlish: 290762 (pass)
Wadebridge: 220463 (Padstow-Bodmin Road pass)
Bodmin Road: 240463 (10.57 Padstow-BR pass (Wadebridge-BR))
Padstow: 260463 (09.03 Padstow-BR pass (Wadebridge-BR))
Gwinear Road: 080763 (shunting)
Newquay: 150664 (stabled)
North Tawton: 250764 (pass)
83D Exmouth Jct: 020864/ 230864
84A: 031064
83D Exmouth Jct: 120765
Barnstaple: 030865 (14.40 Barnstaple Town-Ilfracombe; 15.50 Ilfracombe-
  Exeter Central)
Bristol TM: 070865 (N'bound 'Devonian' (to Bristol), with D6329)
82A: 080865
Bristol TM: 080865 (1N37 pass, with D6339)
Halwill Jct: 210865 (11.05 Paddington-Bude pass)
Braunton: 290865 (banker between Braunton and Mortehoe for 'Mystery'
  special to Ifracombe hauled by D7021)
Barnstaple Jct: 290865 (rescued failed D7021 on 'Mystery' special ex-
  Ilfracombe from Wrafton; hauled train solo from BJ to Exeter)
83A: 190965   **81D:** 281165
81A: 080366/280366
81F: 240466

Swindon Wks: ?

81D: 190666 (recently ex-Wks)
81A: 170766/171266/ 251266
Leamington Spa: 150367/ 050467
85B: 300667
Coleford Branch: 170767 (freight)
85B: 220767
Parkend: 100967 (engineer's train)

Swindon Wks: 251067/ 031267 ('A' Shop). N/listed 211067 & 260168.
  Derived Rcds: xxxxxx-xx1267 C.

82A: 150368
85B: 090468/020668/ 080668/090668
Dursley: 280668 (shunting)
Gloucester: 250768/ 310768
82A: 040868/191068

Withdrawn: 1we211268 (211268)

85A: 260169/ 020269/ 120469/ 200469/ 270469/ 040569/ 250569

STN Booked Transfer: No info found; may have travelled with
  D6321/4/5/9 85A-Newport on 290569.

Received J. Cashmore, Newport: 290569 (with D6324/5/9)
J. Cashmore, Newport: 310569/ 010669 (by Wall)/ 070669/ 090669
Disposal: 05/69 (D&ELfS).

D6342, Parkend,
10 September 1967. Just
a few weeks prior to
being called into works
for a Classified repair and
repaint into blue livery.
(John Cosford)

D6343

NBL Order: L97/38, Progressive No.: 27916.

D6343, 81A Old Oak Common, 24 July 1967. Looking in a bit of a state. One week later in Swindon Works for Classified body repair.
(Peter Groom)

Swindon Wks: 060562 ('A' Shop Yard). N/listed 040362 & 270562.

Date New: 100562

Moretonhampstead branch: 080962 (freight)
Exeter StD: 080363 (pass)
Exeter Riverside Yard: 080763
Bampton: 051063 (pass to Exeter, last day)
84A: 251263
Paddington: 110664/ 110764 (e.c.s.)
81A: 190764/ 020864
Paddington: 100864/ 260964/ wc021164/ 060265
81A: 270265

Swindon Wks: 100465. N/listed 030465 & 090565.

Paddington: 150565
81A: 300565/080865
Old Oak West Jct: 071165 (freight)
81A: 090166/160166/110466/100766/170766/020966/261166/010167

Paddington: 280267
81A: 090467/150767
XX: 200767 (severe fire damage) (FDTL)
81A: 240767 (Factory Yd)

Swindon Wks: 300767/ 030967 ('A' Shop)/ 130967/ 111067 ('A' Shop)/ 211067. N/listed 251067. Derived Rcds: xx0767-xx1067 C+Fire damage reps.

81F: 301267
81A: 070168/270368/ 020668/ 030668
Royal Oak: xx0668 (parcels) (either 050668 or 130668)
Paddington: 220668
High Wycombe: 180768 (LE)
81D: 250868
81A: 290968/081268/ 050169/ 250569/ 120769/ 170869/ 011169/ 221169/ 231169/ 071269/ 250170/ 280270/ 260370/ 050470/ 260470
Didcot: 200670 (hauling exhibits from GWS Didcot to Wallingford OD & return)
XX: 300670 (fire damage) (FDTL)

D6343, Exeter s.p., 7 May 1971. (Norman Preedy [Jim Binnie Collection])

81A: 220870 / 031070
Cholsey & Moulsford/Wallingford: 161070
Reading: 311070 / 021170
81A: 060271   **81F:** 200371
81A: 170471
Exeter: 020571 (with D6308 / 28 / 48 @ 15.22)
84A: 020571 (ex-81A with D6308 / 28 / 48)
Exeter s.p.: 070571 / 080571
Exeter Riverside: 220571 (vans)
Tiverton Jct: 260571 (Hemyock-Exeter milk)
Exeter StD: 060671 (milk to Hemyock)
Exeter s.p.: 260671
Tiverton Jct: 080771 (milk)
84A: 250771
Exeter s.p.: 310771

84A: 080871 / 220971 / 250971
Instow: 300971 (freight to Torrington)

Withdrawn: 1we091071 (031071)

84A: 041071

Transfer 84A-Swindon Wks: 061071 (with D804, D6326 / 56, hauled by D841, noted at Dawlish in transit)

Swindon Wks: 111071 ('A' Shop Yd, whole)/ 181071/ 311071/ 021171/ 041271/ 121271 (Dump, gutted bodyshell, on bogies)/ 231271 (ConYd Cutting Area, being cut-up)/ 291271. N/listed 050172.
Disposal: By 070172 (BR).

D6344

NBL Order: L97/39, Progressive No.: 27917.

Crewe: 100562 (with D6345)

Date New: 180562

Brent: 280762 (down pass, piloting D861)
Newton Abbot: 040862 (down pass, piloting 'Castle' 5056)
84A: 061062
Lostwithiel: 220463 (freight)
Devonport Kings Road: 120863 (16.00 Plymouth-Waterloo pass [to NA?])
84D: 200864   **84A:** 031064
Wadebridge: 170465 (Freight)
Chard: 020865 (freight)
83A: 040865

Swindon Wks: 130366 ('A' Shop). N/listed 230166.

81C: 130466   **81F:** 240466
81A: 170766
Paddington: 020966
81A: 100966/261166/ 171266/ 010167/ 020367/ 110367/ 030667
Kensington Olympia: 150767 (single coach)
81A: 141067/020368/ 080368/ 060468/ 050568/ 120568
Reading General: 010668 (LE)
81C: 020668

Stored: 1we100868 (xx0868)

81A: 060868/170868/ 080968

Withdrawn: 1we140968 (140968)

81A: 290968/201068/ 221068/ 071268/ 151268/ 040169/ 050169/ 190169/ 280169 (Factory Yd)/ 020269 (Factory Yd)/ 160269/ 220269/ 020369/ 140369 (Factory Yd)/ 300369/ 060469 (Factory Yd)/ 200469/ 030569/ 250569

STN Booked Transfer: 0Z33 11.45 290569 (Thursday) 81A-Newport ADJ (with D6335/41)

Reading/Burnham: 290569 (hauled by D7073, with D6335/41)

Received J. Cashmore, Newport: 300569 (with D6335/41)
J. Cashmore, Newport: 310569 (part-cut)/ 010669 (part-cut, cutting area)
Disposal: 05/69 (D&ELfS).

D6344, Reading, 1 June 1968. (Jim Binnie)

D6345

NBL Order: L97/40, Progressive No.: 27918.

Crewe: 100562 (with D6344)

Swindon Wks: 160562 (WksYd). N/listed 060562 & 270562.

Date New: 190562

Gwinear Road: 040762 (Helston-GR pass)
Exeter West Yd: 150663
83F: 080763
Bodmin Road North/Padstow: 281263
Bodmin-Wadebridge: 060664 (pass)
84B: 031064   **84C:** 031064
84B: 120765
Exeter Central: 050865 (e.c.s.)
Bude: 210865 (pass [ex-London], from Exeter?)
83A: 190965
81A: 271165/090166/ 170766

Swindon Wks: ?

81A: 140866 (ex-Wks)/020966/ 300966/ 131166/ 111266/ 251266/ 010167/
020367/ 110367/ 090467/ 230467
West Ealing: 050667 (milk)
Paddington: 060767

81A: 070168/020368/ 080368/ 090368/ 270368/ 120568/ 030668

Store: 1we170868 (xx0868)

81A: 060868/170868/ 080968

Withdrawn: 1we140968 (140968)

81A: 290968/221068/ 071268/ 151268/ 040169/ 050169/ 190169/ 280169
(CSdgs)/ 020269/ 220269/ 140369 (CSdgs)/ 260369 (CSdgs, accident
damage)/ 300369/ 060469/ xx0469 (Factory Yard)/ 200469/ 030569/
290669/ 050769 (CSdgs)/ 120769. Not listed 250569.
81D: 220769 (cab damage)

STN <u>Booked</u> Transfer: 8F89 17.05 250769 (Friday) Swindon-STJ; 8O71
04.10 260769 (Saturday) STJ-Newport Ebbw Jct. N.B. No STN info
found for movement 81A-Reading/ Swindon.

Ebbw Jct: 260769 (listed as D6353)

Received J. Cashmore, Newport: 290769
J. Cashmore, Newport: 290769/ 310769/ 130869 (cabs+side panels).
Not listed 040869.
Disposal: 07/69 (D&ELfS).

D6345, 81A Old
Oak Common,
Undated. (Colour-Rail)

D6346

NBL Order: L97/41, Progressive No.: 27919.

82C: 270562 (SS).
Swindon Wks: 030662 (WksYd)
Swindon: 040662 (13.55 Paddington-Pembroke Dock [Swindon-Cardiff, running-in turn])
Swindon Wks: 050662 (WksYd). N/listed 170662.
Date New: 080662

XX: 170762 (fire damage) (FDTL)

Swindon Wks: 120862 ('A' Shop)/ 190862 ('A' Shop, fire damage)/ 090962 ('A' Shop)/ 211062 ('A' Shop)/ 041162 ('A' Shop). N/listed 181162.
BR Rcds: 300762-131162 HC.

Plymouth NR: 291262
Bere Alston: 090663 (pass)
Exeter West Yard: 150663 (LE)
84A: 251263

Swindon Wks: 260764 ('A' Shop). N/listed 210664 & 160864.

84A: 031064
Bristol TM: 070865 (Plymouth-Newcastle pass, to Bristol, then 06.55 Wolverhampton-Paignton pass [from Bristol], both with D6336)
83A: 190965   **81D:** 241065
81C: 020166   **81F:** 200266
81A: 160366   **Paddington:** 130466
30A: 220466 (for tyre-turning)
81A: 240466

Swindon Wks: ?

Warwick: 150666 (oil tanks, ex-Wks)
81A: 030766/020966/ 131166/ 261166/ 111266/ 110367/ 180667
81F: 250568
81A: 060868/250868/ 270868/ 080968/ 201068/ 221068
Paddington: 081268
81A: 081268/ 050169

Stored: 1we250169 (xx0169)

81A: 190169/280169 (Factory) / 020269 (Factory Yd)/ 160269/ 220269/ 020369/ 140369 (Factory)/ 300369/ 060469 (Factory Yd)/ 200469

Withdrawn: 1we260469 (260469)

81A: 030569/290669/ 050769 (Carriage Sdgs)/ 120769. N/listed 250569.

STN <u>Booked</u> Transfer: At Swindon, to connect with 8F75 15.45 020869 (Saturday) Gloucester-STJ; 8F51 05.35 MO 040869 (Monday) STJ-Newport Ebbw Jct. N.B. No STN info found for movement 81A-Swindon, or, Swindon-Gloucester. Pencil annotation suggests departure from 81A on 240769.

Received J. Cashmore, Newport: 040869
J. Cashmore, Newport: 040869/ 130869 (cabs+side panels)
Disposal: 08/69 (D&ELfS).

D6346, Swindon Works (Timber Yard), 3 June 1962. After less than two months in service, D6346 underwent Heavy Classified Repairs at Swindon from July to November 1962 following fire damage. (Noel Machell)

D6347

NBL Order: L97/42, Progressive No.: 27920.

82C Swindon: 270562 (SS)

Date New: 020662

St. Mary's Crossing Halt: 090662 (pass, piloted by D7008)
82A: 051062
Plymouth Friary: 080763 (freight)
Barnstaple Jct: 310364 (16.21 Exeter Central-Torrington pass (from BJ))
84A: 090564
Bodmin General: 270564
84B: 200864
Yarde/Dunsbear: 160165 (china clay empties)
84A: 040865   **83A:** 190965
81D: 241065
81E: 141165/281165
81A: 090166/160166
Paddington: 220166

Swindon Wks: ?

81A: 130466/010566 (recently ex-Wks)
Paddington: 300566
81A: 030766/140866/ 131166
Witney Goods Yd: 231166 (shunting)
81A: 111266/171266/ 251266/ 020367/ 030667
Paddington: 030867

81A: 141067   **81D:** 031267
81A: 070168/020368
Paddington: 080368

Stored: 1we230368 (xxxxxx)

81A: 270368

Withdrawn: 1we060468 (310368)

81A: 030468/060468/ 090468/ 150468 (Factory Yd)/ 050568/ 120568/ 020668/ 030668/ 090668/ 060868/ 170868/ 080968/ 290968. N/listed 040568.

STN Booked Transfer: 8F00 22.50 051168 (Tuesday) Reading-STJ; 8O71 04.10 061168 (Wednesday) STJ-Newport Ebbw Jct. N.B. D6347 appears to have only moved from Reading to Swindon on 051168; rescheduled as follows:
STN Booked Transfer: 8F89 16.08 071168 (Thursday) Swindon-STJ; 8O71 04.10 081168 (Friday) STJ-Newport Ebbw Jct.

Received J. Cashmore, Newport: 081168
J. Cashmore, Newport: Nil
Disposal: 11/68 (D&ELfS).

D6347, 81A Old Oak Common, 1 May 1966. (Rail-Online)

D6348

NBL Order: L97/43, Progressive No.: 27921.

D6348, 85B Gloucester
Horton Road, Undated.
(Norman Preedy [Kidderminster
Railway Museum])

D6348, Exeter s.p.,
13 March 1971. Air-
intake apertures in the
aluminium castings still
just about visible through
the front-end circular
grilles, despite Classified
body repair work
undertaken in 1970. Like
D6338, plating-over would
have been expected.
(John Medley [Rail-Photoprints])

Swindon Wks: 030662 ('A' Shop Yd, newly delivered ex-NBL, with D6349). N/listed 270562.

Date New: 140662

Castle Cary: 140662 (LE Swindon-83D, with D6349)
Plymouth NR: 250862 (pass, with D6352, piloting D837)
Boscarne Jct: 310862 (14.48 Bodmin General-Wadebridge pass)

Swindon Wks: xx1162 ('A' Shop). N/listed 041162/ 181162/ 091262.

Falmouth: 040663 (freight)
Par: 070763 (Penzance-Paddington pass (Par-Plymouth), piloting D804)
Bodmin Road/Padstow: 281263
XX: 090664 (fire damage) (FDTL)
Royal Oak: 140664 (e.c.s.)
84B: 031064   **83A:** 030865
83D Exmouth Jct: 190965
81D: 281165
81A: 090166/280366
Wheatley (near Oxford): 280466 (B1 61023 assisting/ rescuing D6348)
81A: 030766/100766/ 170766

Swindon Wks: 310866/ 040966 ('A' Shop)/ 140966/ 021066. N/listed 221066.

81A: 131166/261166/ 111266/ 010167/ 110367/ 030667/ 180667
Paddington: 131067
81F: 301267
84A: 230668/310768/ 080968
81C: 290968
81A: 051068/201068
Paddington: 081268
81A: 081268/190169/ 220269
84B: 030569

Stored: 1we100569 (050569)

84A: 100569/140569

Reinstated: 1we140669 (xx0669)

85B: 270669/120769/ 170769
Gloucester Yd: 310769 (tanks)
Gloucester: 111069 (freight)
85B: 291169/ 161269
82A: 180170/250170

Stored: 1we070270 (xxxxxx)

82A: 220270

Reinstated: 1we070370 (xx0370)

Bristol TM: 020370/ 110470
82A: 170570

Swindon Wks: 290770 ('A' Shop)/ 120870. Derived Rcds: xxxxxx-xx0870 C. Paint Date: SWN (W) 7.70.

82A: 020970/260970/ 151070
Bristol TM: 171070 (freight)
82A:131270
Bristol area: 281270/ 220271
Exeter s.p.: 130371
82A: 190471
Exeter: 020571 (with D6308/28/43 @ 15.22)
84A: 020571 (ex-82A with D6308/28/43)
Exeter s.p.: 290571/ 310571
Newton Abbot: 020771 (St.Blazey-Acton freight (Plymouth-NA), assisting D827)

Stored: 1we170771 (130771) (replacement transmission required)
Withdrawn: 1we240771 (240771)

84A: 250771/280771 (sdgs between depot and main line)/ 290771/ 080871/ 250871/ 220971/ 250971/ end-0971

Transfer 84A-83A: ?
Hackney Yd, NA: (101071). See note.
Transfer 83A-BMJ: ?

BMJ: 211071/ 221071 (CPS)/ 271071/ 301071 (CPS)/ 031171 (CPS)/ 141171/ 041271 (VS) / 121271/ 181271/ 241271 (VS)/ 291271/ 040172/ 150172 (VS)/ 260172 (VS)/ 130272/ 190272/ 220272/ 260272 (VS)/ 040372/ 120372

Transfer BMJ-Swindon Wks: 130372 (with D6308/34/7)

Swindon Wks: 150372 ('A' Shop, being stripped)/ 180372 ('A' Shop Yd)/ 220372 ('A' Shop Yd, gutted bodyshell, on bogies)/ 260372 (ditto)/ 050472 (ConYd)/ 100472/ 150472 (ConYd)/ 110572 (ConYd Cutting Area, being cut-up). N/listed 170572.
Disposal: By 190572 (BR).

Note:
1. Photo: D6319/28, Hackney Yard (NA), 10 October 1971 (MLI197). '..... there were seven Class 22s spread around the vicinity', i.e. D6318/22/3 already in the NA area, D6319/28 recently ex-84A, plus D6308/48?

D6349

NBL Order: L97/44, Progressive No.: 27922.

Swindon Wks: 030662 ('A' Shop Yd, newly delivered ex-NBL, with D6348). N/listed 270562.

Date New: 140662

Castle Cary: 140662 (LE Swindon-83D, with D6348)
Newton Abbot: 070762
Penzance: 150862 (up pass, with D6327)
82A: 111162
Clifton Bridge: 280563 (freight from Portishead, with D6353)
82A: 280763
Plymouth: 060964 (18.45 Plymouth-Exeter Central pass)
Instow: 041064
Newquay: 310765 (10.05 Newquay-Paddington, with D6322, piloted by D6325 to Par)
83A: 190965   **81D:** 281165
81A: 160166/160366/ 280366
Paddington: 130466
81C: 240466   **81A:** 030766
81C: 070866
81A: 280866/251266/ 010167/ 090467
Leamington Spa: 030567
81A: 030667   **81D:** 031267
Transfer 81A-84A: 070168 (with D830)
82A: 090668
Bristol Marsh Jct: 110668
82A: 300668/040868

Store: 1we170868 (xxxxxx)

84A: 160868/080968 (Steam depot sdgs)

Withdrawn: 1we140968 (140968)

84A: 290968/171068/ 021168/ 281268 (old steam shed)/ 220269/ 050369/ 120469/ 130469/ end-0469/ 100569/ 140569/ 250669/ 220769/ 290769/ 020869/ 060869/ 200969

Transfer 84A-Exeter StD Carriage Shed Sdgs: 041069 (with D802/30)

Exeter StD Carriage Shed Sdgs: 041069/ 111069/ 310170

Transfer: Exeter StD Carriage Shed Sdgs-Exeter s.p.: 030270

Exeter s.p.: 060270/ 070270/ 130270/ 160270. N/listed 200270.

Transfer: Exeter s.p.-82A: ?

82A: 220270/280270/ 020370/ 180470/ 170570/ 280670/ 090870/ 020970/ 260970/ 171070 (OD)/ 301070/ 131270/ 140271/ 220271

Transfer 82A-Swindon Wks: By 030371

Swindon Wks: 030371/ 080371/ 150471/ 010671/ 300671/ 020871 (TmbrYd, whole)/ 110871 (TmbrYd)/ 140871 (TmbrYd, whole)/ 180871 (TmbrYd)/ 181071 (ConYd, Cutting Area, being cut). N/listed 311071.
Disposal: By 221071 (BR).

D6349, Didcot, January 1968. (Richard Vitler Collection)

D6350

NBL Order: L97/45, Progressive No.: 27923.

Swindon Wks: 240662 (WksYd). N/listed 170662 & 010762.

Date New: 270662

Wadebridge: 200862 (pass)

Swindon Wks: xx0962 (radiator grille removed). N/listed 090962, 300962/ 041162/ 181162/ 091262. BR Rcds: xxxxxx-201162 HC.

82A: 200163
Bristol TM: 170363 (LE)
St. Philip's Marsh: 190463 (LE)
82A: 280763
XX: 300863 (fire damage) (FDTL)
Padstow: 250764 (pass ex-Bodmin)
83B: 041064
Exeter StD: 090665 (freight, to Exeter Central)
84A: 120765
81A: 271165/281265

Swindon Wks: ?

81A: 110466/240466/ 010566 (ex-Wks)/ 030766/ 100766
Paddington: 260866
81A: 300966/261166/ 111266/ 251266
Leamington Spa: 080267
81A: 020367/090467

Leamington Spa: 120467
XX: 130467 (fire damage) (FDTL)
81D: 230467
81A: 141067/020368/ 080368/ 090368/ 120568/ 020668/ 030668
Reading: 050768 (LE)

Stored: 1we100868 (xx0868)

81A: 170868/250868/ 270868/ 080968. N/listed 080868.

Withdrawn: 1we140968 (140968)

81A: 290968/201068/ 221068/ 071268/ 151268/ 040169/ 050169/ 190169/ 280169 (CSdgs)/ 020269/ 170269 (CSdgs)/ 020369/ 140369 (CSdgs)/ 300369/ 060469/ 200469/ 030569/ 250569/ 300569 (towed away for scrap, with D6351/5)

STN Booked Transfer: 0Z33 11.45 300569 (Friday) 81A-Newport ADJ (with D6351/5)

Reading/Swindon: 300569 (hauled by D7073, with D6351/5)
Ebbw Jct: 010669 (with D6351/5)

Received J. Cashmore, Newport: 040669 (with D6321/51/5)
J. Cashmore, Newport: 070669/ 090669
Disposal: 06/69 (D&ELfS).

D6350 and D6355, 81A Old Oak Common, 1 May 1966. (Rail-Online)

D6351

NBL Order: L97/46, Progressive No.: 27924.

Swindon Wks: 240662 (Works Yard). N/listed 170662 & 010762.

Date New: 270662

Swindon Wks: Nil. BR Rcds: 201262-140163 LC. N/listed 091262.

82A: 200163
Bristol West Depot: 080763
82A: 280763
Bristol TM: 210764 (freight)
81A: 200964/ 111064
Paddington: wc021164

Transfer 81A-Swindon Wks: 191164 (for boiler mods)
Swindon Wks: 221164 ('A' Shop)/ 291164 ('A' Shop)
82C: 131264 (ex-Wks)

Swindon Wks: 240165 ('A' Shop). N/listed 170165 & 310165.

Paddington: 270265
81A: 030465
Paddington: 150565
81A: 300565
Paddington: 150865
81A: 281265/090166/ 110466/ 300466

Swindon Wks: 070566/ 050666 ('A' Shop)/ 260666

81A: 100766
Leamington Spa: 220966 (oil tanks ex-Warwick)
81A: 171266/251266/ 010167/ 110367/ 150767/ 070168
Paddington: 080368
81A: 270368
Reading: 290368 (LE)
81A: 050568   **81C:** 020668
81A: 060868   **81F:** 250868
81A: 080968/290968/ 201068

Stored: 1we091168 (xxxxxx)
Withdrawn: 1we301168 (301168)

81A: 071268/040169/ 050169/ 190169/ 280169 (CSdgs)/ 020269/ 170269 (CSdgs)/ 020369/ 140369 (CSdgs)/ 260369 (CSdgs)/ 300369/ 060469/ 200469/ 030569/ 250569/ 300569 (towed away for scrap, with D6350/5). N/listed 151268.

STN Booked Transfer: 0Z33 11.45 300569 (Friday) 81A-Newport ADJ (with D6350/5)

Reading/Swindon: 300569 (hauled by D7073, with D6350/5)
Ebbw Jct: 010669 (with D6350/5)

Received J. Cashmore, Newport: 040669 (with D6321/50/5)
J. Cashmore, Newport: 090669. N/listed 070669.
Disposal: 06/69 (D&ELfS).

D6351, 82C Swindon, 13 December 1964. Original D6306-33 style gangway doors albeit with discs removed. (Rail-Online)

D6352

NBL Order: L97/47, Progressive No.: 27925.

D6352, 85B Gloucester Horton Road, 30 July 1969. No D-prefix.
(Rail-Online)

D6352, 85B Gloucester Horton Road, 19 March 1970. (Norman Preedy [Kidderminster Railway Museum])

Birmingham Snow Hill: 100762 (LE NBL Glasgow-Swindon, with D6353)

Date New: 120762

Plymouth NR: 250862 (pass, with D6348, piloting D837)
Bristol TM: 050163 (freight)
82A: 200163

Swindon Wks: 170363 (WksYd). N/listed 100263 & 240363. BR Rcds: 110363-190363 HC.

Portishead: 080763
82A: 280763
Cheddar: 170863 (10.49 (SO) Witham-Yatton pass)

Swindon Wks: 200964 ('A' Shop)/ 270964 ('A' Shop)/ 111064 ('A' Shop). N/listed 130964 & 181064.

Paddington: wc021164 (ex-Wks)
81A: 221164
Paddington: 231264
81A: 300565/080865/ 180965
Old Oak Common: 071065
81A: 271165/160166/ 280366/ 110466
81F: 170466/240466
81A: 100766/170766

Swindon Wks: 140966/ 021066. N/listed 040966 & 221066.

81A: 131166/111266/ 251266/ 080167
Leamington Spa: 150267
81A: 020367

Leamington Spa: 240567
81A: 180667/150767/ 141067/ 070168/ 020368/ 060468/ 050568/ 020668/ 170868/ 250868/ 080968/ 290968/ 051068/ 201068/ 071268/ 081268
81C: 040169   **81D:** 180169
81A: 200269
Didcot s.p.: 230269
81A: 200469   **81D:** 180569

Stored: 1we140669 (xxxxxx)
Reinstated: 1we140669 (xx0669)

85B: 120769/300769 / 091069
82A: 201169   **85B:** 161269

Swindon Wks: xx0170. N/listed 220270. Derived Rcds: xxxxxx-xx0270 C.

85B: 190370 (ex-Wks)/140470

82A: 170570/100670/ 140271/ 200271/ 220271/ 150471/ 190471

Withdrawn: 1we080571 (020571)

BMJ: 010671 (Albert Road Yd). N/listed 180671.

Transfer BMJ-Swindon Wks: 220671 (with D6307/9/12)
Chippenham: xxxx71 (with D6307/9/12, D6352 not listed, hauled by D853)

Swindon Wks: 250671/ 300671/ 020871 (TYd, whole)/ 110871 (TYd)/ 140871 (TYd, whole)/ 180871 (TYd)/ 181071/ 311071/ 151171. N/listed 121271.
Disposal: By 191171 (BR).

D6352, Swindon Works (Timber Yard), 14 August 1971. Sandwiched between D6309 and D6312. (Anthony Sayer)

D6353

NBL Order: L97/48, Progressive No.: 27926.

Birmingham Snow Hill: 100762 (LE NBL Glasgow-Swindon, with D6352)

Date New: 120762

Newton Abbot: 280762 (down pass, with D6301)

82C: 091262

Clifton Bridge: 280563 (freight from Portishead, with D6349)
82A: 080763/280763
Cheddar: 170863 (Witham-Yatton pass)/ 070963 (Witham-Yatton pass)
82A: 150364
Bristol TM: 210764
82A: 181064
Paddington: wc021164

Swindon Wks: 170165. N/listed 291164 & 240165.

81A: 270265/030465
Scrubs Lane (Old Oak): 010565
Paddington: 150565
81A: 080865
Paddington: 220166
81F: 200266
Abingdon: 140366 (shunting car-flats)
81C: 280366
81A: 240466/100766/ 170766

Paddington: 170766

Swindon Wks: 021066/ 221066. Not listed 140966 & 131166.

81A: 111266/251266/ 020367/ 090467/ 230467/ 030667/ 150767/ 070168/ 020368/ 050568/ 030668
Paddington: 030868
81F: 250868

Stored: 1we070968 (xx0968)
Withdrawn: 1we280968 (230968)

81F: 280968/230269/ 200469/ 030569/ 180569/ 050769 (prepared for despatch to Newport)/ 060769

STN Booked Transfer: 8F45 02.45 170769 (Thursday) Reading-STJ; 8F45 12.45 SX 170769 (Thursday) STJ-Newport Ebbw Jct. N.B. No STN info found for movement 81F-Reading.

Severn Tunnel Jct: 190769 (listed as D6345)

Received J.Cashmore, Newport: 220769 (with D800/63, D6314)
J.Cashmore, Newport: 220769/ 240769 (whole, in cutting area)/ 120869/ 130869 (cabs+side panels). N/listed 290769/ 150869.
Disposal: 07/69 (D&ELfS).

D6353, 82A Bristol Bath Road, 15 March 1964. (Rail-Online)

D6354

NBL Order: L97/49, Progressive No.: 27927.

D6354, 82A Bristol Bath Road, Undated. (Richard Vitler Collection)

West Bromwich: 180762 (on delivery)

Date New: 020862

82A: 280763
Bristol TM: 130864 (LE)
Paddington: 120964

Swindon Wks: xx0964. N/listed 130964/ 200964/ 270964.

81A: 111064
Paddington: wc021164

Swindon Wks: 310165/ 070365 ('A' Shop)/ 140365 ('A' Shop).
 N/listed 240165 & 280365.

81A: 030465

West Ealing: 030465 (LE, ex-Wks)
Paddington: 220465
81A: 300565
Paddington: 091065
81A: 281265/090166/ 160166
Paddington: 220166
81A: 240466/030766/ 100766
Paddington: 170766
81A: 131166/261166/ 251266/ 010167
Leamington Spa: 140167
81A: 020367

Swindon Wks: 050467 ('A' Shop Yard, accident damage)/ 190467/ 070567
 ('A' Shop). N/listed 020467. Derived Rcds: xxxxxx-xx0567 C + accident
 damage repairs. Paint date: 16/5/67.

81A: 180667

Paddington: 060767/080767 (ex-Wks)
81A: 150767/141067
Paddington: 041167 (p.way)
81A: 020368
Southall/Paddington: 080368
81F: 070468
81A: 050568/030668/ 170868/ 250868
81F: 280968   **81A:** 071268
81C: 151268   **81D:** 180169
82A: 260169
Exeter StD: 220369 (vans)
Exeter s.p.: 030469
83A: 130469
Exeter s.p.: 100569
83A: 100569
82A: 240769/020869/ 010969/ 140969/ 150969/ 181069/ 201069
85B: 131169/291169/ 161269/ 250170/ 110470/ 140470
82A: 170570/100670/ 280670
84A: 020870
82A: 250970/260970/ 171070
Marsh Sdgs, Parkend: 261170 (shunting)
82A: 131270

Bristol area: 281270
Cardiff: 120371 (parcels)

Stored: 1we080571 (020571)

85B: 050571/130571
82A: 150571

Withdrawn: 1we220571 (220571)

BMJ: 010671 (Diesel Depot [SPMCS?])/ 160671 (SPMCS)/ 270671 (SPMCS)/ 020771/ 290771 (SPMCS)/ 310771 (SPMCS)/ 130871/ 300871 (SPMCS)/ 250971 (SPMCS)/ 260971 (SPMCS)/ 221071/ 271071/ 301071 (SPMCS)/ 031171 (SPMCS)/ 141171 (SPMCS). N/listed 301171.

Transfer BMJ-Swindon Wks: 021271 (with D6315/ 27/31)

Swindon Wks: 121271 ('A' Shop Yd, complete)/ 050172 (Dump/Yds)/ 090172/ 210172/ 260172/ 120272 (ConYd Cutting Area, rems). N/listed 270272.
Disposal: By 110272 (BR).

0854B. D6354 and D6320, 85B Gloucester Horton Road, 11 April 1970. The paintwork on many Class 22 locomotives suffered badly from engine coolant corrosion inhibitor aggravated by incessant mechanical cleaning whilst on e.c.s. duties; the issue was most acutely apparent at Old Oak Common. D6354 was repainted blue in May/June 1967 and was allocated to Old Oak up to January 1969 and it was probably during this period that it acquired the disfiguring damage illustrated here. (Norman Preedy [Jim Binnie Collection])

D6355

NBL Order: L97/50, Progressive No.: 27928.

82C Swindon: 120862 (SSYd)
Swindon Wks: 190862 (WksYd). N/listed 010762 & 090962.

Date New: 240862

82A: 200163/280763
84A: 090564

Swindon Wks: 181064 (WksYd)/ 251064/ 041164/ 081164 ('A' Shop).
   N/listed 111064 & 221164.

Paddington: 270265/130365
81A: 030465/300565/ 180965/ 090166/ 240466/ 010566/ 131166/ 261166/
   171266
81C: 251266
Reading: 281266
81A: 010167
Leamington Spa: 080367
81A: 230467/180667
81D: 070468
Chinnor Cement Works-Princes Risborough: 110468 (engine+van)
81A: 050568/120568/ 030668

Stored: 1we100868 (xx0868)

81A: 060868/170868/ 080968

Withdrawn: 1we140968 (140968)

81A: 290968/221068/ 071268/ 151268/ 040169/ 050169/ 190169/ 280169
   (CSdgs)/ 020269/ 020369/ 140369 (CSdgs) / 300369/ 060469/ 200469/
   030569/ 250569/ 300569 (towed away for scrap, with D6350/1)

STN <u>Booked</u> **Transfer:** 0Z33 11.45 300569 (Friday) 81A-Newport ADJ
   (with D6350/1)

Reading/Swindon: 300569 (hauled by D7073, with D6350/1)
Ebbw Jct: 010669 (with D6350/1)

Received J. Cashmore, Newport: 040669 (with D6321/50/1)
J. Cashmore, Newport: Nil
Disposal: 06/69 (D&ELfS).

D6355, Paddington, 22
August 1965. (Fred Castor)

D6356

NBL Order: L97/51, Progressive No.: 27929.

D6356, 30A Stratford, April 1967. Presumably at Stratford for tyre-turning. (Rail-Online)

D6356, Exeter s.p., 4 May 1971. (John Medley [Rail-Photoprints])

Dumfries: 120962 (trials)

Swindon Wks: 250962 (WksYd)

Date New: 270962

82A: 141062/280763

Swindon Wks: 111064 ('A' Shop)/ 181064 ('A' Shop)/ 251064/ 041164/ 081164 ('A' Shop)/ 221164 (WksYd). N/listed 270964 & 291164.

81A: 191264/270265
Paddington: 130365
West Ealing: 210465 (freight)
Paddington: 220465/150565/ 150865
81A: 180965

Swindon Wks: 051265 (Weigh Shop)/ 121265 ('A' Shop)/ 230166 ('A' Shop). N/listed 101065 & 130366.

81A: 160366/110466/ 030766/ 100766/ 300966/ 251266
81D: 250167/250267
81F: 120367
Leamington Spa: 210367 (oil tanks ex-Warwick)/ 290367

30A Stratford: xx0467

Paddington: 230467/060767
81A: 150767/060468/ 050568/ 120568/ 020668/ 030668/ 170868
Reading General: 100968 (freight)/ 110968
81A: 290968/051068/ 221068/ 050169
Paddington: 150169
81A: 200269/220269/ 200469
Plymouth NR: 100569
84A: 100569
Truro: 140569
Lostwithiel: 290769
Bodmin General: 200869 (freight)
84A: 200969

Stored: 1we140669 (xxxxxx)
Reinstated: 1we140669 (xxxxxx)

Stored: 1we130969 (xx0969)
Reinstated (to Wks): 1we061269 (041269)

Swindon Wks: 051269/ 071269 ('A' Shop)/ 101269 (repainted)/ 311269/ xx0170. N/listed 041069. Derived Rcds: xx1269-xx0170 C.

Maidenhead: 220170 (LE towing Class 47, ex-Works)

Reinstated (to Traffic): 1we070270 (xx0270)

81C: 070370/140370
81F: 180470
81A: 220870/241070/ 251070/ 311070/ 031170/ 030171/ 200271
81F: 200371
Reading: 240371 (breakdown train/ 070471)
81A: 170471
84A: Arrived 020571 (with D6336); D6331 (apparently hauling D6336/56) removed from consist at Exeter after catching fire at Sampford Peverell)
Exeter s.p.: 040571
84A: 150571
84B: 130671/ 190671
Newham Yd, Truro: 020771 (shunting)
Lostwithiel: 220771
84A: 280771
Exeter s.p.: 300771
Newton Abbot: 020871 (parcels)/ 130871
Exeter s.p.: 220871/ 040971
Par: 100971 (Drinnick Mill-St.Blazey Yard china clay, assisting D825)
St. Austell: 130971 (Parkandillack-St Blazey freight, with D6330)
Truro: 290971 (freight)

Withdrawn: 1we091071 (031071)

84A: Nil

Transfer 84A-Swindon Wks: 061071 (with D804, D6326/43, hauled by D841, noted at Dawlish in transit)

Swindon Wks: 071071/ 111071 ('A' Shop Yd, whole)/ 181071/ 311071/ 041271/ 121271 (Dump, gutted bodyshell, on bogies)/ 291271/ 050172 (ConYd Cutting Area)/ 090172 (ConYd Cutting Area, being cut-up). N/listed 210172.
Disposal: By 210172 (BR).

Additional information regarding D6356's 1969/70 Classified Repair prior to reinstatement to traffic:

"Swindon Works Intake Report No.209 dated 05/12/69: D6356: Ex-Store, to receive Intermediate Repair.

Details: Body - Intermediate; Engine No.141 (5650hrs since GR) - General (No.7 piston seized); Transmission No.16879 (10450hrs since GR) - General (output casing fractured); Bogies (55 & 56) (105,000 miles since new) and Boiler No.20211 (11 months) - No attention."

D6357

NBL Order: L97/52, Progressive No.: 27930.

Swindon Wks: 231062 (delivery date)/ 041162 ('A' Shop). N/listed 300962 & 181162.

Date New: 131162

Westbury: 081262 (07.15 Filton Jct-Westbury: 09.55 Westbury-Yatton pass)
82A: 200163/ 280763
Paddington: 230564 (e.c.s.)

Swindon Wks: 060964/ 130964 ('A' Shop)/ 270964 (Weigh Shop). N/listed 160864 & 200964.

Paddington: wc021164
81A: 221164
Paddington: 231264/ 070365

Swindon Wks: 300565 (WksYd). N/listed 090565 & 200665.

81A: 150865
Paddington: 100965
81A: 180965/271165/ 160166
Paddington: 220166
81D: 240466
81A: 170766/020966
81C: 131166   **81A:** 261166

81F: 181266   **81A:** 251266
Paddington: 281266
81A: 010167/020367/ 110367
81D: 230467
Paddington: 230567
81A: 180667/150767
Kensington Olympia: 181167 (milk)
81A: 020368/ 060468/ 020668/ 060868/ 051068

Stored: 1we141268 (xx1268)

81D: 081268/121268

Withdrawn: 1we211268 (211268)

81D: 180169/260169/ 020269/ 130469/ 170569/ 180569/ 080669/ 270669 (despatched to Newport)

STN Booked Transfer: No information

Gloucester: 270669 (en route J. Cashmore, Newport, hauled by 'Hymek')

Received J. Cashmore, Newport: 020769
J. Cashmore, Newport: Nil
Disposal: 07/69 (D&ELfS).

D6357, Swindon Works, 1965. Possibly end-May/ early-June. Shed plate on buffer-beam. (Rail-Online)